PATTERNS OF
PERSUASION

IN THE GOSPELS

PUBLISHED VOLUMES

Robert W. Funk,
The Poetics of Biblical Narrative

Burton L. Mack and Vernon K. Robbins,
Patterns of Persuasion in the Gospels

PATTERNS OF PERSUASION

IN THE GOSPELS

BURTON L. MACK &
VERNON K. ROBBINS

POLEBRIDGE PRESS

SONOMA, CALIFORNIA

Design & composition: Polebridge Press, Sonoma, California
Printing & binding: McNaughton & Gunn, Inc., Saline, Michigan
Display type: Palatino Italic Swash
Text type: Palatino

Library of Congress Cataloging-in-Publication Data
Mack, Burton L.
     Patterns of persuasion in the Gospels.

     (Foundations & facets. Literary facets)
     Bibliography: p.
     Includes index.
     1. Bible. N.T. Gospels—Criticism, interpretation,
etc. 2. Bible. N.T. Gospels—Language, style.
3. Jesus Christ—History of doctrines—Early church,
ca. 30–600. 4. Sociology, Biblical. I. Robbins,
Vernon K. (Vernon Kay), 1939-   . II. Title.
III. Series.
BS 2555.2.M254   1989   226'.066   89–3832
ISBN 0-944344-08-9

Printed in the United States of America

To B. J. & Deanna
we express our sincere gratitude.

Contents

Preface

|G| This book grew out of a sustained exchange of ideas and research during the spring semester of 1982. Vernon Robbins was an SBL-Claremont Fellow at the Institute for Antiquity and Christianity where Burton Mack was involved in the Claremont Chreia Project. A very constructive conversation developed, Robbins representing the work of the SBL Seminar on pronouncement stories, and Mack the work of the Claremont project on the chreia in ancient rhetoric. We exchanged papers and ideas through the year, wrote first drafts of the studies during 1983–84, and completed our writing and research for this volume during 1986. The volume has been cited as forthcoming in footnotes and bibliographies under the provisional title *Rhetoric in the Gospels: Argumentation in Narrative Elaboration*. We hope that the present title is preferable.

The rhetorical theories of Theon (*Progymnasmata*) and Hermogenes (*Progymnasmata* and *Peri ton Staseon*) that we have used in the experimental exegetical chapters have attracted widespread attention since drafts of our work began to circulate three years ago. The patterns of persuasion discussed in these educational texts from the Greco-Roman world have shed much light on the compositional logic of synoptic materials. We do not claim to have seen all the light there is to see, nor even to be right in every exegetical judgment. But we dare to think that we have seen enough correctly to make the case and to interest other scholars in the approach we are suggesting. We have discussed each other's work along the way, shared portions with colleagues and students for critique, and have worked hard to craft a workable nomenclature for such analyses of synoptic pericopae. Working together in this way has been a very enjoyable and productive engagement; we hope the excitement of fresh and perhaps significant discoveries is evident in the finished product.

We have not discussed the pertinent books, articles, and papers that have appeared since 1986, although we have added some publications to the bibliography. We hope to acknowledge in this way a growing interest in the rhetoric of the New Testament and to provide the reader with a place to begin, should one want to join us in this very interesting field of exploration.

Mack would like to express his appreciation to the Chreia Project team, especially to Edward N. O'Neil, Ronald F. Hock, and James R. Butts, whose collective *intelligence* and *esprit* first marked the texts for this adventure and made the work seem most worthwhile. He is deeply indebted as well to careful and critical readings of first drafts of chapter 2 by Chuck Young, Claremont Graduate School, Tom Conley, University of Illinois, and David Seeley, University of Montana. Students at Claremont helped to hone the method of application to early Christian texts by able performance in their roles of advocate, prosecutor, and judge. Shawn Carruth, Sterling Bjorndahl, and Zachary Maxey have each played their parts with enviable finesse. Stan Stowers at Brown has freely shared his remarkable erudition on many occasions when Mack has posed leading questions. And Ron Cameron has put the icing on the cake with a remarkable essay that used our method of rhetorical analysis to unravel the logic of a very important New Testament text (See bibliography).

Robbins would like to express his sincere appreciation to the members of the SBL-Claremont Fellowship board for granting the fellowship during Spring 1982 when the research began for this volume. Also, he records with pleasure his deep indebtedness to the staff at the Institute for Antiquity and Christianity at Claremont, California, and its Director, James M. Robinson, for the warm hospitality, the generous use of resources, and the monthly colloquies. Special thanks to Edward N. O'Neil and Ronald F. Hock for the meetings of the Chreia Project. These meetings started a a substantive, new phase of research for Robbins.

With a touch of nostalgia, Robbins expresses gratitude to the Research Board of the University of Illinois at Urbana-Champaign for supporting this work with a Study in a Second Discipline Grant during the Fall of 1981. In addition, it was opportune that Thomas M. Conley came to the University of Illinois at just the right time to serve as guide and mentor in the field of rhetorical literature and theory. His friendship, knowledge, and creative spirit were a welcome boon. In addition, William R. Schoedel, David L. Petersen, and Gary G. Porton at the University of Illinois provided encouragement and information that nurtured my scholarship and productivity in ways unknown even to me.

Robbins is also deeply grateful to the US Educational Foundation in Norway and the Religionsvitenskapelig Institutt at the University of Trondheim for that unique year as Fulbright Professor during 1983–84. Peder Borgen is surely unsurpassed in his ability to host a Fulbright Professor. In addition, I must thank Eirik Lien and many people at NTH (the technical campus of the University of Trondheim) who made it possible for me to make use of excellent computer facilities.

Dean David Minter of Emory University has supported this research unstintingly. I am also grateful to Leah Jones, to Adrienne Freeman and to Lyn Schechtel for their superb work.

To James R. Butts goes the credit for extensive editing and bibliographical work. And finally, to Helen Melnis for the elegant cover design, and to Stephanie Funk, Char Matejovsky, and Robert W. Funk for seeing the volume through its final stages we express our sincere gratitude.

Vernon K. Robbins   Burton L. Mack
Emory University   Claremont Graduate School
March 1989

ONE

Chreia & Pronouncement Story in Synoptic Studies

Vernon K. Robbins

The synoptic gospels tantalize us with a variety of traditions about Jesus of Nazareth. We would like to know how these traditions developed, what features in them reliably portray the activities of Jesus, and what settings provided the milieu for their transmission. Scholars have accurately observed that this tradition is characterized by small units, which they have called pericopae.[1] These units contain a variety of phenomena including summaries, scripture quotations, sayings, and stories.

Since the nineteenth century, scholars have used various methods to study these units. Textual criticism has revealed their distinctive wording and language in each gospel. Philology and source criticism have uncovered complex relationships of dependence and independence among them. And form criticism and redaction criticism have probed the interplay of oral and written traditions in them. Even though these disciplines have advanced the analysis of the units in many ways, significant dimensions of the formulation and transmission of the Jesus tradition remain essentially mysterious. Interpreters refer to certain sayings as "free-floating" traditions, certain stories as Palestinian or Galilean in formulation, and certain groups of stories or sayings as collections prior to the composition of the gospels we possess. But only a few studies have explored the logic at work in the abbreviation or expansion of units, or the arrangement of units in a sequence to interpret or defend a particular point of view. It would be beneficial if we could discover the

---

1. Aland, *Synopsis*, divides the units in all four gospels into 367 pericopae.

1

logic at work in the growth and development of the saying and story, since this logic might help us to understand the issues at stake in the expansion, abbreviation, and recasting of traditions in literature available to us from early Christianity.

Already in antiquity teachers of rhetoric had discussed the inner logic of certain forms of oral and written discourse. The most widely discussed form was the speech. The ancient rhetoricians developed an intricate program for analyzing previously given speeches and for composing new speeches. This program explained the inner progression of the speech, its interweaving of thought, character, and emotion, and its function in different kinds of rhetorical settings.[2] And several scholars have profitably applied this information about the speech to the analysis of letters in the New Testament during recent years.[3] During this same period, a number of interpreters have sought to explain the inner unity and organization of various forms of the Jesus tradition. Some of these analyses have probed the feasibility of aretalogy as a genre for the portrayal of Jesus as a divine man.[4] Others have used collections of the sayings of the wise to explain the gathering of sayings together in early Christianity.[5] Still others have used structures, patterns, and genres in Hellenistic and Roman biography to explore the composition and function of the gospels in early Christianity.[6] Only a few have attempted, however, to employ rhetorical literature, either ancient or modern, to explain the inner logic, development, and function of stories and sayings about Jesus in earliest Christianity.[7]

1. Martin Dibelius and Rudolf Bultmann

If an interpreter contemplates the use of rhetoric for analysis of the synoptic tradition, a few issues in previous research call for special

2. See Clark, *Rhetoric*; Kennedy, *Art of Persuasion, Art of Rhetoric, Classical Rhetoric*; and Bonner, *Education*.

3. See Betz, *Der Apostel Paulus*, "Literary Composition," "In Defense of the Spirit," and *Galatians*; Church, "Rhetorical Structure"; Jewett, "Romans as an Ambassadorial Letter"; and Wuellner, "Paul's Rhetoric of Argumentation," "Der Jakobusbrief," and "Greek Rhetoric."

4. See Betz, "Jesus as Divine Man"; Hadas and Smith, *Heroes and Gods*; Tiede, *The Charismatic Figure*; Georgi, "The Records of Jesus"; Holladay, *Theios Aner*; Kee, "Aretalogy and Gospel"; and Smith, "Prolegomena."

5. See Robinson and Koester, *Trajectories*.

6. See Talbert, "The Concept of Immortals," *What Is a Gospel?*, "Biographies of Philosophers and Rulers," "Prophecies of Future Greatness"; and Shuler, "The Greisbach Hypothesis."

7. See Betz, "The Sermon of the Mount"; Spencer, "Form and Function of the Biographical Apophthegms"; Tannehill, *The Sword of His Mouth*, "Introduction: The Pronouncement Story," "Varieties," "Types and Functions of Apophthegms"; Robbins and Patton, "Rhetoric and Biblical Criticism"; and Robbins, "Classifying," and "Pronouncement Stories."

discussion. Among these issues is the function of the stories and sayings in the articulation of the Christian message during the first century.

1.1 Martin Dibelius

Dibelius presupposed that the stories and sayings functioned within a larger rhetorical unit, namely, the early Christian sermon. His understanding of the sermon was similar to the ancient rhetoricians' understanding of the speech. Taking his cues from the reference to "eyewitnesses and ministers of the word" in Luke 1:2, the repetition of content in the speeches in Acts, and the formulaic structure of 1 Cor 15:3–5, Dibelius proposed that Christian preachers and missionaries regularly delivered sermons containing an established, traditional content within a four-part structure:

(1) introduction;
(2) kerygma or message;
(3) scriptural proof;
(4) exhortation to repentance.[8]

Dibelius intended this proposal to be a model for understanding the transmission of stories and sayings in early Christian tradition. He claimed simply to be following the logic of the material in 1 Corinthians and Luke-Acts. But a close reading of his analysis reveals his awareness of the basic parts of the speech as taught by the ancient rhetoricians. According to their analysis, the standard speech has four essential parts:

(1) introduction (προοίμιον, *exordium*);
(2) statement of the case (διήγησις, *narratio*);
(3) proof or argument (πίστις, *argumentatio*);
(4) conclusion (ἐπίλογος, *peroratio*).[9]

The formal similarity between the two patterns, and Dibelius's comments on each part of the early Christian sermon, suggest the influence of standard rhetorical theory on his analysis. In rhetorical theory, the four-part pattern of the speech had emerged as the most appropriate format to use in the courtroom and the political assembly. In each instance, the speaker asked the hearers to make a decision on the basis of his statement of the facts, his arguments about the nature of past or future events, and the participation of certain people in those events. In Dibelius's application, the kerygma—that is, the account of the death and resurrection of Jesus—presented the facts of the case. In turn, the argument was based on scriptural proof. With this structure, the sermon, according to Dibelius, functioned as a vehicle of persuasive communication during the first century, winning converts to the newly formed

---

8. Dibelius, *From Tradition to Gospel*, 17–23.
9. Lausberg, *Handbuch*, pars. 263–442.

group and nurturing believers who had already committed themselves to this new way of life.[10]

In this schema, the stories about Jesus before the passion events and the sayings of Jesus which did not quote Old Testament scripture were incidental to the central message of Christianity.[11] The incidental stories, according to Dibelius, included legends, tales, and paradigms. Legends, revealing personal interest in individual people, were truly peripheral to the tradition.[12] They had the form of "'religious' stories as they were known and loved in the world."[13] This kind of story arises in every group of religious people, and it was inevitable that it should emerge in early Christianity. Tales, in contrast to legends, were not quite so inevitable. Even though they contain detailed description that reflects worldly interests, they were essential forms for the narrative content of the synoptics.[14] Surely storytellers and teachers transmitted them among the early Christians.[15] But we cannot describe the setting for their transmission, since "the sources have nothing to say of tellers of tales."[16] The most important narrative forms in the synoptic tradition, according to Dibelius, were the paradigms, since they functioned as examples that supported the main argument of the early Christian sermon.[17] Their place, however, was still subsidiary to scriptural proof.

Because Dibelius viewed the paradigms as subsidiary to scriptural proof in the argumentation of early Christians, he had little interest in the rhetoric internal to the stories themselves. His interests focused entirely on characteristics of the paradigms that accompanied their function in the sermon. Accordingly, he described five attributes of the paradigm:

(1) "rounding off" at the beginning and ending of the paradigm as the preacher made a transition from the sermon to the story and back again to the sermon;[18]

(2) "brevity" within the paradigm that "makes the material subject to the purpose of the preacher, hinders wandering, and silences the unessential";[19]

(3) "religious (i.e., realistic unworldly) coloring of the narrative" that edifies rather than entertains;[20]

10. Dibelius, *From Tradition to Gospel*, 21.
11. Dibelius, *From Tradition to Gospel*, 24.
12. Dibelius, *From Tradition to Gospel*, 133.
13. Dibelius, *From Tradition to Gospel*, 104.
14. Dibelius, *From Tradition to Gospel*, 133.
15. Dibelius, *From Tradition to Gospel*, 70.
16. Dibelius, *From Tradition to Gospel*, 70.
17. Dibelius, *From Tradition to Gospel*, 37–69.
18. Dibelius, *From Tradition to Gospel*, 44–48.
19. Dibelius, *From Tradition to Gospel*, 53.
20. Dibelius, *From Tradition to Gospel*, 56, 58, 69.

(4) "a word of Jesus" in which the paradigm reaches its point and comes to a conclusion;[21]

(5) "a thought at the end useful for preaching purposes."[22]

Among these attributes, only the assertions about rounding off, brevity, and the presence of a word of Jesus at or near the end are truly rhetorical observations. Rounding off points to the inner completeness of the story, brevity indicates a lack of rhetorical elaboration, and the presence of a word of Jesus at or near the end suggests a rhetorical goal toward which the story moves. The comments about religious coloring and a thought at the end useful for preaching indicate Dibelius's interest in the compatibility of the stories with a Christian sermon. But religious coloring points to subject matter rather than rhetorical form, and a thought at the end useful for preaching is a feature external to the story itself.

Even though Dibelius identified three rhetorical attributes of the paradigm, he did not present a thorough analysis of any story to test his theory. He cited various items and their parallels to discuss external rounding off, brevity, religious coloring, the concluding word of Jesus, and an ending that is useful for preaching.[23] His theory runs into difficulty, however, when actually applied to the stories. First, the paradigms are rounded off at the beginning and end simply because this is a characteristic of popular stories. This attribute is not evidence for their function in a sermon. Secondly, comparison of synoptic paradigms with forms outside the gospels shows that the synoptic stories are not as brief as Dibelius asserted. Almost all the synoptic paradigms are moderately elaborated forms, and the elaboration points to a function outside the setting of a sermon. Thirdly, Dibelius's emphasis on the word of Jesus at or near the end of paradigms led him away from the interrelation of setting, action, and speech within the paradigms. In contrast to Dibelius's conclusion that the settings and actions are incidental to the halakic, didactic, or edificatory speech of Jesus in the paradigms, the detailed features in the stories transmit the authority and role of Jesus on their own terms. But Dibelius analyzed details only as an aid in identifying stories that presently or previously existed in the form of a paradigm. These stories are reliable, and thus important for the interpreter, he suggested, but they remain incidental to the central message of Christianity.

Dibelius's identification of a significant number of stories in the synoptic tradition as paradigms depended on the explanation of details that, according to his theory, should not be in them. He noticed that some paradigms describe individual people and situations. The story of

21. Dibelius, *From Tradition to Gospel*, 56.
22. Dibelius, *From Tradition to Gospel*, 58.
23. Dibelius, *From Tradition to Gospel*, 44–58.

the rich young man (Mark 10:17–22), for instance, is too long and contains too much detail in its present form to be a paradigm. Yet in its original form, he reasoned, it existed as a paradigm. A general concern about rich people in the Kingdom of Heaven (Mark 10:25) led to its expansion rather than a personal interest in the people in the story.[24] Likewise, the stories of the Sons of Zebedee (Mark 10:35–40) and the blind man at Jericho (Mark 10:46–52) contain too many details. The expansion, however, occurred as the result of religious interests rather than interest in personal lore.[25] The actual length and nature of the stories in the synoptic gospels, therefore, do not conform to Dibelius's theory as well as he thought. His proposal for their function within early Christian communication, however, was generally convincing in the absence of a better explanation.

1.2 Rudolf Bultmann

While Dibelius wrestled with the function of stories and sayings in the early Christian sermon, Rudolf Bultmann probed the relation of stories to sayings. Committing his analysis to the synoptic tradition in and of itself, rather than a theory about a larger rhetorical form in which the stories and sayings had functioned, Bultmann introduced a type of literary-historical research that has since dominated both friend and foe of form criticism. In order to explain the origin and transmission of the synoptic tradition, Bultmann claimed, the interpreter must make literary and historical judgments at the same time. He or she must determine not only if individual features in a saying or story are original or added. The interpreter must also determine if a saying or story is genuine, formulated by analogy to another saying or story, or imported in an adapted form from Jewish or Greek tradition.[26] As Bultmann carried out this program of analysis, he introduced a long list of formal designations to describe the variety within the synoptic tradition. The forms included conflict saying, didactic saying, prophetic saying, apocalyptic saying, legal saying, "I" saying, biographical apophthegm, controversy dialogue, scholastic dialogue, similitude, parable, healing miracle, nature miracle, Easter narrative, and infancy narrative. With these formal designations, Bultmann bequeathed nomenclature that guided New Testament research as it advanced and flourished during the second and third quarters of this century. But the nomenclature was only part of his contribution. As he discussed each form, he distinguished between early, primary units and later, secondary additions. Whereas Dibelius

---

24. Dibelius, *From Tradition to Gospel*, 50.
25. Dibelius, *From Tradition to Gospel*, 51–53.
26. Bultmann, *History of the Synoptic Tradition*, 6.

only pointed to certain instances of expansion in units, Bultmann distinguished between "primary" and "secondary" features in every unit, and between entire units that were "primary" (that is, original) or "secondary" (formed by analogy to other units in the tradition). For him, the verses in a unit that contain a "unitary conception" (that is, all of them are part of a consistent, coherent presentation) are the earliest form of the unit. Thus, in unit after unit he looked for verses that appear to be complementary parts of a unified presentation and then decided whether the unit itself was primary or secondary.

The frontispiece of Bultmann's analysis of the sayings and stories in the synoptic tradition was the apophthegm. Defining the apophthegms as "sayings of Jesus set in a brief context,"[27] Bultmann began to determine if the saying in a literary unit originally existed as an isolated saying (γνώμη or *sententia*) or an "organic ἀπόφθεγμα." The apophthegms are especially pertinent to his analysis, since they contain both narrative and speech, and his approach to the apophthegm established the model for his analysis of the other forms. For Bultmann, the saying is the primary phenomenon in the apophthegm. Any information in the narrative is subsidiary to the saying. Thus, a saying in an apophthegm may originate with Jesus, or it may be a secondary saying that someone later developed from another saying in the tradition. In either case, however, the narrative depends on the saying. If the narrative is essential for understanding the saying, the saying and the narrative are an organic apophthegm that presents early tradition about the life of Jesus. A narrative may not be essential for understanding the saying, however. In this instance, someone probably artificially constructed the narrative to provide a setting for the saying. This procedure pervades the entire program of interpretation. Only sayings have a natural potential for being primary. Actions, if necessary in the setting of the saying, may be genuine. Otherwise, actions are contrived or derived.

Bultmann's choice of the term apophthegm was important for subsequent analysis. Various people used the term in antiquity to refer to brief units that attribute a saying to some person in the past.[28] But the ancient rhetoricians did not give the term ἀπόφθεγμα a prominent place in their discussions of units featuring the speech and action of famous people. For this reason, Bultmann was free to analyze the apophthegms in the synoptic tradition without reference to classical rhetorical theory. He could make the rules as he himself applied his analysis.[29] But there is another matter of importance also. An apophthegm is a brief unit.

---

27. Bultmann, *History of the Synoptic Tradition*, 11.
28. Spencer, "Form and Function of the Biographical Apophthegms," 169–313.
29. In the second edition of his *History of the Synoptic Tradition*, 11, Bultmann

Calling synoptic stories apophthegms predetermined the existence of a unitary conception within or behind the synoptic unit. Neither a rhetorician nor a literary critic would naturally think of a moderately lengthy apophthegm as an original form. Bultmann's terminology exhibits its inadequacy in some of the moves he made during his analysis. Chief among them is his use of rabbinic tradition but not Hellenistic tradition as a source for analogies to the synoptic units. This move was natural, after he had decided to limit his interest in Hellenistic tradition to brief apophthegms rather than more elaborated forms. But this decision led him away from Hellenistic literature, resulting in a comparative approach concerned only with rabbinic tradition. Also, this decision led Bultmann away from Hellenistic rhetoric, so that he rarely described rhetorical characteristics of synoptic units or identified the features in the primary units that called forth the secondary features. It was natural, from his perspective, not to include this kind of discussion, since he was not trying to suggest that the origin and transmission of the synoptic tradition were integrally linked with its rhetorical characteristics.

The closest Bultmann came to a rhetorical analysis emerged as he compared the synoptic controversy dialogues with rabbinic controversies. Without reference either to rhetorical theory or to kinds of rhetorical discourse, he observed some of the techniques in the controversy dialogues that rhetoricians in antiquity had associated with judicial rhetoric. In a judicial situation, the issue is whether a certain action has left a person guilty or not guilty before the law. The most typical form of interchange occurs when the act stands in the past, and the point of contention is whether the act deserves punishment or chastisement of some sort.[30] As Bultmann described the controversy dialogues, he called forth the judicial situation:

> The starting-point of a controversy dialogue lies in some action or attitude which is seized on by the opponent and used in an attack by accusation or by question. Clearly the typical character of a controversy dialogue is most marked when a single action like plucking corn or healing on the Sabbath constitutes the starting-point rather than when the opponent merely fastens on some general attitude of the person he criticizes. This fact also explains why an effort is made to describe some particular action, even when it is obvious that only a general attitude is under discussion.[31]

Here Bultmann described the kind of situation the rhetoricians considered judicial. After introductory comments, someone states a case

---

cited Gemoll, *Das Apophthegma*, and criticized his "lack of conceptual clarity." Bultmann considered himself to be the one providing the clarity to the discussion of the apophthegm.

30. Lausberg, *Handbuch*, par. 61,1.
31. Bultmann, *History of the Synoptic Tradition*, 39.

against someone.[32] This statement features an opponent who forces another person to defend himself or herself against a charge of wrongdoing. After the speaker has presented and argued the case, the accused person or a person representing the accused presents a refutation.[33] This procedure may be followed during an initial hearing of a case or during an actual trial before a judge or jury. Bultmann's discussion evokes this kind of situation, and his discussion continues with a description of the phenomena within the refutation:

> The reply to the attack follows more or less a set form, with special preference for the counter-question or metaphor, or even both together. Nevertheless—like the attack—it can also consist of a scripture quotation.[34]

When Bultmann compared the synoptic controversy dialogues with rabbinic disputes, he observed phenomena in the response that lent themselves to analysis according to principles discussed by the ancient rhetoricians. Unfortunately, Bultmann did not use information in the rhetorical treatises to guide his analysis. Instead, he simply cited examples of counter-questions containing a metaphor,[35] detailed parable,[36] a demonstration or symbolic action,[37] or a scripture quotation,[38] and he argued that all except the last instance were designed to lead the opponent *ad absurdum*.[39] With this observation, Bultmann was at the threshold of a full-fledged rhetorical analysis. He did not, however, cite rhetorical discussions of judicial situations, nor did he explore the possibility that certain apophthegms developed into controversy dialogues when someone added sayings that provided additional judicial argumentation.

After analyzing the controversy dialogues, Bultmann turned to the scholastic dialogues.[40] The discussion is very brief and builds on the close relationship between the scholastic and controversy dialogues.[41] For Bultmann, the scholastic dialogues differ by not having "some particular action as the starting-point but for the most part the Master is simply questioned by someone seeking knowledge. That leads to an answer which is sometimes in question form, as in Luke 12:13–14; 13:1–

32. Cf. Quintilian, *Inst. Orat.* IV. ii.1ff.
33. Cf. Quintilian, *Inst. Orat.* V. xiii.1ff.
34. Bultmann, *History of the Synoptic Tradition*, 41.
35. Bultmann, *History of the Synoptic Tradition*, 42.
36. Bultmann, *History of the Synoptic Tradition*, 42–45.
37. Bultmann, *History of the Synoptic Tradition*, 44–45.
38. Bultmann, *History of the Synoptic Tradition*, 45.
39. Bultmann, *History of the Synoptic Tradition*, 45.
40. Bultmann, *History of the Synoptic Tradition*, 54–55.
41. Bultmann, *History of the Synoptic Tradition*, 54.

5, but not with a view to taking the questioner *ad absurdum.*"[42] Bultmann noticed a similarity between controversy dialogues and scholastic dialogues, but he did not suggest that a shift had occurred from judicial rhetoric to deliberative rhetoric, where the goal is to give advice about future action.[43] If he had employed insights from ancient rhetorical treatises, he might have shown how the scholastic dialogues contain rhetorical procedures that the rhetoricians considered part of a rhetorical situation quite different from one containing judicial accusation and refutation. Instead, he simply distinguished two major features in the dialogues—the presence or absence of *argumentatio ad absurdum* and the presence of a question or action at the beginning. In neither instance, however, did he use ancient rhetorical descriptions of discourse and argumentation that occur in different kinds of rhetorical situations.

1.3 Dibelius, Bultmann, and Ancient Rhetoric

In conclusion, both Dibelius and Bultmann used some principles of rhetoric in their analysis of the synoptic tradition. Dibelius used his rhetorical understanding to describe the early Christian sermon and to find a place for the development and use of paradigms in the tradition. Bultmann, on the other hand, described some of the judicial dynamics in controversy dialogues. Neither Dibelius nor Bultmann emphasized their use of rhetorical principles, however, because of their interest in the transmission of Christian traditions among common folk in the Mediterranean world. In this vein, Dibelius referred explicitly to "the lowly folk" who used a style "independent of the individual personality"[44] and recommended that the interpreter put aside "all evaluations derived from literature proper, and certainly everything from the classics."[45] Bultmann's disclaimers resided primarily in footnotes—for example, his criticism of Gemoll's "lack of conceptual clarity" as he analyzed the apophthegm.[46]

Dibelius's and Bultmann's analyses, therefore, systematically guided interpreters away from ancient rhetorical discussions as they immersed themselves in the details of the synoptic tradition. Dibelius' approach suggested that rhetorical discussions applied only to speeches in early Christian literature and made it most natural to carry rhetorical analysis further with the speeches in Acts.[47] Bultmann, on the other hand, cre-

---

42. Bultmann, *History of the Synoptic Tradition*, 54.
43. See Lausberg, *Handbuch*, par. 61,2 and cf. Quintilian, *Inst. Orat.* III.viii.1ff.
44. Dibelius, *From Tradition to Gospel*, 7; cf. 156–58.
45. Dibelius, *From Tradition to Gospel*, 6.
46. Bultmann, *History of the Synoptic Tradition*, 11.
47. Recently, several scholars have pursued rhetorical analysis of the speeches in Acts with great interest. See, for example, Veltman, "The Defense Speeches," and Long, "The *Paulusbild*."

ated a detailed system of classification with no reference to standard rhetorical analysis.

2. Chreiai and Synoptic Units

In spite of Dibelius's and Bultmann's particular applications of rhetorical principles, the belated discovery of Hellenistic rhetoric as a resource for interpreting the synoptic tradition is something of an anomaly. A few well-placed studies have been available to synoptic researchers for many years, and these studies even pointed the interpreter in the direction that probably is the most productive to follow. Martin Dibelius himself pointed the way in the second edition of *Die Formgeschichte des Evangeliums* (1933), and it is the purpose of the studies in this volume to follow this lead. In a chapter devoted to analogies to synoptic forms in rabbinic and Greek literature, Dibelius cited a number of synoptic units that contain close affinities with the rhetorical chreia.[48] A chreia, according to the ancient rhetorician Aelius Theon, is:

σύντομος ἀπόφασις ἢ πρᾶξις μετ' εὐστοχίας ἀναφερομένη εἴς τι ὡρισμένον πρόσωπον ἢ ἀναλογοῦν προσώπῳ

A brief statement or action with pointedness attributed to a definite person or something analogous to a person.[49]

Among the chreiai Dibelius quoted in his discussion are three from Diogenes Laertius' *Lives of the Eminent Philosophers* and two from Philostratus' *Lives of the Sophists*:

To the question how the educated differ from the uneducated, he (Aristippus) replied, "Like a tamed from an untamed horse." (Diogenes Laertius 2.68)[50]

To one who boasted that he belonged to a great city his (Aristotle's) reply was, "That is not the point to consider, but who it is that is worthy of a great country." (Diogenes Laertius 5.19)[51]

---

48. Dibelius, *From Tradition to Gospel*, 152–64.
49. All references to Theon in this volume are to the Greek text edition of Walz, *Rhetores Graeci*. For an English translation of Theon's chreia chapter, see Hock and O'Neil, *Chreia in Ancient Rhetoric*. The most recent critical edition of Theon's *Progymnasmata* is Butts, "*Progymnasmata* of Theon," which also contains an English translation of the entire work and a commentary. All references to Aphthonius are to the Greek text edition of Rabe, *Aphthonii Progymnasmata*. The most recent English translation of Aphthonius' chreia chapter is Butts and Hock, "Chreia Discussion of Aphthonius."
50. Cited by Dibelius in *From Tradition to Gospel*, 153.
51. Cited by Dibelius in *From Tradition to Gospel*, 153.

When someone expressed astonishment at the votive offerings in Samothrace, his (Diogenes') comment was, "There would have been far more, if those who were not saved had set up offerings." (Diogenes Laertius 6.59)[52]

And he (Lucius) saw some slaves at a well that was in the house, washing radishes, and asked them for whose dinner they were intended. They replied that they were preparing them for Herodes. At this Lucius remarked: "Herodes insults Regilla by eating white radishes in a black house." This was reported indoors to Herodes, and when he heard it he removed the signs of mourning from his house, for fear he should become the laughing-stock of wise men. (Philostratus, *Lives of the Sophists* 2.1)[53]

The Emperor Marcus was greatly interested in Sextus the Boeotian philosopher, attending his classes and going to his very door. Lucius had just arrived in Rome, and asked the Emperor, whom he met going out, where he was going and for what purpose. Marcus answered: "It is a good thing even for one who is growing old to acquire knowledge. I am going to Sextus the philosopher to learn what I do not yet know." At this Lucius raised his hand to heaven, and exclaimed: "O Zeus! The Emperor of the Romans is already growing old, but he hangs a tablet round his neck and goes to school, while my Emperor Alexander died at thirty-two!" (Philostratus, *Lives of the Sophists* 2.1)[54]

With these examples, Dibelius exhibited rhetorical units in Greek tradition that are highly analogous to synoptic units. Some examples are brief, while others are only moderately brief. The longer ones contain a series of independent clauses connected with δέ or καί, and participial clauses enrich the main clauses by describing the circumstances of the action and the speech. The close analogy is evident from the following examples Dibelius cited from the synoptic tradition:

Now when Jesus saw great crowds around him, he gave orders to go over to the other side. And a scribe came up and said to him, "Teacher, I will follow you wherever you go." And Jesus said to him, "Foxes have holes, and birds of the air have nests; but the Son of Man has nowhere to lay his head." (Matt 8:18-20)

Another of the disciples said to him (Jesus), "Lord, let me first go and bury my father." But Jesus said to him, "Follow me, and leave the dead to bury their own dead." (Matt 8:21-22)

John said to him (Jesus), "Teacher, we saw a man casting out demons in your name, and we forbade him, because he was not following us." But Jesus said, "Do not forbid him; for no one who does a mighty work in my name will be able soon after to speak evil of me. For he that is not against us is for us. For

---

52. Cited by Dibelius in *From Tradition to Gospel*, 153.
53. Cited by Dibelius in *From Tradition to Gospel*, 154.
54. Cited by Dibelius in *From Tradition to Gospel*, 155.

truly, I say to you, whoever gives you a cup of water to drink because you bear the name of Christ, will by no means lose his reward." (Mark 9:38–40)

The Pharisees came and began to argue with him (Jesus), seeking from him a sign from heaven, to test him. And he sighed deeply in his spirit, and said, "Why does this generation seek a sign? Truly, I say to you, no sign shall be given to this generation." (Mark 8:11–13)

In these examples from the synoptic tradition, there is a similar approach to composition and a similar approach to the portrayal of speech and action. Also, the units vary in length from brief to only moderately brief.

Dibelius's discussion of the chreia has not influenced many interpreters of the gospels, and an innocent observer may wonder why. Undoubtedly there are many reasons, but two are important to observe here. First, Dibelius did not discuss the rhetorical chreia until the second edition of *Die Formgeschichte des Evangeliums* in 1933. As a result, his insights had not influenced his original analysis in 1919, and he never revised the analysis on the basis of his later insights. Second, Dibelius's understanding was not based on the discussions of the chreia in the *progymnasmata*—the handbooks containing the "preliminary exercises" that the rhetoricians wrote for teachers to use during the final stage of grammar school. As a result, his discussion subtly misconstrued both the nature of the saying and the significance of the action in a chreia. Even though Dibelius quoted the definition of a chreia in Theon's *Progymnasmata* in a footnote,[55] in his own discourse he defined the chreia as

the reproduction of a short pointed saying of general significance, originating in a definite person and arising out of a definite situation.[56]

With this definition, Dibelius limited the statement in a chreia to a saying "of general significance." In contrast, Theon's definition does not limit the statement to a saying of a particular kind. When Dibelius described the statement as a pointed saying *of general significance*, he limited chreiai to stories containing sayings that could function as independently circulating maxims ($\gamma\nu\hat{\omega}\mu\alpha\iota$). In fact, chreiai may contain sayings of general significance or short remarks understandable only in the situation in which they occur. Also, Dibelius limited chreiai to units containing sayings, while Theon asserted that a chreia could contain either "a brief statement" or "an action" or both a statement and an action (Theon 202,18–206,8). Rhetoricians like Theon, therefore, discussed action-chreiai as well as sayings-chreiai. Since actions are either active or passive, depending on one's point of view as the action occurs,

55. See Dibelius, *From Tradition to Gospel*, 152, note 1.
56. Dibelius, *From Tradition to Gospel*, 152.

there are active and passive action-chreiai. The following are active action-chreiai:

> Diogenes the Cynic philosopher, on seeing a boy eating delicacies, struck the paidagogus with his staff. (Theon 205,22–24)

> Diogenes the Cynic philosopher used to seek a man with a lighted lamp during the day. (Diomedes 310,22–23, Walz; cf. Diogenes Laertius 6.41)

In both instances, the action in the chreia points the reader's thinking in a particular direction and encourages the reader to reflect on the meaning of the action. In the light of such chreiai, interpreters must give more attention to Jesus' action in a unit like Mark 9:33–37 and parallels, where Jesus places a child before the disciples as part of the answer to a question about greatness. Even though the sayings vary in the parallel units, Jesus' action of placing a child before the disciples is common to all three versions. Moreover, Jesus' action provides the essential answer to the question about greatness, whereas the sayings provide alternative explanations of the action. In this instance, then, an action-chreia may represent the primary form of the unit, while the units containing sayings represent particular interpretive uses of the unit.[57]

In contrast to active action-chreiai like the units cited above, the following unit is a passive action-chreia:

> Didymon the flute-player, on being caught in adultery, was hanged by his namesake. (Theon 205,24–206,1)

Passive actions also exist in units in the synoptic tradition, as exhibited by Luke 3:21–23:

> Now when all the people were baptized, and when Jesus also had been baptized and was praying, the heaven was opened, and the Holy Spirit descended upon him in bodily form as a dove, and a voice came from heaven, "Thou art my beloved Son; with thee I am well pleased."[58]

The descent of the Holy Spirit as a dove is an action upon Jesus, and the saying from heaven is a laudatory supplement. The interpreter will give a proper interpretation of this unit only if he or she explains the significance of both the action and the saying.

In the above-cited synoptic units containing an action, both an action and a saying are present. The ancient rhetoricians called such a unit a mixed-chreia (cf. Theon 206,1–207,5; Aphthonius 4,8). It was common practice for a narrator to interpret the meaning of the action in a chreia, as this chreia about Pythagoras shows:

---

57. The complete analysis of these synoptic texts appears in Robbins, "Pronouncement Stories," 43–74.

58. Cf. Dibelius, *From Tradition to Gospel*, 161.

> Pythagoras the philosopher, on being asked how long the life of men is, went up to his bedroom and looked back out for a short time, showing thereby its brevity. (Theon 206,3–6)

In this chreia, an editorial comment explains that the action showed the brevity of a man's life. It is also informative to compare a chreia Theon cites about a Laconian and his spear with three versions of the tradition in Plutarch:

> A Laconian, when someone asked him where the Lacedaimonians had the boundaries of their country, showed his spear. (Theon 206,6–8)

> Being asked once how far the boundaries of Laconia extended, he (Agesilaus) said, with a flourish of his spear, "As far as this can reach." (*Moralia* 210E,28)[59]

> Being asked how much land the Spartans controlled, he (Archidamus, son of Agesilaus) said, "As much as they can reach with the spear." (*Moralia* 218F,2)

> Is it that Romulus placed no boundary-stones for his country, so that Romans might go forth, seize land, and regard all as theirs, as the Spartans said, "which their spears could reach?" (*Moralia* 267C,15)

Only Theon's chreia and the first version in Plutarch contain an action by the Laconian with his spear. The other two versions contain only a saying about a spear, with no reference to an action with it. On the basis of these traditions, it would seem as plausible to suggest that an action was primary and produced the saying as to suggest that the saying is primary and produced the action. The last version, which uses a truncated form in a discussion about Romulus, shows how the saying may dominate over the action once the saying is part of the tradition. A mixed-chreia, then, contains both action and speech. The interpreter should be on the alert for the possibility that the action in such a unit is primary and the saying is a supplementary, explanatory feature in the unit.

Dibelius's discussion of the chreia therefore identified a rhetorical unit that is analogous to many units in the synoptic tradition. He limited the reader's perspective of the form and function of the chreia, however, not only through a definition that limited the chreia to units containing sayings, but also through a predisposition for units containing sayings "of general significance." When Dibelius supported his view with units he construed to be chreiai in Xenophon's *Memorabilia*, Lucian's *Demonax*, Philostratus' *Lives of the Sophists*, and *Philogelos*,[60] rather than with units the rhetoricians cited as chreiai in their *progymnasmata*, he gave the

---

59. All references to and translations of Plutarch's *Moralia* are from the Loeb Classical Library editions.

60. See Dibelius, *From Tradition to Gospel*, 153–57.

reader little hint of the range of rhetorical features and the type of flexibility within the chreia. A close reading suggests that Dibelius's discussion of the chreia was influenced by Bultmann's discussion of the apophthegm.[61] As a result, subsequent interpreters continually have returned to Bultmann's analysis of synoptic units as ἀποφθέγματα, after reading Dibelius's discussion of the chreia, rather than turning to the analyses of the chreia by the rhetoricians. In the discussions by the rhetoricians, the interpreter discovers that ἀποφθέγματα often provided material for chreiai, but the chreia was not limited in all the ways Dibelius assumed.

In 1946, R. O. P. Taylor expanded and corrected the discussion of the chreia for use as a guide in interpreting the gospels.[62] On the basis of his research, he considered it strange that form critics had not used the careful studies of literary form available to them in the progymnasmata.[63] Observing that the rhetoricians gave priority of place in the exercises to the chreia, he presented an accurate translation of Theon's definition of a chreia as

> a concise and pointed account of something said or done, attributed to some particular person,

and asserted that

> the definition exactly fits the detachable little stories, of which so much of Mark consists.[64]

Then Taylor pursued the significance of the chreia in the Hellenistic educational system. He noted the difference between the chreia, which is attributed to a particular person, and a maxim (γνώμη), which gives a general statement. The Hellenistic teachers considered the chreia to be of central importance within education as a means of persuading and giving guidance for conduct. And, he suggested, perhaps our view of the chreia versus the maxim is the reverse of what their view was:

> We view a maxim as if it had an existence and authority of its own, apart from its author. If we approve of it, we may be interested to find who was its author, and willing to value him for its sake. But, to them, the maxim, however impressive, had to come from an accredited person to carry the greatest weight. In short, the maxim was required to be a dictum."[65]

I have quoted this statement in its entirety, since it identifies a major

61. See Dibelius, *From Tradition to Gospel*, 156.
62. Taylor, *Groundwork of the Gospels*.
63. Taylor, *Groundwork of the Gospels*, 75.
64. Taylor, *Groundwork of the Gospels*, 76.
65. Taylor, *Groundwork of the Gospels*, 79–80.

problem in the approach of Dibelius and Bultmann, and, as a result, in gospel research. An essential rhetorical attribute of the paradigm for Dibelius was the saying at or near the end, and for Bultmann the primary element in an apophthegm was a saying that may have existed independently or may have been part of a tradition that included action in the setting. But for both Dibelius and Bultmann, most sayings could serve their purpose outside of stories, since the saying provided the halakic, didactic, or edificatory matter of significance. Dibelius and Bultmann were confronting, of course, literary units that presented speech in settings characterized by actions. But these details were embarrassing to Dibelius, because they occurred in paradigms in which there should be no detail. In turn, the details simply presented a challenge for Bultmann to find the primary form underlying all the secondary additions.

Taylor saw that the details of setting and action, the "secondary" features in Bultmann's analysis, contain a central concern of the Hellenistic teachers and represent a matter that interpreters should investigate from an angle different from Dibelius's and Bultmann's approaches. If an integral relation exists between speech and action in the tradition, possibly both the longer and the shorter forms result more from rhetorical usage than from the existence of primary or secondary items in the tradition. For this reason, a tradition may be articulated in a longer or shorter form without clearly presenting "secondary" features in the longer form. In other words, the presence of longer and shorter forms may show quite a different process at work than Dibelius and Bultmann presupposed. Theon's *Progymnasmata* shows that the ability of a person to present a chreia in a long and short form was one of the fundamental skills a person learned prior to rhetorical training. In his discussion of the basic compositional exercises with the chreia, Theon used a tradition about Epameinondas. First, he exhibited a short form of the chreia:

’Επαμεινώνδας, ἄτεκνος ἀποθνῄσκων, ἔλεγε τοῖς φίλοις, δύο θυγατέρας ἀπέλιπον, τήν τε περὶ Λεύκτραν νίκην, καὶ τὴν περὶ Μαντίνειαν

Epameinondas, as he was dying childless, said to his friends: "I have left two daughters—the victory at Leuctra and the one at Mantineia." (Theon 213,14–17)

Here the chreia is presented in one sentence containing a nominative participial clause and a saying in direct quotation. Then he presented a longer form of the chreia as follows:

’Επαμεινώνδας, ὁ τῶν Θηβαίων στρατηγὸς, ἦν μὲν ἄρα καὶ παρὰ τὴν εἰρήνην ἀνὴρ ἀγαθὸς, συστάντος δὲ τῇ πατρίδι πολέμου πρὸς Λακεδαιμονίους, πολλὰ καὶ λαμπρὰ ἔργα τῆς μεγαλοψυχίας ἐπεδείξατο· βοιωταρχῶν μὲν περὶ Λεύκτρα ἐνίκα τοὺς πολεμίους, στρατευόμενος δὲ ὑπὲρ τῆς πατρίδος καὶ ἀγωνιζόμενος

ἀπέθανεν ἐν Μαντινείᾳ. ἐπεὶ δὲ τρωθεὶς ἐτελεύτα τὸν βίον, ὀλοφυρομένων τῶν
φίλων τά τε ἄλλα, καὶ διότι ἄτεκνος ἀποθνήσκοι, μειδιάσας, παύσασθε, ἔφη, ὦ
φίλοι, κλαίοντες, ἐγὼ γὰρ ὑμῖν ἀθανάτους δύο καταλέλοιπα θυγατέρας, δύο
νίκας τῆς πατρίδος κατὰ Λακεδαιμονίων, τὴν μὲν ἐν Λεύκτροις, τὴν πρεσ-
βυτέραν, νεωτέραν δὲ τὴν ἄρτι μοι γενομένην ἐν Μαντινείᾳ.

Epameinondas, the Theban general, was of course a good man even in time
of peace, but when war broke out between his country and the Lacedaemonians, he performed many brilliant deeds of courage. As a Boeotarch
at Leuctra, he triumphed over the enemy, but while campaigning and fight-
ing for his country, he died at Mantineia. While he was dying of his wounds
and his friends were particularly grief-stricken that he was dying childless,
he smiled and said: "Stop grieving, friends, for I have left you two immortal
daughters: two victories of our country over the Lacedaemonians, the one at
Leuctra, who is the older, and the younger, who has just been born to me at
Mantineia. (Theon 213,17–214,4)

Here the chreia contains a series of clauses paratactically constructed
with the use of δέ and καί. This form is comparable to many synoptic
units in length and compositional approach. Using the approach of
Dibelius or Bultmann, the interpreter would probably assert that the
short form of the unit represents an earlier, purer form of tradition about
Epameinondas, whereas the longer form reveals secondary interests
imposed by a redactor. What this approach misses is an awareness that
both forms are the result of composition according to some person's
interests. And such a procedure governed both oral and written composition of this tradition from its beginnings.[66] The shorter version,
which appears to be earlier and purer, results from a desire to tell the
tradition in the shortest and most poignant form possible. The longer
version, in contrast, includes detail in the description of events and
actions, and incorporates exhortation, personal address, and descriptive
appositional statements in the saying. In this instance, as in many
others, it is highly speculative to assume that the shorter form is earlier
and more reliable, since often the longer forms in a piece of literature
were the source for shorter forms that a teacher or author composed.

If an approach is devoted primarily to a distinction between primary
and secondary tradition, it runs the risk of ignoring features of the
tradition that may be highly informative to the interpreter. The presentation of an epideictic rhetorical situation guides both versions of the
Epameinondas chreia. Epideictic rhetoric features praise and censure as
a means of exhibiting already-held beliefs and attitudes.[67] Rhetorical
situations governed by epideictic rhetoric, therefore, are different from

66. See Kelber, *Oral and Written Gospel*, 14–32.
67. See Lausberg, *Handbuch*, par. 61,3.

those governed by accusation and defense (judicial rhetoric) or by advice and exhortation (deliberative rhetoric). These two versions of a tradition about Epameinondas evoke the rhetorical situation of a funeral oration. In such an oration, the speaker revives and strengthens the beliefs, attitudes, and values of the assembled mourners through a rehearsal of the past activities of the dead person governed by a strategy of praise and censure. The nature of a chreia is that the narrator may move toward the rhetorical goal in both the narrative and the speech, rather than simply through narrative or through speech. In the shorter version, the tradition is told with no enriching details in the narrative and with as few words as possible in the saying. A speaker would probably use such a version in the setting of an overarching rhetorical form in which this unit played a small role. The longer version, in contrast, mentions titles of honor, attributes of character, past events, emotions, and circumstantial actions in the narrative, and it features exhortation, personal address, descriptive adjectives, and comparison (on the basis of age) in the saying. It functions much more like a complete rhetorical form with its own introduction, statement, and conclusion. An analysis of primary and secondary features in the two units, therefore, may not be as informative for understanding the transmission of this kind of tradition as an analysis of the rhetorical dynamics governing the composition of each version. The constraints on the composition operate out of rhetorical dynamics internal to the situation as well as recitations of the tradition external to the composition. Primarily, the author pursues his own rhetorical goals. His degree of submission to an oral or written version available to him depends on many factors, including his own personal inclinations. He develops or alters the rhetorical dynamics of the story and imposes his own style and length on the unit as these dimensions further his rhetorical goals. To the extent that an earlier version fits his purposes, he may use it in that form. But he will not hesitate to compose it according to his own style and rhetorical interests.

We find a similar process at work among the synoptic authors. These authors appear to have composed units as they wished to compose them. In some instances, they only slightly revised a version that existed in another written document, a practice followed by many authors outside the biblical tradition. In other instances, they presented the unit in quite a different form, either following the lead of another written or oral form of the tradition or composing it differently for their own rhetorical purposes. For example, when Mark decided to begin Jesus' Galilean ministry with a summary of Jesus' teaching, he composed a unit in one, paratactically-constructed sentence containing double components in both the narrative and the saying (Mark 1:14–15):

> After John was arrested Jesus came into Galilee
>> *preaching* the gospel of God
>> and *saying*,
>>> "The time *is fulfilled*
>>> and the kingdom of God *is at hand*;
>>>> *repent*
>>>> and *believe* in the gospel."

When Matthew, in contrast, decided to present Jesus' Galilean ministry as a fulfillment of a prophecy of Isaiah, he composed a unit which is integrated through repetition of key words (Matt 4:12–17):

> Now when he heard that John had been arrested,
>> he withdrew into *Galilee*;
> and leaving Nazareth he went and dwelt in Capernaum by the
>> *sea*, in the territory of *Zebulun* and *Naphtali*,
> that what was spoken by the prophet Isaiah might be fulfilled:
> "The land of *Zebulun* and the land of *Naphtali*,
>> toward the *sea*, across the Jordan, *Galilee* of the Gentiles—
>>> the people *who sat in* darkness
>>>> have seen a great *light*,
>>> and for those *who sat in* the region and shadow of death
>>>> *light* has dawned."
> From that time Jesus began to preach, saying,
> "Repent, for the kingdom of heaven is at hand."

In both instances, the authors have composed units according to their compositional style and rhetorical interests. For Mark, an interest in formulating a rich, poignant summary of Jesus' preaching, defined as the "gospel of God," provided the strategy for the composition. For Matthew, in contrast, the desire to ground Jesus' Galilean ministry in a substantive scripture quotation provided the strategy for the composition. Only a brief exhortation to repent, with the imminence of the kingdon of heaven as a rationale for the exhortation, was necessary, since Matthew was setting the stage for an elaborate account of Jesus' message about the kingdom in the Sermon on the Mount (see Matt 5:3).

The compositional strategy exhibited in Luke indicates an interest noticeably different from Mark's and Matthew's interests. Luke also used a scripture quotation from Isaiah. But his strategy was to open Jesus' entire ministry in his home town of Nazareth. Jesus' entry into Galilee, therefore, is simply a preparation for his dramatic reading of the Isaiah passage in the synagogue at Nazareth (Luke 4:18–19). For this purpose, Luke composed a summary of Jesus' ministry in Galilee in the following manner (Luke 4:14–15):

> And Jesus returned in the power of the Spirit into Galilee, and a report

concerning him went out through all the surrounding country. And he taught in their synagogues, being glorified by all.

This unit contains no speech by Jesus, because it is a summary statement leading to the scene in Nazareth where Jesus reads a passage from Isaiah (Luke 4:18–19), comments on the passage (4:21), and presents a series of statements after the people respond to his initial statement (4:23–27).

Luke's rhetorical goals govern his version of Jesus' entry into Galilee (4:14–15), therefore, as fully as Mark's and Matthew's govern their versions. In Luke's case, his composition produces units about both Jesus and John the Baptist that do not contain a pointed announcement, "Repent, for the kingdom of God (heaven) is at hand." Luke approached both John the Baptist's ministry (3:1–20) and Jesus' ministry (4:14–30) by featuring a lengthy scripture quotation that grounded their ministries in ancient testimony (3:4–6; 4:18–19). After the composition had fulfilled this interest, Luke presented a sequence of sayings by both John the Baptist and Jesus that criticized the conventional thought and behavior of the audience as it presented central dimensions of the speaker's attributes and role (3:7–17; 4:21–27). After presenting the teaching, Luke composed a brief series of clauses which told about a sharp conflict that arose as a result of the speaker's activity (3:18–20; 4:28–30). This compositional procedure produced a gradual elaboration of thoughts and actions in a setting of extended composition that does not emphasize exact repetition of previous words or phrases.

In contrast, Matthew's compositional procedure emphasized continuity through exact or nearly exact repetition of words and phrases. We noted above how Matthew's introduction to the Isaiah passage contains key words that appear in the quotation itself, producing the following repetitive chain: Galilee (4:12); sea (4:13); Zebulun and Naphtali (4:13); Zebulun and Naphtali (4:15); sea (4:15); Galilee (4:15). This pattern is supported by the *parallelismus membrorum* in the last part of the scripture quotation that repeats "those who sit in" (ὁ καθήμενος . . . τοῖς καθημένοις) and "light" (φῶς). Matthew established similar continuity in his account of John the Baptist by referring to the Baptist's preaching "in the wilderness" (3:1) prior to its exact repetition in the quotation (3:3). Matthew followed a similar pattern of repetition to establish continuity between the ministries of John the Baptist and Jesus. Instead of varying the statement that introduces the Isaiah quotation as Luke does (3:4; 4:17), Matthew referred in each instance to "that which was spoken through Isaiah the prophet saying" (3:3; 4:14). But Matthew's interest in continuity goes much deeper, influencing his actual formulation of the speech of John the Baptist and Jesus. Following his rhetorical technique of repetition, he produced exact summaries of the teaching of John the

Baptist and Jesus: "Repent, for the kingdom of heaven is at hand" (3:2; 4:17). Matthew's rhetorical interests, therefore, imposed themselves on the direct speech of John the Baptist and Jesus, just as Luke's rhetorical interests influenced his presentation of the speech of John the Baptist and Jesus.

Mark's rhetorical procedures produced yet a third way of presenting the accounts of John the Baptist and Jesus. Using words and phrases he introduced from the beginning verse of his composition—gospel (1:1); Jesus (1:1); God (1:1); John (1:4); preaching (1:4); repentance (1:4); he preached saying (1:7); Jesus came . . . Galilee . . . into (1:9)—he composed a unit that gathered these themes together and produced a rich, succinct summary of Jesus' teaching:

> After the arrest of *John, Jesus came into Galilee preaching the gospel of God* and *saying*: "The time is fulfilled and the kingdom *of God* is at hand; *repent* and believe in *the gospel.*" (Mark 1:14–15)

Using a compositional technique that integrates previous words and phrases into a new account, Mark introduced new themes (the arrest, the fulfillment of time, the imminence of the kingdom, and belief) in a setting of familiar words, phrases, and actions.[68] The end result is significant, because Mark's rhetorical procedures influenced his formulation of the speech of Jesus, making it different both from Matthew's version and from Luke's version.

3. Inaugurating a New Approach

During the past thirty years interpreters have explored many items observed above using redaction criticism and composition criticism. The question is whether it might be possible, using an approach informed by Hellenistic rhetoric, to explore the inner dynamics and logic of such abbreviation, expansion, and elaboration. The authors of this volume think such a possibility is on the horizon. The research recounted above as well as other more recent studies have set the stage. One of these more recent studies appeared in 1962, when William R. Farmer explored five sections in Luke and one in Matthew containing a sequence of units that have a close relation to one another.[69] Much of our discussion above concerned a process of internal expansion or abbreviation of units. The pioneering dimension of Farmer's study lay in its identification of external elaboration in which the addition of related units supplemented, complemented, or extended the thought and action in an initial unit. His

---

68. See Robbins, *Jesus the Teacher*, 29–30.
69. Farmer, "Notes on a Literary and Form-Critical Analysis."

knowledge of exercises performed with the chreia in Hellenistic education enriched and guided his study. As he analyzed Luke 15 and 13:6–9,
he observed that both sections contain an introductory unit followed by
two relatively short sayings that are closely parallel in structure and
highly similar if not identical in meaning. These sayings begin with a
rhetorical question, end with a pronouncement introduced by λέγω ὑμῖν
("I say to you"), and are connected by the conjunction ἤ ("or"). The third
unit is a story that illustrates the point made in the first two sayings.[70]

As Farmer sought an explanation for this structuring of the material,
he posited a pre-Lukan source. This document must have been "created
to meet the needs of the catechetical and homiletical needs of some early
Christian community,"[71] he reasoned, since the final story was meant to
"be viewed in the light of the situation set forth in the introduction to the
literary unit, and in the light of the two parallel sayings of Jesus which
follow the introduction and precede the story."[72] In an attempt to explain
how such a procedure may have developed in the Christian community,
Farmer cited the Hellenistic practice of quoting, paraphrasing, illustrating, and expounding chreiai, a practice that included the use of parables
at the end of units to illustrate chreiai.[73] But, Farmer asserted, the practice of using a parable to illustrate a chreia is also evident in Matt 18:21–
35 and Luke 12:13–21, and possibly Luke 16:14–15, 19–31.[74] Possibly,
therefore, this activity was not limited to one source alone in early
Christianity. This exploratory study stands as a promising beginning for
further analysis. Even though very little work has built upon this exploratory study, other analyses have produced results that support the
fruitfulness of such an approach.

David E. Aune, for example, while describing the characteristics of
units in Plutarch's "Banquet of the Seven Sages," identified and discussed units which he called "wisdom stories" in a manner that encourages further analysis along the lines we have been discussing.[75] A
wisdom story, according to Aune's definition, contains two basic parts.
The first part presents a problem, question, or problematic situation, and
the second part contains a solution presented by a sage.[76] These stories
may contain two additional elements, a false solution (before the real
solution) and an acclamation. Among the wisdom stories in Plutarch's
treatise concerning the seven sages, Aune identified three distinct types:

70. Farmer, "Notes on a Literary and Form-Critical Analysis," 305.
71. Farmer, "Notes on a Literary and Form-Critical Analysis," 306.
72. Farmer, "Notes on a Literary and Form-Critical Analysis," 306.
73. Farmer, "Notes on a Literary and Form-Critical Analysis," 307–8.
74. Farmer, "Notes on a Literary and Form-Critical Analysis," 309.
75. Aune, "Septem Sapientium Convivium."
76. Aune, "Septem Sapientium Convivium," 66.

(1) the gnomic wisdom story, (2) the agonistic wisdom story, and (3) the paradigmatic wisdom story.[77] The two following stories present what Aune called "gnomic wisdom stories." Both stories feature the solicitation of an opinion by a friendly and admiring interlocutor and an instantaneous response by the sage. The first story was composed according to the principle of abbreviation:

> For example, he was told that, when you (Thales) were asked by Molpagoras the Ionian what was the most paradoxical thing you had ever seen, you replied, "A despot that lived to be old." (*Moralia* 147B)

Another story was composed in an elaborated form:

> When this discussion had come to an end, I said that it seemed to me to be only fair that these men should tell us how a house should be managed. "For," said I, "but few persons are in control of kingdoms and states, whereas we all have to do with a hearth and home."
>
> Aesop laughed and said, "Not all, if you include also Anacharsis in our number; for not only has he no home, but he takes an immense pride in being homeless and in using a wagon, after the manner in which they say the sun makes his rounds in a chariot, occupying now one place and now another in the heavens."
>
> "And that, I would have you know," said Anacharsis, "is precisely the reason why he solely or pre-eminently of all the gods is free and independent, and rules over all and is ruled by none, but is king, and holds the reins.
>
> "Only you seem to have no conception of his chariot, how surpassing it is in beauty, and wondrous in size; else you would not, even in jest, have humorously compared it to ours.
>
> "It seems to me, Aesop, that your idea of a home is limited to these protective coverings made of mortar, wood, and tiles, just as if you were to regard a snail's shell, and not the creature itself, as a snail.
>
> "Quite naturally, then, Solon gave you occasion to laugh, because, when he had looked over Croesus's house with its costly furnishings, he did not instantly declare that the owner led a happy and blessed existence therein, for the good reason that he wished to have a look at the good within Croesus rather than at his good surroundings.
>
> "But you, apparently, do not remember your own fox. For the fox, having entered into a contest with the leopard to determine which was the more ingeniously coloured, insisted it was but fair that the judge should note carefully what was within her, for there she said she should show herself more ingenious.
>
> "But you go about, inspecting the works of carpenters and stonemasons, and regarding them as a home, and not the inward and personal possessions of each man, his children, his partner in marriage, his friends, and servants; and though it be in an ant-hill or a bird's nest, yet if these are possessed of

77. Aune, "Septem Sapientium Convivium," 66.

sense and discretion, and the head of the family shares with them all his worldly goods, he dwells in a goodly and a happy home.

"This then," said he, "is my answer to Aesop's insinuation, and my contribution to Diocles." (*Moralia* 154F–155C)

These stories vary decisively in length. Yet, as Aune properly saw, they are related to one another. The first unit features one poignant statement in response to a question. The second unit expands the response of Anacharsis into a sequence of units that present and argue a point of view. The unit could have ended after the initial statement by Anacharsis. Instead, like many synoptic units (e.g., Plucking Grain or Beelzebul Controversy), the initial response begins a sequence of sayings that produce an extended argument. Aune offered no analysis of the rhetorical features in these units beyond the observation of the two essential parts, the possibility of a false solution and an acclamation. But his observation of a similar "gnomic" quality in each unit opens the door for detailed rhetorical analysis of the inner dynamics and logic at work in the story.

Aune also identified stories which he called "agonistic." These stories feature a special test in the first part that is met successfully by the sage in the second part. There is a similar variation in length among these units. Also, in relation to our discussion above, two of the shorter ones contain the ingredients of action-chreiai, as follows:

"The king," said he, "sent to Bias an animal for sacrifice, with instructions to take out and send back to him the worst and best portion of the meat. And our friend's neat and clever solution was, to take out the tongue and send it to him, with the result that he is now manifestly in high repute and esteem." (*Moralia* 146F)

"In your case (Thales), for instance, the king finds much to admire in you, and in particular he was immensely pleased with your method of measuring the pyramid because, without making any ado or asking for any instrument, you simply set your walking-stick upright at the edge of the shadow which the pyramid cast, and two triangles being formed by the intercepting of the sun's rays, you demonstrated that the height of the pyramid bore the same relation to the length of the stick as the one shadow to the other. (*Moralia* 147A)

These stories, exhibiting a sage's successful response to a test, are only two of the five agonistic stories Aune identified in Plutarch's treatise on the seven sages (cf. *Moralia* 150ff.; 152E–153E; 153E–154C). In addition, he found one story which he called "paradigmatic" because the sage exemplifies his theoretical wisdom through practical action or conduct (*Moralia* 148E–149B). This story is quite long, much like the second example of gnomic wisdom stories cited above. Without quoting it here, perhaps we have discussed Aune's analysis sufficiently to show that he was interpreting units similar to those found in the synoptic gospels. Also, we should see that Aune found, in a treatise composed close to the time of the composition of the gospels, both abbreviated units and units in which the response is expanded into a sequence of statements by the sage.

During the same period of time in which Aune was writing his study of Plutarch's "Banquet of the Seven Sages," the Pronouncement Story Group, under the leadership of Robert C. Tannehill, was gathering units of tradition analogous to those studied by Aune.[78] Using Vincent Taylor's term "pronouncement story,"[79] Tannehill defined a pronouncement story as:

> a brief narrative in which the climactic (and often final) element is a pronouncement which is presented as a particular person's response to something said or observed on a particular occasion of the past. There are two main parts of a pronouncement story: the pronouncement and its setting, i.e., the response and the situation provoking that response. The movement from the one to the other is the main development in these brief stories.[80]

This definition is highly similar to Aune's definition of a wisdom story, except for the special emphasis on the movement from the situation to the response. Building on this special emphasis, Tannehill developed a typology of stories based on the rhetorical feature that appeared to be central for the movement from the first to the second part of the story. Without claiming that his typology was comprehensive for all Mediterranean literature during the Hellenistic period, he described six types of stories: description, inquiry, correction, objection, commendation, and quest.[81] The movement in the description is based on initiative by the sage to describe a situation or person, whereas the inquiry features a solicitation of the sage's response by a question. In neither instance does the response evaluate or present a critique of a person or situation. Rather, the response is simply striking, witty, or apt. The correction features a critique of a person or situation, whereas the commendation features a positive response to a situation or person. The objection story features initiative against the sage in the situation, whereas the quest gives a prominent role to a secondary character who seeks from the sage, either successfully or unsuccessfully, an answer or solution important for his well-being in life.

This approach, as well as Aune's, gleaned longer and shorter stories from literature and approached them in an informative manner. The

---

78. Tannehill, *Pronouncement Stories.*
79. Taylor, *Formation of the Gospel Tradition*, 29–30, 63–87.
80. Tannehill, "Introduction: The Pronouncement Story," 1.
81. Tannehill, "Introduction: The Pronouncement Story"; "Varieties"; and "Types and Functions of Apophthegms."

avowed goal of the approach was a rhetorical description of the stories. It produced good initial results[82] and was an important stimulus for the approach in this book.[83]

Now that these others have made these beginnings, the question is whether interpreters can take the analysis to another level of precision. Even more pressing is the issue of whether it is possible to develop a systematic method for analyzing both short and long units containing narrative and speech in Mediterranean literature. The studies in this volume attempt to move toward a systematic approach through a special insight into rhetorical composition that Burton L. Mack observed and developed in the context of the Chreia Project at the Institute for Antiquity and Christianity at Claremont. While analyzing the chreia sections in the rhetorical manuals entitled progymnasmata, he noticed references to an elaboration exercise (ἐργασία) in addition to the set of exercises that included abbreviation and expansion referred to above. After initial exploration, he produced a detailed analysis of Hermogenes' illustration of the elaboration exercise and applied it to Philo's *De Sacrificiis*.[84] In order to use these observations for analysis of synoptic tradition, Mack explains this exercise in chapter two and suggests its importance for analysis of literature during the Hellenistic period.

Chapter two exhibits the strategy of the authors in interpreting sayings and brief stories in the synoptic gospels. Using insights especially from the *Rhetorica ad Herennium* and Hermogenes' *Progymnasmata*, the authors have in view a rhetorical scenario in which a writer or speaker launches an argument with an *introduction* (which usually is a description of a situation); a *chreia* (which presents a proposition, thesis, or statement of the case); and a *rationale* or reason (usually in the form of an authoritative saying). When an *introduction, chreia,* and *rationale* are present, the initial ingredients are present for an argument. An additional rhetorical figure or topic must be present, however, for a complete argument to occur.

According to this scenario, gleaned from the ancient rhetoricians, once the initial ingredients for an argument are present, a complete argument may occur by using a combination of one or more of the following: a *contrary* statement (which clarifies or restates the initial proposition, thesis, or statement of the case); an *analogy* (which introduces another sphere of human life or nature); an *example* (which introduces an authoritative person as a paradigm or model); a *judgment* (which is an authoritative saying or principle gleaned from written documents or well-known sayings) and a *conclusion* (which intensifies

---

82. For a fuller appreciative response to Tannehill's approach, see Schneider, "Jesu Überraschende Antworten," 322.

83. See Robbins, "Classifying" and "Pronouncement Stories."

84. Mack, "Decoding the Scriptures."

and focuses emotions and thoughts through summary, exhortation, and other techniques). The ancient rhetoricians insist, and analysis in this volume shows, that the sequence, as well as the presence or absence, of rhetorical figures may vary. There appears to be a consensus among the rhetoricians, however, that a speaker or writer must use one or more of these figures in order for a complete argument to occur (cf. *Rhet. ad Her.* II.xix.28–30).

Since most of this is new to the field of New Testament interpretation, it may be appropriate to make some additional comments about the ingredients necessary for the occurrence of a complete argument. Perhaps the most important observation is that every discrete move in an argumentative discourse may combine internally a multiple number of rhetorical figures and topics. For example, a *contrary* argument may use *analogy* to make its point and present the decisive *rationale*. Since the goal is to exhibit aspects of internal argumentation in synoptic units, the interpreter should keep an eye on multiple rhetorical features in a unit and maintain an openness and regard for multiple nuances in the argumentation.

In addition, something must be said about *analogy* (παραβολή; *simile*) and *example* (παράδειγμα; *exemplum*). An *analogy* may come from outside the human sphere, for example, from the animal kingdom; or it may be found in arenas of human life and culture, like a "kingdom" or a "house." But an analogy may present a type of person, like a farmer, a shepherd, or a woman who does basic work in a household. When an analogy refers to a type of person, it is a "social example." The social example is not what the rhetoricians meant by *example*; rather a social example is an *analogy*. The term *example* as the rhetoricians used it is meant to refer to a specific person like Demosthenes, Socrates, or Alexander. There is in the synoptic gospels, however, the general example—"whoever," "anyone who," or "the one who." Since sayings that introduce specific examples are rare in the synoptic gospels, but sayings that introduce general examples are numerous, the authors of this volume have had to reflect on the relation of the general example to the specific example in the argumentative discourse of the members of the early Jesus movements. Our studies will explore this circumstance and make some suggestions at the end why this may have occurred.

One additional feature the reader will encounter in the scenario of the complete argument is the *judgment* (κεκριμένον; κρίσις; *iudicatio*). In a legal environment, a judgment is a decision by a judge or jury, and this decision introduces a principle to which people could appeal in the future. In philosophical, educational, or ethical environments of thought, however, judgments can have a much wider reference. A line or two from well-known literature (usually poetry) or a well-known saying in the culture may function as a *judgment* about some aspect of life and its challenges. Some early Christian literature uses quotations or allusions from scripture as judgments, but we will see that sayings of Jesus appear to be the primary resource for judgments about life and its responsibilities in the synoptic tradition. The authors of this volume have reflected on this issue also, and they will make suggestions in the studies concerning the dynamics in the Jesus movements that may have accompanied this phenomenon.

In subsequent chapters the authors analyze various synoptic units from a perspective guided by the major rhetorical phenomena in a complete argument as rhetoricians discuss it. The authors offer these studies as a supplement or complement to other forms of analysis now being pursued in biblical studies. It is inevitable that this approach will challenge some conclusions within the discipline, but it also may help some interpreters to pursue with greater precision and detail some aspects of the synoptic tradition in which they have been interested for some time.

TWO

Elaboration of the Chreia in the Hellenistic School

Burton L. Mack

New Testament scholars now recognize the marked similarity between the pronouncement stories of the synoptic tradition and the Greek form of the anecdote that teachers of literature and rhetoric called a chreia. This similarity has immediate significance for questions of a form-critical nature about the synoptic materials, as chapter one points out. The importance of the discovery of the chreia for synoptic studies, however, is not limited to making more precise the formal definition of these little stories. Functionality can now be clarified, since the Greco-Roman discussions of the chreia occur within educational texts that give us considerable information about the ways in which Greco-Roman writers and teachers understood these small units of speech. This information introduces the chreia's own cultural context, a culture that was highly conscious of its rhetorical and literary orientation. This material also displays a kind of hermeneutical theory about the chreia's effectiveness that must have been broadly shared and understood during this time. This information proves to be of some consequence for approaching the synoptic materials, since it offers an alternative, if not a challenge, to interpretive readings based only upon recent theories of criticism taken from studies of modern literature.

The educational context for discussions of the chreia is available in teachers' handbooks that came to be called *progymnasmata* ("preliminary exercises"). Students who had completed their secondary education used these exercises to prepare for advanced instruction in rhetoric. All of the extant progymnasmata contain a chapter on the chreia, complete with discussions of its formal characteristics, topics for analyzing its rhetorical aspects, and exercises that students were to perform with a chreia in order to learn basic rhetorical skills. These discussions describe the chreia as a fundamental unit of literary and rhetorical composition that contains within itself the principal elements of the speech-situation as defined by classical rhetoric. For instance, the saying (λόγος) of a chreia can be analyzed in terms of rhetorical theory about figures, tropes, and arguments. The attribution of a saying to a specific person is also important since a chreia may be analyzed with respect to the speaker's character (ἦθος), and can function therefore as a rhetorical paradigm in a larger narrative or speech context. These discussions also indicate that the chreia can be expanded internally by amplifying its narrative aspects, or expanded upon (externally) by developing its theme or logic into a literary unit known as an "elaboration" (ἐργασία). Thus the chreia turns out to be a most interesting speech-form, recognized by Greco-Roman educators as a unit of composition with both literary and rhetorical characteristics, and capable of development in larger narrative and discursive formations.

The purpose of this chapter is to introduce New Testament scholars to the discussions of the chreia in the progymnasmata as a preparation for the exegetical exercises on synoptic materials to follow. The first two sections of this chapter contain a summary discussion of the progymnasmata for those unfamiliar with these handbooks. Section 2 gives a fairly comprehensive review of the several kinds of chreia exercises that Theon gives in the earliest extant handbook. Primary emphasis, however, will fall upon one particular kind of chreia exercise that Hermogenes called the elaboration (section 6). The discovery of the significance of this classroom exercise for understanding the compositional and rhetorical aspects of certain kinds of Greco-Roman literature (section 7), including the synoptic gospels (section 8), made possible the exegetical studies in this volume. The discussion of the elaboration exercise will require some information about chreia types (sections 3–4) and the major categories and classifications of the art of rhetorical persuasion (section 5).

The chreia and the elaboration are forms of composition that bridge between rhetorical speech on the one hand and discursive, narrative literature on the other. They are also rhetorical and literary activities that combine interpretation with composition. Only by gaining some grasp of the theory and practice of rhetoric in a culture dominated by literary education is it possible to understand the rhetorical effectiveness for Greco-Roman ears of compositions like the gospels that were crafted in keeping with its rules. That, at any rate, is the thesis that has guided the presentations in this volume.

1. The *Progymnasmata*

Most New Testament scholars will have a general familiarity with the standard handbooks of the rhetorical tradition, called *technai* in keeping with their theoretical classifications and discussions of techniques pertaining to the craft.[1] These handbooks were compendia of rhetorical theory for teachers, rhetors, and other theoreticians advanced in their professions. They assumed readers with a general knowledge of rhetorical practice and thus are slim on preliminary matters having to do with the learning of rhetoric. There is, to be sure, an occasional example of a composed unit of rhetorical speech to illustrate the theory under discussion, but most illustrative references are small snippets taken from works of well-known poets, historians, and rhetors. Thus these handbooks presupposed not only an advanced level of proficiency in rhetorical training, but a high level of general education and readership in the canons of literature as well.[2]

The progymnasmata belong to this tradition of writing handbooks for the practice of rhetoric, but they are structured differently, since they grew out of the pedagogical concern to introduce the study of rhetoric to beginners. They assumed that the student had completed basic literary studies at the secondary level of general education. Building upon these skills, and taking up at first literary material with which the student already was familiar, these handbooks provided the teacher with a graded curriculum of lessons and exercises with which to make the transition from literary studies to rhetoric.

Progymnasmata probably began to appear in the first century B.C.E., although the earliest text extant is from Theon in the first century C.E.[3] In addition to Theon's handbook, there are two others of importance. The first is attributed to Hermogenes (second century),[4] a text that appar-

---

1. The major extant τέχναι of the classical periods are the *Rhetorica ad Alexandrum* of Anaximenes, the *Ars Rhetorica* of Aristotle, the *Rhetorica ad Herennium* of Pseudo-Cicero, several works by Cicero including the *De Inventione*, the *De Optimo Genere Oratorum*, the *Topica*, the *De Oratore*, the *De Partitione Oratoria*, and the *Orator*, Quintilian's *Institutio Oratoria*, and the Τέχνη ʿΡητορικῆς of Hermogenes.

2. The standard secondary studies that summarize classical rhetorical theory are Clark, *Rhetoric*; Kennedy, *Art of Persuasion* and *Classical Rhetoric*; Lausberg, *Handbuch*; Perelman and Olbrechts-Tyteca, *New Rhetoric*; and Volkmann, *Die Rhetorik*.

3. The most recent critical edition of Theon with an English translation is Butts, "*Progymnasmata* of Theon." Earlier critical editions include those of Spengel, *Rhetores Graeci* and Walz, *Rhetores Graeci*. All references in this volume to the Greek text of Theon will be to the page and lines in Walz's edition.

4. The most recent critical edition of Hermogenes is Rabe, *Hermogenis Opera*. All references in this volume to the Greek text of Hermogenes will be to the page and lines in Rabe's edition. Baldwin, *Medieval Rhetoric*, 23–38 contains an English translation of Hermogenes' *Progymnasmata*.

ently came to be preferred in the Latin tradition of rhetoric via its translation by Priscian. The other is that of Aphthonius[5] (fourth century) which became the standard progymnasmata in the Byzantine tradition.

The number of chapters in these progymnasmata range from ten in Theon to fourteen in Aphthonius. Chapters were added and slightly re-arranged in the course of the first few centuries. Taking Theon as an early example, the chapter titles are as follows: fable ($\mu\hat{\nu}\theta_{OS}$), historical episode ($\delta\iota\acute{\eta}\gamma\eta\mu\alpha$), anecdote ($\chi\rho\epsilon\acute{\iota}\alpha$), commonplace ($\tau\acute{o}\pi_{OS}$), praise and blame ($\grave{\epsilon}\gamma\kappa\acute{\omega}\mu\iota_{O\nu}$, $\psi\acute{o}\gamma_{OS}$), comparison ($\sigma\acute{\nu}\gamma\kappa\rho\iota\sigma\iota_{S}$), speech-in-character ($\pi\rho_{O}\sigma\omega\pi_{O}\pi_{O}\iota\ddot{\iota}\alpha$), description ($\grave{\epsilon}\kappa\phi\rho\alpha\sigma\iota_{S}$), thesis ($\theta\acute{\epsilon}\sigma\iota_{S}$), and introduction of a law ($\nu\acute{o}\mu_{OS}$). The titles show that each chapter contains a discussion of a particular form of composition. The typical chapter begins with a definition of the speech-form that points to essential characteristics in comparison and contrast with other closely related forms. Then follows a loosely diairetic schema of the form's major types. Examples may be given, as well as suggestions to the teacher for constructing one's own anthology of good examples from the canons of literature and rhetoric. With the speech-form in place, the discussion then turns to the classroom exercises to be performed in each case. A closer look at the kinds of exercises appropriate to the chreia occurs in section 2.

Several observations should be made about the list of chapters in the progymnasmata as a whole. The first is that the earlier chapters work with small units of popular and literary material not technically rhetor-ical. This orientation is in keeping with the design of the curriculum which built upon the secondary level of education where instruction in reading, writing, and grammar used these same literary forms. But it also reflects the integration of rhetoric with literary studies that was taking place in the Greco-Roman period in general. Rhetorical theory, it was found, could be used to analyze and interpret literary material, and the methods for doing this were taught in the schools. This fact may prove to be of some significance for exploring what might be called a rhetorical hermeneutic of the gospel materials. It is also the case that certain kinds of literary activity during our period followed rhetorical as well as liter-ary rules of composition (see section 7 below).

The second observation is that the collection ranges from small liter-ary units, through sub-units of the rhetorical speech, to exercises having to do with complete speech forms. This range indicates that graded sequencing was involved in the organization of the material. The move from more literary to more specifically rhetorical forms of composition is

---

5. The most recent critical edition of Aphthonius is Rabe, *Aphthonii Progym-nasmata*. All references in this volume to Aphthonius will be to the page and lines in Rabe's edition. Nadeau, "Progymnasmata," contains an English translation of Aphthonius.

one principle of sequencing. Another, not obvious from the chapter titles themselves, was the progression from more mimetic and analytical exercises to those that required compositional skills. This principle of grading comes to light in the kinds of exercises suggested for each speech form, as well as in the general sequencing from smaller and easier speech forms to larger and more complex ones. It may have been the case, in fact, that the handbook was graded in two ways. The sequence of speech types (chapters) would have been one. The other may have been given with the kinds of exercises proposed. Theon (216,8–10), for example, makes the suggestion that advanced students could return to the chreia, an early analytic exercise, in order now to compose a thesis, one of the more difficult exercises in the curriculum (see section 2 below).

A third observation about the progymnasmata as a whole is also important. Analyzing the several chapters, and guided by the introductory chapter that Theon gives, the pedagogical strategy becomes clear. These graded lessons allowed for learning through memorization, imitation, and practice as an introduction to the whole system of rhetorical theory and technique. Basic skills in the analysis of issues (*quaestio*; στάσις), the building of a persuasive case (*inventio*), practice in composing material appropriate to the various parts of the speech (*prooemium, narratio, argumentatio, conclusio*), exercises in argumentation (κατασκευή) and rebuttal (ἀνασκευή), considerations of style (including *figura*), diction (λέξις), and delivery—all would be engaged. And each of the three major speech types with their characteristic outlines and objectives would eventually be proposed as assignments for composition and delivery. The deliberative speech, for example, appears as the declamation of a thesis and the introduction of legislation. The judicial speech takes its classroom form as the commonplace, and the epideictic speech comes clothed as an encomium. This pedagogy is crucial for understanding the treatment of the chreia in this curriculum. Rhetorical purpose governed every exercise, even the more simple ones such as learning to paraphrase and amplify a stock anecdote: students were to learn the means by which speech was effective or persuasive.

2. Exercises on the Chreia in Theon

In the extant manuscripts, Theon's chapter on the chreia comes in third place, following those on the fable and the narrative. This order is in keeping with the standard outlines already established by the time of Hermogenes and Aphthonius. But in Theon's introduction to the *Progymnasmata* (157,3–5) he lists the chreia in first place and gives reasons for beginning the curriculum with it. The discussion indicates that during this period first century teachers used the chreia to introduce the basic notions and skills necessary for the practice of rhetoric. The chreia functioned in this way because it had to do with a particular case in which a specific person was challenged to respond to a certain situation. The saying or action of that person could therefore be viewed rhetorically. It was an address to, or an assessment of, or a judgment upon the situation. Its way with words was open for analysis. The chreia could be seen, in other words, as a mini-speech situation complete with speaker, speech, and audience, and evaluated as to its use of rhetorical forms of argumentation. It could also be viewed as a maxim, or a saying from an approved authority, or as an example—all customary forms of argumentation or "proofs" ($\pi i \sigma \tau \epsilon \iota s$; $\dot{\epsilon} \pi \iota \chi \epsilon \iota \rho \dot{\eta} \mu \alpha \tau \alpha$) when taken up into a larger speech context. Thus Theon displays a wide variety of exercises on the chreia, all of which had value for training in rhetorical skills.

These exercises Theon (210,3–6) lists as follows: (1) *Recitation* ($\dot{\alpha} \pi \alpha \gamma$-$\gamma \epsilon \lambda i \alpha$), (2) *Inflection* ($\kappa \lambda i \sigma \iota s$), (3) *Commentary* ($\dot{\epsilon} \pi \iota \phi \omega \nu \epsilon \hat{\iota} \nu$), (4) *Critique* ($\dot{\alpha} \nu \tau \iota \lambda \dot{\epsilon} \gamma \epsilon \iota \nu$), (5) *Expansion* ($\dot{\epsilon} \pi \epsilon \kappa \tau \epsilon i \nu \epsilon \iota \nu$), (6) *Abbreviation* ($\sigma \upsilon \sigma \tau \dot{\epsilon} \lambda \lambda \epsilon \iota \nu$), (7) *Refutation* ($\dot{\alpha} \nu \alpha \sigma \kappa \epsilon \upsilon \dot{\eta}$), and (8) Confirmation ($\kappa \alpha \tau \alpha \sigma \kappa \epsilon \upsilon \dot{\eta}$). The list consists of eight exercises that may, however, be reduced to four sets of complementary pairs. Of these four sets, two have to do generally with basic skills in style and delivery (recitation/inflection; expansion/abbreviation), and two sets have to do with basic skills in analysis and argumentation (commentary/critique; refutation/confirmation). The first pair (recitation/inflection) appears at first glance merely to repeat customary exercises in memorization and grammar practiced at the level of general secondary education. But they are quite appropriate as well for training in rhetoric where skills in delivery were telling. Theon (210,7–9) emphasizes that the recitation should aim at clarity—a mark of good delivery frequently mentioned in technical discussions on style. He suggests that the student could freely paraphrase the chreia if that would be helpful—another commonly used stylistic skill. Theon illustrates the inflections exercise at some length (210,9–212,12). This exercise amounts to a series of recitations that (1) conjugate the main verbs by changing the number of the persons referred to in the chreia, and that (2) decline the proper nouns into the five cases by making changes in the phrasing that introduces the chreia. The ability to do inflections well was a stylistic skill needed for inserting bits of traditional material into a longer speech context with its demands upon stylistic variations.

The second pair of exercises (expansion/abbreviation) are also skills related to composition and style. If the longer speech-context demanded it, a brief chreia might thus be expanded by adding descriptive details of the circumstance, or explaining in more detail who the characters were, or even expanding the dialogue into a little story with dramatic traits of its own. But if the larger speech-context required a pointed chreia, one also had to be able to reduce longer stories (ἀπομνημονεύματα) in order to make that point. (See Theon 213,11–214,4.)

Classroom practice was probably quite demanding, both for teacher and students. The teacher was responsible for supplying appropriate materials and knowing how they might best lend themselves to various exercises. He also had to be capable of giving a precise and technical critique of student performance. The instructor would select the chreia for a certain exercise and call upon a student to perform. Correction, explanation, and performance by the teacher might intervene. Then another chreia and another student, and so forth. Memorization and repetition were basic, and the codes of style were firm. Students achieved the skills necessary to apply the prescribed techniques to these small bits of speech material through long and difficult practice.

The first exercises in argumentation required an even more difficult and demanding set of skills. In order to perform here, the student needed to have some knowledge of the major types of rhetorical arguments or proofs.[6] Argumentation theory was extremely complex, and facility in rhetorical logic required a very long and detailed study. First steps toward gaining such facility involved only the more obvious, general, and single ways of making a telling point. Theon's lists of arguments, for instance, for use in the first exercises on the chreia, are brief composites of various kinds of proofs. (See Theon 214,4–7.) There was also a tendency to include the most general and easily recognized proofs capable of illustrating the several technical classifications. The student was provided only with a basic introduction to the main types of proof and their use in constructing an argumentation. The emphasis in the chreia exercises, moreover, seems to have been at first inductive and analytical. Focusing on a chreia proposed by the teacher, the student would run down the list of proofs showing whether the speaker in the chreia had made use of them and how well.

For the third pair of exercises (commentary/critique), Theon (212,11–213,2) suggests looking at a chreia to see whether its statement is true (ἀληθής), honorable (καλόν), and expedient (συμφέρον), and whether a similar saying by some other person of distinction has expressed its thought. This list of four items appears at first glance to be innocent enough, a harmless suggestion about how to begin a series of reflections upon the meaning of a chreia's saying. But those acquainted with the rhetorical handbooks will know that, in fact, this list is deliberately selective and highly structured. It significantly combines representative categories from two major types of persuasion or argumentation.

6. Discussions of the major types of rhetorical proofs were available to teachers in the advanced handbooks on rhetorical theory. For the beginning student, various lists were probably copied out, judging from the itemized discussions given in the progymnasmata. The various types of rhetorical proof are discussed in section 5.

The first type carried the designation "final categories" (τελικὰ κεφάλαια), and referred to a set of very general, conventional values which was of concern to every rhetorical speech. According to Aristotle (*Rhet.* I.iii.5), the judicial speech as a whole was an argumentation determined ultimately by the category of "what was right" (δίκαιον); the deliberative speech by "the expedient" (συμφέρον); and the epideictic speech by "the honorable" (καλόν). The idea was that persuasion finally rested upon the correlation between the construction that the speaker put upon a particular case and those general cultural codes of conduct and value shared by the audience. The cultural codes that concerned rhetoric ranged from actual legal codes, through accepted social conventions, to popular ethical philosophical ideals. The rhetors knew that and reduced the theory of the "final court of appeal" to shorthand lists of the "final categories" which referred to these codes and values. In the ancient handbooks, the standard listings of these final categories include anywhere from three to eight items.[7] Anaximenes' (*Rhet. ad Alex.* I.1421b,21–1422b,12) list of the eight categories of persuasion is as follows: that which is right (δίκαιον), lawful (νόμιμον), expedient (συμφέρον), honorable (καλόν), pleasant (ἡδύς), easy (ῥάδιον), feasible (δυνατόν), and necessary (ἀναγκαῖον). In the course of rhetorical tradition the final categories came to be associated primarily with the deliberative speech as a way to codify its particularly challenging objectives, and thus to control theory about it. With the judicial and epideictic speeches, there were other ways to structure a theory of persuasion, but, of course, even with these speeches the final categories continued to apply. In cases where a conflict of categories occurred, there were ways to rank them, or otherwise adjudicate the tension. What Theon did, then, was to supply the student with a list of the three most general categories belonging to rhetorical theory of persuasion. He substituted "true" for "right" because he treats the chreia as a maxim or philosophical judgment, not as a judicial judgment.

To the three final categories Theon added an example of another type of rhetorical proof. The citation of an ancient authority was known as a "witness" (μαρτυρία, κρίσις) or "previous judgment" (κεκριμένον), and belonged to a class of arguments (ἐπιχειρήματα) used to support a position or thesis.[8] It is important to note in this connection that the citation of authority frequently occurs at the end of lists of supporting arguments. Some of these listings are intentionally sequential, so that Theon may have had a concluding and therefore conclusive argument in mind. In a judicial speech the citation of authority referred most naturally to precedent decisions. But in a deliberative speech, or a thesis,

---

7. Lausberg, *Handbuch*, par. 375.
8. See section 5 for a review of several lists of these supporting arguments.

the authority was more properly taken from the canons of ethical and philosophical literature. We use the term judgment to refer to all arguments of this type.

Students could easily memorize the list of four categories. But their application to a given chreia, whether to support or criticize it, required considerable ingenuity. The worked-out example Theon gives for the commentary on a saying of Euripides, "that the mind of each of us is a god,"[9] illustrates just how difficult this exercise was. Not only must the pupil give reasons to show how the saying was true, expedient, and honorable. It was also necessary to find a theme that could unite all of the considerations together in a small paragraph. This commentary can be reconstructed from Theon's discussion of the exercise and the illustrations given for each of the four items. This reconstructed paragraph reads as follows (Theon 212,16–213,2):

> Euripides the poet said that the mind of each of us is a god.
>
> For the mind in each of us is *truly* (ὄντως) a god, encouraging us toward things that are *advantageous* (συμφέρον) and keeping us away from things that are injurious.
>
> For it is *noble* (καλόν) that each considers god not to reside in gold and silver but in himself.
>
> So that, by supposing that punishment is not far distant, we might not have much tolerance for wrong doing.
>> 'For the mind of earthly men is like the day
>> Which the father of men and gods sends them' (*Od* 18.136–7).

The italics show how Theon used the categories. He also used the theme of the god within as a conscience to string the statements together. Because this exercise combines analytical operations with invention or composition, and treats the chreia as a thesis to be supported, it is clearly a precursor of the more elaborate ἐργασία found in Hermogenes. (See sections 4 and 5.)

For the exercises in refutation/confirmation, Theon (214,4–7) provides a much larger list of nine items that now combine dictional, logical, and ethical categories. Since the only list he gives is for the refutation, it is therefore composed of "fallacies." For the confirmation exercise, the list would contain the "opposites" of these "fallacies." The dictional are: (1) obscure (ἀσαφόν), (2) loquacious (πλεονάζον), (3) elliptical (ἐλλεῖπον). The logical are: (4) impossible (ἀδύνατον), (5) implausible (ἀπίθανον), and (6) false (ψεῦδος). The ethical are: (7) unsuitable (ἀσύμφορον), (8) useless (ἄχρηστον), and (9) shameful (αἰσχρόν). From the discussion that follows, it is clear that the teacher expected the student to have this list clearly in mind when presented with a chreia. The student's task was to run down the list, analyzing the chreia with each in

---

9. Nauck, *Tragicorum*, frag. 1018 of Euripides.

mind, and say whether and how the category might apply. The exercise is purely analytical and the procedure *ad seriatim*. There is no indication here that one was to construct a coherent paragraph by using this list of topics.

Theon does suggest at the end of the chapter on the chreia (216,8–10) that advanced students might take a chreia as a thesis and develop it as a thesis exercise. And later on in the chapter on the thesis (243,13–17), Theon indicates that not only chreiai, but maxims, proverbs, apophthegms, stories (ἰστορίαι), and encomia may be used in this way. Theon (244,19–246,9) also gives a very long list of twenty-three topics which includes (1) a full set of the final categories, (2) a fairly full set of traditional items known as supporting arguments, plus (3) random selections from other, less organized, frequently lengthy lists of argumentative topoi and devices found in the handbooks on rhetorical theory and technique. Clearly, then, fuller lists of ever more specialized and intricate categories for inventing arguments confronted the more advanced student who was now expected to come up with a sizable number of telling arguments to support the chreia as the statement of a thesis.

The time must have come for a student to present a full and polished speech in support of a thesis. All of the necessary ingredients for the construction of a coherent and comprehensive argumentation are there in the list of twenty-three topics. But Theon does not, either in his discussion or in his illustrations of the exercise, say that this was to happen, or what such a chreia-thesis-speech might have looked like. At the end of the chreia chapter (215,10–15), however, he does mention that, if the chreia is used as a thesis, there should be an appropriate "introduction" (προοίμιον), after which the chreia itself should be set forth, followed by "the arguments in order" (τάξις), and the use of elaborations, digressions, and character delineations as opportunity presented itself. This notice contains references to most of the major parts of what was known as a "complete argumentation" (see section 5 below), and it presents them in a sequence that correlates rather closely with the standard outline. Thus, it is very close to the outline for the elaboration of the chreia in Hermogenes.

The evidence from Theon, then, is that the chreia was found to be helpful for a wide range of preliminary exercises in basic rhetorical skills, graded, as it appears, from very elementary practices to quite advanced compositions. Teachers of rhetoric viewed the saying primarily as a rhetorical statement itself that they could subject to analysis and critique in keeping with rhetorical theory. There is a decided emphasis upon refutation of chreiai in Theon, even though the list of exercises does strike an even balance between negative and positive analyses. For the most part, the material gives the impression of ad hoc and *ad seriatim* procedures, chreiai tossed up one after the other for analysis as to their rhetoricity in keeping with the prescribed topics and categories of persuasion. But in the case of the commentary, and in the chapter on the thesis, the discussions suggest that teachers and students also used chreiai as statements for which several supporting arguments were to be invented. And at the end of the chreia chapter it seems that a speech-outline is in the making. The discussion in section 5 below pursues further the significance of this speech-outline.

3. The Preference for Approved Chreiai

Before turning to Hermogenes, however, there is an important matter to consider regarding Theon's preference for "approved" chreiai. The commentary, he says, "is possible for those who approve (ἀποδέχεσθαι) of what has been said properly" (οἰκείως; 212,12–13). In the thesis chapter (243,16), he cautions that the sayings (ἀποφθέγματα) appropriate for theses are those that are "helpful" (χρήσιμος); those appropriate for citation as supporting arguments are from "approved" persons (δεδοκιμασμένοι; 212,15). The exercise in critique cannot use some chreiai, because "many have been expressed properly and faultlessly"; and some cannot be praised at all, because they involve "outright absurdity" (213,8–11).

The issue here is quite complex. Theon is using at least two criteria to make distinctions between or among types of chreiai. One criterion is the basis upon which approval is granted; the other has to do with a chreia's appropriateness for certain kinds of exercises. Both criteria apparently involve judgments which assign approved chreiai to exercises in commentary (ἐπιφωνεῖν), confirmation (κατασκευή), and thesis development. The impression is given that other chreiai, not acceptable for these exercises, may still be used for exercises in analysis, critique (ἀντιλογία), and refutation (ἀνασκευή). This division of chreiai is important and needs further exploration. The first step is to look at a first-century set of notions that explains why only approved chreiai should be used for confirmation. Then the next task is to ask about the nature of other chreiai that might be appropriate for analysis and critique, but not for confirmation.

That maxims and citations are to be taken from approved authorities is a dictum belonging to the tradition of rhetorical theory. Anaximenes (*Rhet. ad Alex.* I,1422a,27) states specifically, for instance, that "previous judgments" (κεκριμένα) should be cited from "men of repute" (ἄνθρωποι ἔνδοξοι). This advice makes good sense, given the general theory of rhetorical persuasion discussed above, and the requirement that arguments appeal to generally accepted canons and conventions. But in Theon this dictum takes on a much more decidedly moralistic tone than was ever intended in the earlier traditions. In the first section of the chreia-chapter (202,1–2 and 8–10) Theon makes the distinction between the chreia that is not always "useful for life" (βιωφελές) and maxims and memorable accounts (γνῶμαι; ἀπομνημονεύματα) that are. There are also other curious remarks throughout the chapter that seem to indicate that Theon considered some chreiai "wholesome," and therefore appropriate for praise and confirmation. In the introductory chapter to the *Progymnasmata* as a whole (148,12–15), moreover, Theon makes the following very revealing statement: "Indeed, the chreia-exercise (γυμνασία) produces (ἐργάζεται) not only a certain facility with words (δύναμις λόγων), but a good character (χρηστὸν ἦθος) as well, if we work with apophthegms of the sages." This statement is a clue to a first century discussion and concern about the influence of literature upon the student-reader. Further discussion will clarify the basis upon which some chreiai were judged as helpful, and their authors approved.

Seneca's concern for ethics is well known, and his statements about the effectiveness of moral maxims are provocative. According to Seneca, a person achieves virtue by imitating models. One should select a model from among men of repute, and cultivate "conversation" (*conversatio*) with their words (Seneca, *Ep*. 11,8). "The frequent hearing of them little by little sinks into the heart and acquires the force of precepts" (*Ep*. 94,40). The mark of a model is that his deeds match his words, that his life is lived in accordance with his words (*Ep*. 52,8). For Seneca, the model of virtue par excellence was Socrates, founder of ethical philosophy, speaker of precepts, who lived his life in keeping with his teaching.[10]

Seneca's advice about taking care in the selection of one's models indicates the first-century concern for ethical guidance that defined the larger arena of discourse for Theon's notion of approved chreiai. The way in which Seneca formulates his advice, moreover, opens this discourse up as one in which much more than discrimination about the ethical quality of philosophers and their maxims is at stake. The words of the sages, according to Seneca, are effective in the formation of the character of the reader who holds conversation with them. This notion is closely related to the theory of μίμησις ("imitation") as the rhetors developed it. It is a notion that appears in much of the literature of the period. Theon refers to it in a statement in his Introduction (151,11–152,1) on the importance of choosing material for the exercise in reading (ἀνάγνωσις): "Since the soul is formed by noble examples (καλὰ παραδείγματα), we should imitate (μιμήσεσθαι) just the finest ones." Μίμησις ("imitation") begins with reading. The notion that reading affects the reader, and that the teacher should take care not to allow

10. Döring, *Exemplum Socratis*, 18–42.

students to regard the speeches of unwholesome characters (e.g., in Homer) as worthy of imitation, govern the literature of the time on teaching poetry to youth. The Pseudo-Plutarchian treatise on this theme offers a good example. This author used literary criticism to demonstrate from the text that the poets had not intended for imitation the words and deeds of unacceptable characters. But, should this literary criticism fail to show why that must be so, the teacher must not fail to use the last recourse, namely outright censure of the unacceptable models. Coming to expression here is a first century fascination with, and fear of, the power of words to form character.

This notion about the effective power of speech to form character is a combination of two insights traditional to rhetorical theory and their application to ethical pedagogy in the early Roman period. The first insight had to do with the requirement that a speaker establish his character as trustworthy in the first few moments of the speech in order to gain the ear and respect of the audience. Only if the audience was convinced that the speaker had a right to speak (ἦθος) could that speaker then move ahead into issues requiring argumentation (λόγος) and conclude with appeals to agree with him (πάθος). The problem was that if the speaker were not already known to the audience, how could he win from them this right to speak (ἦθος)? The answer was that he could achieve it by the way in which he began to speak, i.e., by careful choice of words and style for entry into the speech situation. Ἦθος, then, could be established through λόγος itself.[11]

As rhetorical theory came to be applied to literary criticism, the scholars of antiquity apparently transferred this dictum about λόγος and ἦθος from the oral speech situation to the speeches and sayings of speakers encountered in literature. Now they began to think that the words of a speaker encountered in written form, or the works of an author, revealed the author's character. In addition to the already quoted citations from Seneca, there is considerable evidence for this notion. Mary Lefkowitz has demonstrated that it was a fundamental assumption enabling the writing of biographies of the poets, for whom, of course, only their works were in hand.[12] And Plutarch offers some fine statements to the effect that the characters of great men are revealed even more clearly in their sayings than in their deeds.[13] This is certainly an exaggeration. The traditional view about deeds revealing character had not been given up, least of all by Plutarch. But the shift from warriors and their deeds to sages and their sayings, a shift that occurred in the fifth and fourth centuries, redefining the ideal of virtue (ἀρετή), is

---

11. Cf. Aristotle, *Rhet.* I.ii.3–4; II.i–ii.
12. Lefkowitz, "The Poet as Hero."
13. Plutarch, *Vita Alex.* 2.

surely at work here, and is not to be discounted lightly. The study of literature now dominates *paideia*, and the theory of rhetoric now informs the study of literature. Psychologized as *conversatio* in Seneca, a literary encounter with the sayings of great men not only reveals their character, but also produces a like character in the reader as well. This, of course, sets the stage for the second rhetorical insight informing this general notion about the effectiveness of speech. It is the theory of μίμησις.

The idea of μίμησις is firmly grounded in rhetorical theory and intends, at first, merely to express the pedagogical effectiveness of learning by copying. The written models set the example and formed the patterns of style which the student learned to follow. Therefore it was necessary to select good examples. The teachers of rhetoric, of course, understood reading itself to be mimetic, as we have seen; but the proper provenance of μίμησις was always in the process of learning both to read and to write by copying. By a series of subtle shifts that led from rote copying-out of letters and sentences (sometimes literally inscribed in the students' tablets), through memorization, nuanced recitation, and paraphrasing, to "original" compositions, imitation eventually produced "inventive" rhetors.

Combined with the theory of λόγος and ἦθος, the mimetic approach to rhetorical composition took some interesting turns. The exercise called speech-in-character (ἠθοποιΐα; προσωποποιΐα) reveals these turns most clearly. This skill was extremely important to rhetorical training, given the practice of writing speeches for others to give, and the notion of advocacy as representing the speech of the defendant himself. It consisted of composing a speech in keeping with the character assumed (ἠθοποιΐα), or even of the creation of a character by means of the kind of speech attributed to it (προσωποποιΐα). In order to do it well, according to rhetorical theory, one had to be able to "imitate the character" (Hermogenes, 20,7). Μίμησις now has shifted from an imitation of the style of the λόγος, to include impersonation of the character of the assumed speaker as well. Quintilian explains how that was to be done:

> Even in the schools it is desireable that the student should be moved by his theme, and should imagine it to be true. . . . Suppose we are impersonating an orphan, a shipwrecked man, or one in grave peril. What profit is there in assuming such a role unless we also assume the emotions which it involves? (*Inst. Or.* II.vii.2–4)

By yet another displacement, occasioned by the moralistic concerns of the time, and rationalized in terms of ethical psychology, imitation became not only a matter of learning style and impersonation, but of assuming "character" in some fundamental way as well. Seneca says that he does not know how that happens in *conversatio* with the sages, but that it happens he does know (*Ep.* 94.40–41).

4. The Cynic Chreia

We have now explored the moralistic concerns and rhetorical-literary theories which determined that only helpful chreiai be chosen for exercises in confirmation. Theon's choice of a religious-philosophical maxim from Euripides for his example of a commentary, and his selection of the proposition "That a sage should participate in government" for his example in the thesis chapter, clearly reflect these interests. We are on the way to the second sophistic and the cultural domestication of rhetoric. With Hermogenes, as we shall see, the chreia to be elaborated is a moralistic saying of Isocrates about education. From that point on, through Libanius, Aphthonius, and into the medieval traditions, all the handbooks prefer chreiai containing ethical maxims, since for these later contexts rhetoric's function was primarily enculturating.

What, then, are we to make of the many other examples of the chreia in Theon that are not moralistic? What of those chreiai that are examples of clever, terse, and telling rejoinders by speakers who set a situation on its ears? This kind of anecdote is actually predominant in Theon's chapter, so much so that one is taken by surprise to see that Euripides' rather banal pronouncement is suggested for the commentary. As a chreia it does fit the minimalist definition, i.e., a maxim attributed to a particular person. But it does not have the flavor of most of the many other chreiai Theon cites as examples of the type.

At this point we are up against the very difficult question of the definition and possible typology of the chreia as a literary form. The term itself means "useful," and apparently was a designation crafted by the teachers of rhetoric to indicate a kind of literary material useful for instructional purpose in rhetoric. But like most technical terms in rhetoric, the shorthand designation is not enough. Definition, classification, and example are necessary in order to know what was intended. This information is available in the progymnasmata, but, as it turns out, it hardly satisfies modern form-critical needs. The definitions of the chreia are actually congeries of descriptive, normative, and genre-critical observations that apparently served several needs at once. One was simply the need for a teacher to recognize a certain form when it was encountered in the reading of literature in order to collect a set for use in the classroom. Another was to indicate aspects of a form which determined its usefulness for classroom exercises. Yet another was to indicate the rhetorical characteristics of the form or the place it might be given in a larger speech-context.

Theon worked out his definition in terms of certain telling distinctions between chreia and maxim on the one hand (a maxim becomes a chreia when it is attributed to a specific person), and chreia and ἀπομνημόνευμα ("memoir") on the other (a chreia is more concise and highlights the aspect of attribution, i.e., what we have called characterization). These distinctions give only a sliding scale from maxim to memorable account within which to place the chreia, hardly adequate for a precise form-critical definition. This may not have been enough even for first century teachers, supposing they were as concerned about generic precision as we are and that they understood the definitions to have only form-critical purpose. But following the introductory section on definition, classification systems occur, and with them the examples. Reading carefully, and looking closely at the examples, the chreia as an object does begin to take recognizable shape.

Turning, then, as teachers would have done, to the literature of the period in order to collect a set of chreiai, our task would be to find material (1) falling within the definitional constraints, (2) analogous to the examples already given, and (3) demonstrating the rhetorical features which determined the chreia's usefulness for the exercises in the first place. This task is manageable. The chreia definition points to actual anecdotes observable in the living tradition of literature.

Working through Diogenes Laertius, for instance, one can distinguish chreiai in most cases from (1) brief accounts of important circumstances and events in the life of the person, (2) brief accounts of a person's typical behavior, characteristics, virtues, nicknames, and so forth, (3) lists of precepts or wise advice attributed to the person, as well as (4) lists of what Diogenes called a person's views ($\delta\delta\xi\alpha\iota$) or doctrines ($\delta\delta\gamma\mu\alpha\tau\alpha$) that cover a wide variety of philosophical and ethical matters. What we are left with for the most part is a large number of brief accounts in which some occasional encounter results in a fresh aphoristic response, or in some suggestive action on the part of the subject of the story. These anecdotes belong to the type Theon used predominantly as examples throughout the chreia chapter. They mention the person. They frequently indicate the occasion by means of a participial construction. They give the action or the statement-response with a finite verb in a secondary tense, although the saying may occur either in direct or indirect discourse. A random example from stories of this type about Diogenes the Cynic illustrates the basic form: "Diogenes, on being asked what was the right time to marry, replied, 'For a young man, not yet; for an old man never at all'" (Diog. Laer. 6.54). Frequently the setting requires description, the import of the question some bit of clarification, the response an additional line or two. But there is great economy always. And the wit and cleverness of the dissimulating response is clearly the point of the story. Theon may actually refer to this "pointedness" of the response in his definition: "The chreia is a concise saying or action (with pointedness) attributed (with aptness) to some specific person . . ." (201,16–17). The phrase $\mu\epsilon\tau'$ $\epsilon\dot{\upsilon}\sigma\tau o\chi\acute{\iota}\alpha s$ is syntactically ambiguous as the two alternative readings in parentheses indicate. If it refers to the response as "sharp" or "well-aimed," there can be little doubt about the literary material in view: that class of anecdotes that have as their chief characteristic a skillful and surprising rejoinder to a challenging encounter or situation.

This characteristic is typical of anecdotes attributed to philosophers of the Cyrenaic and Cynic schools. Noticing this fact, Von Fritz proposed that the chreia originated in the rough and tumble of Cynic debate and practice in the late fourth century B.C.E.[14] He argued that the form of the anecdote was most compatible with Cynic style and that the typical themes reflected Cynic views. It is not the case, of course, that anecdotes of this type deal only with Cynics. The clever rejoinder was something of an ideal and delight for Greeks in general. There is a remarkable class of chreiai with Spartan subjects and themes. And the Aristotelian tradition of writing biographies (βίοι) apparently used, and possibly expanded, the application of anecdotal material to philosophers of all types as a way to characterize them and make distinctions among their schools with their different life-styles. Nevertheless, it is also the case that Theon as well as Diogenes Laertius attribute the majority of examples of this type of anecdote to Cynics, Cyrenaics, and others associated with what might be understood loosely as the Socratic-sophistic tradition and debate.

This being the case, it is possible to talk about a Cynic chreia that, even if it turns out not to define the chreia per se, certainly constituted a sizeable class. It is important to see that chreiai of this class are quite different from those that contain a moral maxim attributed to a philosopher, poet, or sage of repute. The two classes differ from one another as markedly as σοφία differs from μῆτις, a distinction documented by Detienne and Vernant.[15] Σοφία is the kind of wisdom appropriate to the orders of perceived reality understood as stable systems; μῆτις is the kind of wisdom appropriate to the contingent and threatening situations of life where survival depends upon a clever sagacity. It is exactly this latter kind of skill that the Cynic anecdote demonstrates. A look at an example of a Cynic chreia will show more clearly how this crafty wisdom works. It is important to our discussion of Theon and Hermogenes. It will also be important to our discussion of chreiai in the synoptic tradition.

We shall look at the anecdote about Demonax in Lucian that Tannehill uses as an example of a correction story.[16] We do this to highlight the issue of edifying intent versus the display of μῆτις in Cynic chreiai. The story goes as follows:

14. K. von Fritz, "Zusatz: Chreia," cited in Horna, "Gnome," 87–89.
15. Detienne and Vernant, *Cunning Intelligence*.
16. Tannehill, "Introduction: The Pronouncement Story," 7.

When one of his students said: "Demonax, let's go to the Asclepium and pray for my son," he replied: "You must think Asclepius very deaf, that he can't hear our prayers from where we are!" (Lucian, *Demonax* 27)

Tannehill does not discuss this story as such, but offers it as an example of the correction story which he does discuss. By definition:

". . . someone has taken a position as to what is right or expedient, and the responder corrects that position. Thus two attitudes are contrasted . . . [T]he attitude (of the responder) is being recommended in contrast to the attitude being corrected. . . . This also opens up a choice for the reader, which can lead to a shift of attitudes and priorities."[17]

If the story about Demonax is read in this way, i.e., with serious edifying intent, the attitude of the friend must have something to do with conventional religiosity and belief. The contrasting attitude of Demonax must then be a correction of conventional religious belief in the direction of some universalizing tendency, i.e., "But the gods are omnipresent and can hear our prayers wherever we are."

The problem with this interpretation is that Demonax was a Cynic. In keeping with Cynic attitude and stance it would be most unusual to find that Demonax would want to be taken seriously as recommending piety or propounding religious teaching. If we look at the story more closely, another reading is much more plausible.

The first observation is that the setting of this story is simply a typical one for Cynic chreiai: the Cynic and his "students." That it is a student instead of an antagonist, or a tyrant, or another philosopher, or an average person on the street, indicates that the nature of the response will be less caustic than usual, i.e., a mild reprimand, and that its critical aspects will be less damning, a bit more playful, or, perhaps, inconsequential. The situation described by the student and his suggestion is thus merely a set-up for the Cynic rejoinder. One need not take it seriously at all, since the Cynic's life-style is such that he can move into any typical human situation, personally apathetic with regard to social conventions, in order to make his typical social critique. Especially provocative situations, those which are particularly vulnerable for social critique, and dangerous for the Cynic's image, were favorites for these stories. These situations include the court of the tyrant, the brothel, the drinking house, and the banquet with the rich. The cultus is not as dangerous as these, but the Cynic's stance when encountering conventional religion will be the same. The description of the situation will highlight some aspect of the social conventions associated with the

---

17. Tannehill, "Introduction: The Pronouncement Story," 7.

situation in order to indicate the normal expectations for behavior that confront the Cynic. The trick, then, was to see if the Cynic's wit and wisdom could get him off the hook unscathed.

The student suggests that they both go to the Asclepium and pray for the student's son. As with most chreiai, this request carefully phrases the situation in order to heighten the sense of entrapment, and to allow for the clever rejoinder. Since it is a student's request, and has to do with his son, the reader's first impression is that Demonax can hardly refuse the invitation. But his response avoids those aspects of entrapment, namely the "let us" and the "for my son." Instead, Demonax picks up on two other aspects of the suggestion, namely "go to the Asclepium" and "pray." He also unveils an unexpressed assumption of the suggestion, namely that the student thinks Asclepius can "hear." This selectivity is typical of Cynic chreiai. By choosing just those aspects of the situation which lend themselves to irony, ambiguity, and contradiction, the Cynic exposes the situation itself as ridiculous and thus frees himself from its demands.

Demonax's retort is: "You must think Asclepius very deaf, that he can't hear our prayers from where we are." If we set this rejoinder over against the suggestion, we can see how it develops its logic:

| Suggestion: | Let us go | to the Asclepium | and pray. |
| Rejoinder: | You think | where we are | he's deaf. |

The rejoinder uses the rhetorical topic of the contrary to develop its logic. It presents three alternatives, the most obvious being that of "there" ("to the Asclepium") and "here" ("where we are"). The second alternative is won by expressing an assumption associated with prayer, namely Asclepius "hears," and by juxtaposing "deaf." The third alternative is less obvious, but is very important, since it contains the bite. It translates the assumption into an ascription of belief ("you think") and contrasts it with the proposal made ("let us go and pray"). This contrast is between practice and belief (or deed and word).

This alignment of three alternatives—one granted and obvious, the second a quickly recognized disclosure of assumptions, the third a subtle but biting conclusion that is left for the student and reader to draw—maps out a rapidly moving series of logical plays that turns the tables on the situation completely. The contrary implication is clear: "The action you propose is not supported by the beliefs you hold." It catches the student in a hopeless contradiction and discloses his suggestion as ridiculous. The logics that it uses are, taken individually, impeccable in terms of rhetorical topics of argumentation. Taken together they amount to a rhetorical syllogism which "proves" that the opposite is the case from that which is proposed. But it is all a ruse, of course. The rejoinder achieves its point by means of the principle of selectivity and partiality—taking up a single aspect of a situation which accords with the overall conventional code and system of values, only to play it off against some other aspect of the same set of assumptions in order to point up a devastating incongruity. This mechanism is not the dialectic of philosophical inquiry at all. It is rather the swerve approach to a contingent situation that Detienne and Vernant have called the μῆτις of the Greeks.[18] The purpose is to escape entrapment by extricating oneself from the social determinants of a situation, and to entrap by throwing the net over the other. The result in the case of the μῆτις of chreiai is to gain space for the Cynic, which is exactly what he wants.

This move does not in any way instruct the student and reader. It silences them. There is no recommendation proffered at all, either about a more adequate understanding of the gods, or about whether or not one should pray, here or there. The setting of the cult is merely one of the typical situations that can be used, as any and all others can, to exhibit the Cynic at work with words, and to add a snippit to his portrayal as one who consistently behaves as a Cynic.

It is now possible to suggest why it was that the teachers of rhetoric found this type of anecdote useful for instruction. Still in touch with sophistic mentality, the Cynic chreia offered fine examples of a way with words that exhibited basic rhetorical devices. One could almost say that the chreiai were examples of primitive rhetoric, and that they put the teachers of rhetoric in touch with the origins of the tradition. The typical scene was a situation of debate in which the major weapon of the individual, contrasted as he was with the need to challenge the tyranny of convention, was his own rhetorical skill.[19]

Theon's reticence to use this type of chreia for exercises in commentary/confirmation is therefore most understandable, given his positive stance toward the value of cultural conventions and ethics. By the time of the second sophistic, rhetoric had changed sides completely in the debate about convention, used now to "confirm" instead of "refute." But for exercises in the analysis of basic rhetorical designs, the Cynic chreia was still most helpful.

A very important section of Theon's chapter documents that Hellenistic teachers understood chreiai as examples of rhetorical devices. In this section (206,8–210,3), Theon lists the twelve ways in which a chreia might be expressed: (1) with a maxim, (2) with proof (ἀποδεικτικῶς), (3) with wittiness, (4) with a syllogism (συλλογιστικῶς), (5) with a rhetorical syllogism (ἐνθύμημα), (6) with an example (παράδειγμα), (7) with a wish,

18. Detienne and Vernant, *Cunning Intelligence.*
19. See Farenga, "Periphrasis."

(8) in a symbolic manner ($\sigma\nu\mu\beta o\lambda\iota\kappa\hat{\omega}s$), (9) in a figurative manner ($\tau\rho o\pi\iota\kappa\hat{\omega}s$), (10) with double entendre, (11) with substitution ($\mu\epsilon\tau\acute{a}\lambda\eta\psi\iota s$), and (12) with combinations of the above. The first six items have to do with classical forms of rhetorical argumentation; the other five (or six) items have to do with matters of rhetorical style, also understood to be important for persuasive speech. It is clear, therefore, that the teachers of rhetoric collected chreiai with a view to illustrating the rhetorical devices they employed and classified chreiai with respect to rhetorical forms of argumentation. The list does not suggest that only Cynic chreiai are in view, since maxims are listed along with wittiness. And for Theon, as we have seen, the saying of Euripides is also a chreia. But the Cynic chreia must have first caught the attention of the teachers of rhetoric. Theon could still use it for analytic purposes and exercises in refutation, though he may stand toward the end of its history of usefulness in the progymnasmata tradition. In section 8 we shall return to the importance of this typology for synoptic studies: Cynic versus edifying and moralistic chreiai. But before we do, the important matter of the elaboration of the chreia in Hermogenes needs to be understood. With it a pattern emerges that we shall rediscover in many synoptic compositions.

5. Elaboration as the Complete Argument

The shift in emphasis that occurs with Hermogenes comes to light in the fact that there is no longer any mention of separate exercises in recitation, inflection, expansion, abbreviation, critique, or refutation. Instead, Hermogenes presents a single exercise in support of the chreia as thesis in a strictly sequential order of argumentation intended to produce a full and coherent confirmation. This single exercise is called the elaboration ($\dot{\epsilon}\rho\gamma\alpha\sigma\acute{\iota}\alpha$), and it manifests considerable interest in matters of style and composition. The text of this section of Hermogenes' chapter on the chreia (7,10–8,14) reads as follows:

> But now let us move on to the next matter, and this is the elaboration. Let the elaboration be then as follows; (1) First, in a few words, an encomium of the one who spoke or acted; (2) then a paraphrase of the chreia itself; (3) then the rationale. For example: *Isocrates said that the root of education is bitter, but the fruit is sweet.*
>
> (1) Praise: "Isocrates was a wise man . . .," and you amplify the topic slightly.
>
> (2) Then the chreia: "He said . . . and so forth." And you do not present it without embellishment, but you amplify the recitation.
>
> (3) Then the rationale: "For the greatest matters usually succeed because of toil, and their successful accomplishments bring pleasure."
>
> (4) Then a statement of the contrary: "For things that happen by chance

do not require labors, and their end is most unpleasant; but in the case of worthwhile matters it is the opposite."

(5) Then the elaboration from analogy: "For just as farmers must work with the soil before reaping its fruits, so also must those who work with words."

(6) Then the elaboration from example: "Only after Demosthenes had confined himself to his room and toiled long did he reap the rewards: wreaths and public acclamations."

(7) It is possible also to give an argument by means of a judgment. For example: "For Hesiod said, 'For gods in front of virtue ordained sweat.' And another poet says, 'Gods sell us every good, our toil their price.'"

(8) At the end you are to add an exhortation, to the effect that it is necessary to heed the one who has spoken or acted.

So much for now: you will learn the more advanced teaching later.

The elaboration of this chreia consists of making eight statements. Hermogenes labels these statements by shorthand technical designations for various rhetorical tropes and arguments as follows: (1) praise for the author, (2) paraphrase of the chreia, (3) a statement of the rationale, (4) a statement of the contrary, (5) an analogy, (6) an example, (7) a judgment, and (8) an exhortation. The set as a whole follows very closely what, judging from the *ad Herennium*, had come to be known as "the complete argument." There are fine discussions of the complete argument in the *ad Herennium* and Cicero. A study of these discussions shows that the ancient rhetorical theorists had reduced the manifold lists of possible topics and arguments to a single set of the basic and major types of proof, arranged in a logical order and correlated with the standard outline of the judicial speech itself. Before analyzing the way in which this set of arguments works in Hermogenes' elaboration, we need to discuss the standard speech outline and its relation to the complete argument.

Rhetorical theory distinguished among judicial, deliberative, and epideictic speeches. According to Aristotle, the judicial speech was concerned with accusation and defense of charges with respect to an action of the past, and the categories of the just and unjust governed it. The deliberative speech had as its purpose to exhort or dissuade with respect to a policy about the future, and the categories of the expedient and harmful governed it. The epideictic speech brought praise or censure to bear upon some occasion in the present, and argued in terms of the noble and the disgraceful (*Rhet*.I.iii,3–5). Theoretically each of the three speech situations (courtroom, assembly, public occasion) confronted the speaker with a particular kind of audience as his judge (κριτής), and required a particular kind of argumentation on the basis of which the solicited judgment could be made. But, of course, the differentiations among the three modes of persuasion were theoretical, and never restricted the use of any means of persuasion which might be found appropriate or helpful to a given rhetorical occasion. To learn how to praise or censure, for instance, would come in very handy at times, even in the judicial situation!

Nevertheless, the teachers of rhetoric carefully reflected upon the means of argumentation most appropriate to each of the three speech situations. They understood the epideictic speech as the least argumentative, dealing for the most part with an audience already agreeable to the proposition that some person or institution was worthy of encomiastic celebration. Reflection on the principal means of persuasion in this case took its lead from the encomium, a rather standardized speech-form that traced the genealogy and history of some person or institution, comparing it advantageously with other competitors in general, in order to demonstrate its virtues. Only in the case of uncertainty about the appropriateness of praise for the subject of the speech would the topic of comparison and the categories of praise and censure lead the speaker into more deliberative or even judicial modes of argumentation. Xenophon's *Apology* is an example of such a mixture of rhetorical types of persuasion in an essentially epideictic writing.

The teachers of rhetoric, then, worked out the theory of argumentation primarily with the judicial and deliberative situations in mind. In the handbook tradition these speech-types dominate the discussion, the judicial speech-situation producing the standard speech-outline and most of the theory about how to establish one's case and develop persuasive arguments or proofs to support it. The deliberative situation gave rise to the theory about the general means of persuasion and the topics used to amplify a given proposal persuasively. The outline of the complete argument that concerns us is a late development (without evidence before the *ad Herennium*, first century B.C.E.) resulting from a correlation and simplification of both judicial and deliberative argumentation theory. It is the function of this outline that we seek to understand (see figure, p. 54).

The standard speech had four sections: (1) introduction (προοίμιον, *exordium*), (2) statement of the (facts of the) case (διήγησις, *narratio*), (3) argumentation or proofs (πίστεις, *argumentatio*), and (4) conclusion (ἐπίλογος, *conclusio*). In the introduction the speaker was to acknowledge the speech-situation in such a way as to establish his right to address the audience about the matter at hand, as we have seen. A persuasive introduction linked the credibility of the speaker to the nature of the theme, and established rapport with a particular audience. Orators called this mode of persuasion "ethical," i.e., the creation of an ἦθος conducive to persuasive communication. In the statement of the case the speaker presented a narrative description of the matter at hand, constructing it in such a way as to highlight the issue as he saw it

Figure 1

1 The Standard Speech Form	2 Anaximenes' Supporting Arguments (*Rhet. ad Alex.*)	3 Hermogenes' Supporting Arguments	4 The Complete Argument (*Rhet. ad Her.*)	5 The Amplification of a Theme (*Rhet. ad Her.*)	6 Hermogenes' Elaboration
1. Prooimion/Exordium					1. Encomium/Praise
2. Diegesis/Narratio		*Propositio*		*Res*	2. Paraphrase/Chreia
			Ratio	*Ratio*	3. Rationale
3. Pistis/Argumentatio		*Confirmatio*		*Pronuntio*	
		Exornatio			
	Contrary	Same/Contrary		*Contrario*	4. Contrary
	Similar	Analogy	*Simile*	*Simile*	5. Analogy
		Example	*Exemplum*	*Exemplum*	6. Example
		Lesser/Greater	*Amplificatio*		
	Judgments		*Iudicatio*		7. Judgment
4. Epilogos/Conclusio			*Conplexio*	*Conclusio*	8. Exhortation

(στάσις, *status, quaestio*), and lead to a specific position on it (εἰκός, ὑπόθεσις, *propositio*). The section on the proofs, then, was the place to present the arguments (ἐπιχειρήματα, *argumenta*) in support of the proposition proposed. The mode of persuasion appropriate to the statement of the case and the argumentation was the appeal to reason (Aristotle's λόγος, *ratiocinatio*) as it applied to probabilities in the arena of human actions and motivations. In the conclusion a summation would appeal for a judgment or decision. The appropriate mode of persuasion was πάθος or the appeal to the emotions.

The history of rhetoric gave major consideration to the theory of argumentation. One of the ways in which rhetors approached the problem was to develop lists of proofs under several classifications and to discuss their relative appropriateness for use in the various sections of the speech or kinds of speeches. We have already discussed the list of final categories that was especially appropriate to the deliberative speech. Lists of tropes and *figurae* were also customary, and the teachers of rhetoric discussed their rhetorical effect in relation to the most appropriate places for their use in the speech. In the case of the judicial speech, proofs tended to be divided into three general classes: (1) Those that the rhetor did not need to invent were the non-technical proofs (ἄτεχνοι), and consisted of such things as basic evidence, sworn testimony, witnesses, documents, laws, and precedent decisions. Those that the rhetor needed to find or invent (εὕρησις, *inventio*) were the technical or artificial proofs (ἔντεχνοι). In turn, the rhetors discussed these technical proofs in terms of (2) primary and (3) supporting arguments. The primary was more important for the *narratio* section of the speech in which the plausibility of the proposition was to be demonstrated. The supportive arguments were more appropriate for the section of argumentation itself. In the handbooks, one encounters various attempts to list and classify the technical proofs. Known as topics or places from which an argument might be devised, some of these lists are very long, revealing the desire to be as comprehensive as possible. Few lists are able to sustain a single set of principles for classification, however, frequently combining logical, descriptive, and functional concerns. And many of the longer lists seem to peter out at the end with some statement about the list being sufficient if not complete. But here and there one finds a short listing of the major ways to develop a supporting argument. It is with these that we are concerned.

An early example of a short list of topics for argumentation is found in Anaximenes (*Rhet. ad Alex.* I.1422a.25–27). He has discussed a list of final categories as the primary mode of persuasion in a deliberative speech. Then he explains that further argumentation might make use of (1) analogy (τὸ ὅμοιον), (2) contrary (τὸ ἐναντίον), and (3) previous judgments (τὰ κεκριμένα). (See figure, column 2.) The rhetorical tradition considered these three topics for inventing a supporting argumentation basic for inference by induction. Taken together they combine major technical and non-technical proofs, provided that we understand previous judgment to be a deliberative form of appeal to authority correlative to the judicial citation of precedent decision. The authorities Anaximenes suggested are, interestingly enough, "the gods, men of repute, judges, or opponents." Anaximenes intends these lists of basic topics to be sufficient for the creation of a persuasive deliberation.

Hermogenes' treatise on Invention contains a late example of a short list of topics where he discusses the "Elaboration of the Arguments" (Rabe, *Herm.* 148–50). The topics to be used are: (1) analogy (ἀπὸ παρα- βολῆς), (2) example (ἀπὸ παραδείγματος), (3) the lesser (ἀπὸ μικροτέρου), (4) the greater (ἀπὸ μείζονος), (5) the same (ἀπὸ ἴσου), and (6) the contrary (ἀπὸ ἐναντίου). (See figure, column 3.) This list expands upon the ways one can develop arguments by analogy and reflects developments in the Aristotelian tradition. According to Aristotle, analogy and example were primary modes of rhetorical induction (cf. Arist. *Rhet.* I.ii.8; II.xx.2–4). But, as with Anaximenes, comparison and contrary remain the rule. Hermogenes intends this as a list adequate for developing arguments in support of the main proposition established in the preceding section of the speech. The speech-type Hermogenes has in mind is judicial.

The *ad Herennium* contains two very important examples, one of the complete argument, the other of the seven parts for the development of a theme or thesis. Here we find reflections on a set of the basic means of argumentation organized with the rhetor's interest in the outline of a speech as a whole. The distinction between judicial and deliberative types of speech has broken down, as a comparison of the two outlines will show. This intermixing has taken place in the interest of reducing and simplifying matters for teaching purposes, as Anaximenes' example of a thesis shows. Declamation is now standard practice. With the *ad Herennium* we have evidence from the first century B.C.E. of classroom exercises for which, in Theon and Hermogenes, the chreia was found useful as a point of departure.

The complete argument consists of the following five items: (1) *propositio*, (2) *ratio*, (3) *confirmatio*, (4) *exornatio*, and (5) *conplexio* (*ad Herennium* II.xviii.28). (See figure, column 4.) The first three items spell out the steps necessary for establishing the proposition. They correspond to the traditional *narratio* section of a speech, plus primary argument. Of particular interest to us here is the special mention of the *ratio*. The speaker is to accomplish it by means of a brief explanation that can show the reasonableness or truth of the proposition proposed. The *ratio* of the *ad Herennium* corresponds to the αἰτία (rationale) in Hermogenes' elaboration, as we shall see. But of more importance is the list of arguments used in the *exornatio*. They are: (1) analogy (*simile*), (2) example (*exemplum*), (3) amplification (*amplificatio*), and (4) judgment (*res iudicata; Rhet. ad Her.* II.xxix.46). This list is a simplified combination of those already given from Anaximenes and Hermogenes. With it we are very close to the ἐργασία-outline in Hermogenes' progymnasmata. Anaximenes included the item called "amplification" in order to indicate that the list is open-ended.

The outline for the development of a theme or thesis is as follows: (1) statement of the theme (*res*), (2) rationale, 3) restatement or paraphrase of the theme with or without the rationale (*pronuntio*), (4) statement of the contrary (*contrario*), (5) analogy (*simile*), (6) example (*exemplum*), and (7) conclusion (*conclusio; Rhet. ad Her.* IV.xliii.56). (See figure, column 5.) The example given develops the thesis that "The wise man will shun no peril on behalf of the republic." It follows the seven steps and results in a coherent paragraph or little speech much the same as Hermogenes' elaboration of the chreia. It was this mini-speech outline resulting from these theoretical simplifications that Hermogenes used for the elaboration of the chreia. The correlations are given in the figure (column 6). Technically, the term elaboration should apply only to items 4 through 7, the first three items having to do with introducing and establishing the thesis, not elaborating it. Neither should it refer, technically, to the last item, which functions rather as the conclusion of the speech. But the discussions of the complete argument had produced a full speech outline, beginning with the statement of the proposition, and ending with a conclusion. It was in keeping with this view of the argumentation-speech as a unit that Hermogenes could designate the whole as an elaboration.

6. The Elaboration in Hermogenes

The chreia chosen by Hermogenes for elaboration is a saying of Isocrates, recognized as the founder of rhetorical education and the Hellenistic school. The saying is about *paideia* (Rabe, *Herm.* 7,13–15):

Isocrates said that the root of education is bitter, but the fruit is sweet.

First there is to be *a brief word of praise* for Isocrates. This corresponds to the introduction of a speech and is in keeping with the usual considerations about the establishment of a speaker's ἦθος, as well as winning audience appeal, both of which are appropriate to it. It also tips us off to the author(ity) of the chreia to be considered.

Then the chreia is to be given, perhaps paraphrased, making sure that its recitation enhances its meaning. This step is important, because its recitation amounts to a statement of the thesis proposed. Chreiai as theses, however, frequently confronted the student with the necessity of explaining or elucidating their point before going on, since they might consist of maxims, make their point by means of figural language, or, as in the case of Cynic chreiai, be purposefully playful if not enigmatic.

Thus the rationale ($\alpha i \tau i \alpha$) must be given:

> For the greatest matters usually succeed because of labors, and their successful accomplishments bring pleasure (7,18–20).

This is a significant move, for it restates the chreia in the form of an assertion that can be argued. There is an interpretive aspect to this move that corresponds to the determination of the issue in a judicial case, or the isolation of the telling point or side to be taken in a thesis proposal. There is also an argumentative aspect to this move, corresponding to the rationale that gives a proposition or thesis plausibility. If the rationale introduces a reason why a generally accepted view is true, it functions as an apodosis, thus constructing a rhetorical syllogism (enthymeme). This addition of a rationale is necessary, according to Aristotle, in the case of using a maxim as protasis (*Rhet.* II.xxi). Taken together, and viewed as argumentation, the combination of chreia plus rationale establishes the primary proof or basic argument. All that follows is then supporting argumentation. In our case the rationale advances the chreia for argumentation in two ways. First, it transposes the figural mode of the chreia into vain discourse. Second, it makes explicit the theme of labor as the issue in need of elaborative argumentation. The transition is achieved by combining the two figures of the metaphor (vine as symbol for agriculture and *paideia*) under the more generic category of greatest undertakings ($\pi\rho\acute{a}\gamma\mu\alpha\tau\alpha$), and by translating the sequence "bitter root/sweet fruit" into the staged sequence of "hard labor at first/pleasant success afterward." The notion of labor or toil is won by (1) association with the term "bitter," (2) the decision to take the vine as a symbol of agriculture, and (3) the correlation of agriculture and paideia as undertakings. The notion of pleasure is won by association with the term "sweet," and with the ideas of success and accomplishment which are the goals of great undertakings. But pleasure ($\acute{\eta}\delta\acute{v}s$) is also one of the conventional values included in the standard lists of the final categories ($\tau\epsilon\lambda\iota\kappa\grave{a}\ \kappa\epsilon\phi\acute{a}\lambda\alpha\iota\alpha$). This status means that Hermogenes has already made a claim for the validity of the chreia, and proposed a very forceful thesis. If it can be sustained through the elaboration, the claim will be supported. Such an outcome means that the chreia is right about the achievement of education as worthwhile.

The argument that follows is called a statement of the contrary. This argument is a standard one, and a test of the validity of arguments. An orator could employ it in several ways. In our case, it inverts the terms of the proposed rationale. If the opposite set of relationships also makes sense, or is recognized as a plausible statement, this judgment serves to support the original contention:

For everyday occurrences do not require labors, and their end is most unpleasant, but in the case of worthwhile matters it is just the opposite (7,20–8,1).

By itself, this argument might not appear as a convincing statement. But it has succeeded in stating a set of relationships that contrasts with the rationale and describes an eventuality "most *un*pleasant." The contrasting of labors with "everyday occurrences" achieves this result. There is a considerable bit of sleight-of-hand here. Hermogenes has assumed the intentional aspect of labor in order to find the contrary, and he has turned the happenstance (τύχη) of chance-events (τυχόντα) into a purely negative factor. But in the context of the speech-situation, the cleverness of the inversion was probably a telling maneuver. Note also that Hermogenes has taken the occasion to advance the discussion about labors as well. He not only defines labor as undertaking with purpose, he also specifies that the greatest undertakings are worthwhile (σπουδαῖος). The category of the worthwhile is closely related to that of the noble (καλόν), and thus evokes surreptitiously yet another of the conventional values as an argument. The effect would not have been lost on second-century ears.

With the analogy that follows we come to an even more basic means of making a supporting argument. The technical handbooks on rhetoric, beginning with the earliest extant one by Anaximenes and Aristotle, contain discussions of the importance of using the analogy for this purpose.[20] By definition the analogy may arise from any of the orders of reality, but the Greco-Roman mind seems to have preferred the natural and social orders. It must be a general statement having to do with a class of objects, illustrating a principle or a relationship that has the potential for being universalized. It makes its rhetorical point by showing that the principle operates not only in the arena of relationships addressed by the thesis but in some other order of activity as well. The correlation by analogy achieves the illusion of the universal truth of the thesis by expanding the contexts to which it applies:

> For just as it must be that farmers reap the fruit only after working the earth, so it must be also in the case of working with words (8,1–4).

Here the analogy of the farmer arises from the metaphor given with the chreia itself, in keeping with the earlier move that established that the vine was a symbol of agriculture. We can now see the significance of that earlier move. By making it, Hermogenes set himself up for this telling analogical proof. It is especially telling because agriculture itself is an arena that conjoins both human endeavor and natural process. By developing just this analogy, then, Hermogenes has succeeded in corre-

---

20. See Lausberg, *Handbuch*, par. 422. Cf. McCall, *Ancient Rhetorical Theories*.

lating not just two, but three orders of process—the natural, the agricultural, and the arena of rhetorical education. The point is that the principle of the sequence, effort/produce, is constitutive in all arenas. The mention of the farmer gives the analogy a new and additional argument, because it specifies the class against which the correlation may be tested. Hermogenes has also taken the opportunity to specify the arena of labor indicated by the other pole of the chreia's metaphor. He now defines paideia precisely as "working with words." This, of course, has been the understanding of paideia all along, but Hermogenes allows it to come into focus only after stacking up the several implicit analogies that previously were in play: natural process, greatest endeavors, worthwhile matters, farming. Now, at the appropriate place—argument by analogy—he combines the several arenas of the analogous in the analogy proper, and specifies the labor of paideia.

The example that follows continues this movement toward specificity. The example and the enthymeme (rhetorical syllogism) are, according to Aristotle, the two primary forms of rhetorical logic and proof (*Rhet.* I.ii.8–19; II.xx.1–4,9; II.xxv.8). By definition the example comes from the arena of history, and is about some well-known person. Its function is to show that a particular instance has actualized the general principle at issue.[21] If the example is well chosen and telling, the argument confirms the validity of the general rule in terms of a specific and precedent case:

> Only after Demosthenes had confined himself to his room and toiled long, did he reap the rewards: wreaths and public acclamations (8,4–7).

Hermogenes has chosen the famous rhetor as the example. The stories about his long hours at the desk were well known. Hermogenes combined a reference to these stories with an allusion to the equally well-known passage of Demosthenes' famous oration "On the Crown" (18,58). This bit of erudition would not have damaged the argument at all. But the telling force of the argument is just that the thesis Hermogenes is developing pertains in a specific and notable case. The clever inclusion of an allusion to the canons of literature is a special touch, introducing as it does the next category of argumentation.

Other authorities may now be cited. In a judicial case, the citation of authorities functioned as precedent judgments or decisions. In the speech in support of a thesis, the teachers of rhetoric still called the citations judgments or witnesses, but they took the authorities from the canons of literature and philosophy, not law. The purpose of the citation was to confirm the truth of the developed proposition by showing that recognized authorities had said much the same thing.

---

21. See Lausberg, *Handbuch*, pars. 410, 412, and 422.

For Hesiod said,
   "For gods in front of virtue ordained sweat."
And another poet says,
   "Gods sell us every good, our toil their price" (8,8–11).

Hermogenes' reader would have considered the finding of an appropriate citation from Hesiod (*Works and Days* 28a) fortunate indeed. Hesiod's authority ranked with that of Homer, and his teachings in general about the importance of work would add weight to a maxim on the subject. The one selected turns out to be quite significant. Not only does it claim Hesiod's authority in support of the chreia as thesis, but it also achieves two additional specifications. The first is that the ordinance of the gods grounds the necessity of labor. The second is that the maxim reveals the pleasurable goal that is at the end of the time of toil. It is none other than ἀρετή itself, the mark par excellence of the highest human achievements. With this citation, then, the speech reaches its climax not only in the confirmation of the thesis, but in its development as a theme. The next citation from Epicharmus,[22] then, serves as a slight denouement before the concluding exhortation is given. It continues the idea of the divine ordinance and sums things up around two terms: "our toil"/"good things" (ἀγαθά).

The exhortation forms the period by referring again to Isocrates: "It is essential to heed him." This is so because the argument has confirmed the truth of his saying. It is also true because the saying, if heard, demands imitation.

The force of the argument as a whole may now be analyzed briefly. Hermogenes used basic rhetorical modes of inventing arguments to establish the chreia as a thesis and support it. He establishes the thesis by translating the chreia's metaphor into an assertion, and by introducing categories from the final categories of persuasive speech. They function now as designations for commonly accepted values, the point of which is to claim them for the proposition of the thesis. This is the first move in the argumentation: "*Paideia* is like all great undertakings. It requires labor, but brings *pleasure*."

Hermogenes makes the second move with his series of supporting arguments, the elaboration in the narrower sense. Their function is to show that the proposition is in agreement with conventional and accepted judgments about the way things go in the several arenas of human observation, experience, and discourse. These include logic or dialectic (argument from the contrary), natural and social science (analogy), history and the institution of rhetoric (example), literary and cultural tradition (judgment), as well as theology and ethics (citations).

---

22. See Kaibel, *Comicorum Graecorum*, frag. 289.

Taken together, there is precious little space left upon which to stand in dissent.

The third move is more subtle, but also more telling. It is the way in which Hermogenes developed the thesis thematically. He achieved this development by the clever choice of terms that picked up on previous statements and moved the topic ahead toward ever greater specificity and concretion. He correlated this thematic development with the sequence of arguments that moved toward the Example as that argument which could use the particular instance in the form of the most basic rhetorical proof.

Analyzed in this way it is clear that the elaboration of the chreia in Hermogenes was a very difficult and demanding exercise. One wonders what has happened to the beginning exercises. The elaboration assignment surely would have required many advanced skills. The recitation-paraphrase of the chreia, and its insertion into a speech setting presupposes something similar to Theon's exercises in recitation, inflection, expansion, and abbreviation. The rationale would require Theon's exercises in commentary and confirmation, and so forth. As it appears, then, the chreia exercise in Hermogenes seems to assume quite an advanced level of rhetorical training.

There is also much more emphasis on style, composition, and facility with the functions of *figurae*. Moralizing is no longer merely a matter of caution and advice, as with Theon. The elaboration builds it into the structure of the speech as its express intention. And the moral that the argument supports has precisely to do with the work at hand: a rhetoric in support of rhetorical training. It is now the saying of Isocrates that the rhetoric confirms. And in what way, ultimately? By heeding him! We are dealing here, then, with the mimetic mentality of the second sophistic. Rhetoric has come full circle, from its origination in the individual's critique of social convention, to its domestication as *apologia* for social convention itself.

For this latter purpose the Cynic chreiai were singularly inappropriate. The Cynics' critical response to the norms and codes of social convention still gave them their flavor. It was characteristic of the Cynic chreia that it achieved this critical response mainly in terms of a telling way with words, subverting conventional assumptions by pointing up the ironies, incongruities, and contradictions in typical human situations. It was probably the rhetorical skill and power manifest in the chreia that attracted the attention of the earlier Hellenistic teachers of rhetoric. Judging from Theon, they valued it at first for early exercises in the analysis of the rhetorical topics, tropes, and devices that made the telling point. But by the time of Theon late in the first century, certain cautions are in evidence that have to do with uneasiness about the implicit critique of conventional moral and cultural values manifest in chreiai of this type. With Hermogenes the cautions are no longer necessary. The rhetorical tradition has been fully domesticated, the chreia tamed by selectivity, and the emphasis placed upon using rhetorical skills to support the accepted views of an enculturated ἀρετή. Rhetoric now is mainly a matter of μίμησις and style. Archaizing and idealization of certain preferred teachers of the past go hand in hand with a new moralizing scholasticism. To put the polish on eulogies and declamations is now the mark of excellence. For this a moral maxim is much better than the Cynic's bite.

7. The Elaboration Pattern in Literature

Before engaging texts of the synoptic tradition, one further matter needs to be discussed. It is the question of the relationship of this classroom exercise to literary composition in the Greco-Roman period.

Readers of first-century literature will know about the influence of rhetoric in general upon literary composition during this period. And a rhetorical reading of early Christian materials is now an accustomed practice among New Testament scholars.[23] It should come as no surprise, therefore, that we can also detect the elaboration pattern under investigation in this present set of studies as a compositional structure in the literature of the period. That it has not been recognized before in just this form is understandable, of course. Scholars have not generally sought clarity about rhetorical and literary patterns by means of studies in the progymnasmata. They have taken their departure primarily from the rhetorical handbooks with their typologies of the larger speech patterns and their cautions about the freedom of the rhetor to invent a creative discourse of his own. The professional ideal was not to adhere woodenly to some required order for the smaller sections of the speech, but to craft an original composition in keeping with sound rhetorical principles. It is also the case that New Testament scholars have more easily seen the influence of rhetoric upon literary composition in discursive and treatise-like materials, for there the signs of the logic of persuasion are close to the surface, and treatises may be recognized as literary forms of (the) rhetorical speech.

The demostration of the elaboration pattern is therefore quite important for literary studies of narrative and sayings material from a rhetorical point of view. The pattern lends itself to the composition of small blocks of material that form periods of very dense rhetoricity and make very large claims to completeness of persuasive argumentation. And it is

23. See Mack, *Rhetoric.*

capable of dealing with aphoristic, gnomological, poetic, and narrative modes of speech. The value of the pattern in the *ad Herennium* is just that it reduces the lengthy theoretical discussions and the interminable lists of topics and devices and their arrangements found in the technical handbooks to a list of the basic and fundamental items needed for a comprehensive argumentation. The value of the pattern in Theon and Hermogenes is just that it uses this pattern to interpret chreiai. All three texts (*ad Herennium*, Theon, and Hermogenes) present us with examples of small, fully worked-out elaborations that conform to the pattern. They are, of course, classroom exercises. One would not expect to find in literary works blocks of material that followed the pattern so simply and transparently. And yet, alerted to the pattern in its form as a classroom exercise, it is possible to see it at work in an amazingly rich variety of literatures of the time.

Studies in this area are only now beginning, so that reference to publications is limited. But work in progress has discovered the pattern in Plutarch's *Lives* and *Moralia*, Sextus Empiricus, Horace, and Philo of Alexandria.[24] In addition, one should not overlook the importance of the fact that the μελέται of Libanius and the subsequent Byzantine tradition of oratory and preaching upgraded the elaboration of the chreia to the status of a refined literary genre.

Two observations may be made about the significance of the elaboration pattern for a fresh reading of certain types of literary material. We can at first understand the incidence of chreiai in the biographies of Plutarch simply as a continuance of the use of chreiai for characterization as found in Diogenes Laertius. But in Plutarch they function more as examples of specific virtues in keeping with the requirements of the generally encomiastic outline and intention of the works as wholes. The chreia is, of course, capable of functioning as an example, both in narrative and discursive literary contexts. But noting its own essential narrativity on the one hand, and its own internal rhetoricity on the other, the possibilities for the expansion and elaboration of a chreia in a larger narrative frame are multiple and complex. An author can create an entire episode by amplification of the scene, the dialogue, and the dramatic aspects of a chreia without losing track of the fundamentally rhetorical point at the core of its simple form. Elaboration of that rhetorical point can occur within the narrativized episode, as well as in discourse that lies outside the narrative scene of the chreia. Through the author's own dissimulation he can even overlook the obvious point of a chreia, not particularly helpful for his *vita*, and change it into a more

24. For indications of work in progress, see Robbins, "Classifying" (Plutarch); Mack, "Decoding the Scriptures" (Philo), and Alexandre, "Argumentação" (Philo). Edward O'Neil has identified elaborations in Sextus Empiricus and Horace.

acceptable proposition by stating a rationale or αἰτία. For this process and purpose the elaboration pattern was also available. Alerted to the pattern, and understanding the rhetorical significance of such things as contrasts, analogies, secondary examples, and citations of gnomological material when they occur in patterned clusters, the essential rhetoricity even of such biographic literature can be observed.

In his commentaries Philo exhibits another employment of the pattern with yet other hermeneutical consequences. Philo divides the allegorical commentaries into sections, each taking its point of departure from a scripture citation. One of the more frequently occurring patterns of periodizing in the compositon of a section is that of the elaboration.[25] The question that this raises concerns the status of the scripture text being elaborated. Has Philo taken it as a chreia, i.e., as a figural or enigmatic saying? It does appear that this is the case. Philo's first move away from the scripture is normally a statement of the true (allegorical) meaning of the text. If we understand this statement as the *ratio* or αἰτία that translates the assumed enigmatic and figural language of the scripture into another mode of discourse, the elaboration pattern in Philo is precisely that of the elaboration of a chreia. Thus the combination of interpretation and composition that determines the elaboration exercise made it possible for a particularly creative form of scribal activity to emerge. If Philo understood the biblical text as chreia-like, the elaboration pattern offered a practical hermeneutic for its elucidation that honored the authority of the text on the one hand, while calling for inventive exegesis on the other. With this in mind we are ready now to address the question of elaboration in the aphoristic materials of the Jesus tradition.

8. Elaboration of Chreiai in the Gospels

We turn now to the synoptic tradition, not in order to ascertain whether chreiai may be found there, for that is now generally acknowledged, but to test our thesis with respect to the elaboration pattern in a narrative and biographic literature rife with aphoristic material and seeming didactic intention. Our study of the chreia in the Hellenistic school sharpens the questions we must address. Having noticed the difference between maxim chreiai and Cynic chreiai, for instance, the question is whether the synoptic chreiai bear more resemblance to the one than the other. We can already anticipate what we shall find in this regard. The chreiai of Jesus bear striking resemblance to the chreiai of the Cynics.

Is it not the case that silence occurs at the end of many of the stories

---

25. See Mack, "Decoding the Scriptures."

about Jesus? We modern readers have failed to grasp their import, so that we cannot say in other words what the saying of Jesus meant. Many of the stories end expressly with the announcement that Jesus' speech silenced or amazed his hearers. Reading more closely we can now see why. They are chreiai in which a μῆτις-like response masters a situation of challenge, introducing a devastating swerve in the place of expectations that would follow more conventional logic. This is especially true of the so-called controversy stories, and it is also true to some degree of all the pronouncement stories. What is the challenge exactly? What is the purpose of the terse response? What ἦθος do these stories portray for Jesus? Why were they told, if silence is the point? And can they be mimetic? Do they square with the picture of Jesus portrayed by the larger Gospel frame? The familiar questions all come tumbling out again, sharpened by learning the teacher's task in the Hellenistic schools of rhetoric. Can the teacher's learning help us?

Taking our lead from the progymnasmata, we must look more closely at the scenes or situations into which Jesus speaks the response. We cannot any longer proceed merely on the assumption of free-floating λόγια eventually attracting (inadequate) narrative settings in the interest of framing, conserving, or historicizing imaginatively some important teaching. Scene and saying go together, and the questions of historicity, authenticity, and developmental tendencies in the formation of this material are as appropriate for scene as for saying, as well as for both together as a recognizable form in which memory, characterization, and mimetic mechanisms could be cultivated.

There is no guarantee that learning to read these stories as chreiai will put us in touch with things we have not known in some way or another all along, much less help us solve the pack of problems with which the synoptic tradition confronts us. But such a reading may clarify certain issues and help to make them more precise. And it may open up certain avenues of investigation that eventually may lead to greater understanding. We are taking one promising approach in the present set of studies. It is the investigation of the patterns of argument that appear in the pronouncement story as an elaborated chreia and in other configurations of the sayings of Jesus found in the synoptic tradition.

We have found that the pattern of elaboration is reflected in synoptic compositions. This means that the early Jesus communities had noticed the essential rhetoricity of chreia-like material, for without that, elaboration according to the pattern would have been impossible. It also means that, if they "received" the chreia, they also made judgments as to its rationale and thesis. If they elaborated received chreiai, then, we can document a stage in the chreia's cultural history. In the case of a chreia with μῆτις-like response, moreover, elaboration should be a wondrous thing to behold. We would be witnessing the attempt to domesticate the enigmatic, to turn the silence at the borders of convention into thesis, or to resolve it in the interest of another λόγος from within the new social formation.

In any case, the newness of those groups that storied Jesus, their sense of being different from others of their past and present will not have made elaboration easy. Where could they go for examples? Whence their "final categories" that must reflect those values shared by all in order to persuade? What kinds of analogies would be available to them, requiring as they would a common consent about the way things were and would go in normal human endeavor? And what would be the canon for judgments cited, if the canons had suffered critique in the violence of the new group's birth? Could elaboration work at all according to its prescribed rules?

That the pattern is in evidence at all is thus the first astonishment that requires a sobered second look. We offer our studies simply to share that astonishment. We shall try to show that the pattern is there, and to carry our reflections as far as we are able. That is all. We have chosen the texts to illustrate the scope of the pattern's incidence and influence. They include a story amplified internally according to the pattern of elaboration (chapter 4), chreiai whose elaboration moves the discourse out into the larger narrative frame (chapters 5 and 7), a cluster of speech material organized along its lines (chapter 3), and evidence that a major block of parables unfolds in keeping with its outline (chapter 6). If we can show that this is so, it will be enough. After the first speech is always, appropriately, the chance for the rebuttal.

THREE

Foxes, Birds, Burials & Furrows

Vernon K. Robbins

In this chapter we return to the synoptic tradition with guidelines from the elaboration exercise in Hellenistic education. In chapter one, we observed basic similarities between synoptic units and chreiai, but we did not look at the dynamics and logic in those units. In this chapter, we will analyze rhetorical features in two well-known chreia-like units in Matt 8:19–22 and Luke 9:57–60 about foxes and birds and burying the dead. These units, individually, are like abbreviated chreiai. Yet, we do not find them separated from one another in the synoptic tradition. The parallel wording, the common sequence of the two units in Matthew and Luke, and the presence of the parallel missionary charge in Luke 10:1–12 and Matt 9:37–38; 10:9–16 suggest that Matthew and Luke found the units together in Q material concerned with discipleship.[1] Yet, the use and presentation of the material differ in Matthew and Luke. In Matthew, the two units stand together with an introductory sentence that establishes a context of travelling to the other side of the sea. Luke introduced the two units in a setting in which Jesus sets his face toward Jerusalem, and he added an additional unit at the end. In both Matthew and Luke, these settings provide an occasion for developing the theme of following Jesus. As the theme emerges through a series of short units, the reader encounters an embryonic stage of the rhetorical elaboration discussed in chapter two. We wish to analyze some of the

---

1. See the discussion in Lührmann, *Die Redaktion*, 58 and Marshall, *Gospel of Luke*, 408.

rhetorical steps involved at this stage, since it may help us in our other attempts to analyze synoptic tradition.

As we begin our analysis, it might be good to remind ourselves that any collection of argumentative tradition in any culture is likely to contain certain basic rhetorical features. Since the Hellenistic rhetoricians were working with actual apophthegmata which they found in the tradition, their observations are likely to help an interpreter with analysis of similar units in any tradition or culture. It is, however, their ranking of certain features above others which may be of special importance. It is too early in our analysis to know if their ranking is distinctive among all cultural traditions. But if we start with the features Hermogenes ranked above others in his elaboration exercise, we may develop an approach which can help us to detect any special rhetorical strategies that might be present in the synoptic tradition.

1.   Matt 8:18–22

We will begin with the passage in Matthew (paralleled in Luke) in which Dibelius found two units that he considered to be remarkably like chreiai:

> Now when Jesus saw a (great) crowd around him, he gave orders to go over to the other side. And a scribe came up and said to him, "Teacher, I will follow you wherever you go." And Jesus said to him, "Foxes have holes, and birds of the air have nests; but the Son of man has nowhere to lay his head."

> Another of the disciples said to him, "Lord, let me first go and bury my father." But Jesus said to him, "Follow me, and leave the dead to bury their own dead." (Matthew 8:18–22)

This passage begins with a sentence which tells the reader that there was a great crowd around Jesus and that Jesus assumed a role of authority over some of them. The opening sentence in 8:18 begins with the participial clause ἰδὼν δὲ ὁ ᾿Ιησοῦς ὄχλον περὶ αὐτὸν ("Jesus, upon seeing a crowd around him") in a manner characteristic of chreiai.[2] But the clause does not lead to a finite verb that introduces direct speech by Jesus. Rather, with the initial sentence the narrator asserts that Jesus is a popular and authoritative person, without letting Jesus himself come to speech. Then two brief units occur that possess the abrupt, aggressive qualities of Cynic chreiai.[3] The initial unit has a simplified chreia style as the participal προσελθών ("came up") is used with the finite verb εἶπεν

2. Cf. Theon, *Progymnasmata* 203,6–8; 205,22–24; 208,2–4; 209,16–210,2; 215, 14–17.

3. Ehrhardt, "Lass die Toten," 131; Wechssler, *Hellas*, 259; Droge, "Call Stories," 254–57; and Butts, "Voyage."

("he said") to introduce the statement of the scribe, and the finite verb λέγει ("he says") with the name ὁ Ἰησοῦς ("Jesus") is used to introduce Jesus' response. If we analyze these chreiai with an approach similar to the analysis of the Demonax chreia in the previous chapter, we observe a skillful use of the contrary in these units as well. The logic of the first unit emerges through the following structure.

| Proposal: | Teacher | wherever | you go I will follow. |
| Rejoinder: | The Son of man | has nowhere | to lay his head. |

Three contrasts or opposites occur. First, whereas the scribe intends to start a joint venture with a teacher, the rejoinder tells him that the person whom he has approached is "the Son of man." Second, while the scribe expects to accompany the teacher to important places, the rejoinder tells him that this person possesses no place. Third, whereas the scribe thinks the person is travelling, the rejoinder tells him that the person cannot lay down his head. This unit frustrates each part of the scribe's statement. It is not clear at the end of the unit whether the scribe should try to accompany Jesus or not. Should the scribe give up his intentions? Should the scribe try a new approach? Only one thing is clear. The prospect of wandering aimlessly around with the Son of man who has no place to relax has replaced the possibility of following a teacher who is travelling toward an established goal.[4] The unit is like a Cynic chreia that thwarts intentions, overturns presuppositions, and at least temporarily stymies actions.

The next unit in Matthew (8:21–22) achieves contrast or the opposite through a technique that skillfully rearranges words and sounds in the statement of the interlocutor in the response of the sage. It is hard to know exactly what the form of the underlying Aramaic was, though scholars have attempted to reconstruct it.[5] The stylistic skill in the Greek version, however, is eminently clear. The statement of the disciple occurs in two clauses connected in the middle with "and" (καί): "Lord, permit me first to go away *and* to bury my father." The skillful use of language and sound occurs as the response of Jesus rearranges both parts. The opening statement of the disciple is: κύριε ἐπίστρεψόν μοι πρῶτον ἀπελθεῖν, ("Lord, permit me first to go") to which the response of Jesus is: ἀκολούθει μοι. ("Follow me.") In this response, Jesus has accepted only one word of the disciple, namely "me" (μοι). The disciple has said "Permit *me*," and Jesus has said, "Follow *me*." In addition, Jesus does not address the disciple with a title, nor does he repeat the alliterative "p" and "r" sounds in ἐπίστρεψόν . . . πρῶτον ἀπελθεῖν ("permit . . . first to go

---

4. See Crossan, *In Fragments*, 239–41.
5. See, for example, Black, *Aramaic Approach*, 207–8 and Schwarz, "Aphes tous nekrous," 272–76.

away"). Rather, Jesus' response changes the last word of the initial clause from ἀπελθεῖν ("to go away") to ἀκολούθει ("follow"). The result in Greek is especially good, since the first part of ἀκολούθει has replaced ἀπ- ("away") with ἀκο . . . υ, which is a combination of the first letter of ἀπελθεῖν (α), the first syllable in κύριε (κυ), and the last vowel in ἐπίστρεψον and πρῶτον (ο). Then, the last part of ἀκολούθει ("follow") has replaced ἐλθεῖν ("go") with λ . . . θει. This means that Jesus makes a statement which incorporates the first sounds of his title and the last sounds of the words concerning permission, priorities, and going, but he does not allow himself to repeat the sounds associated with actions he will not allow the disciple to do. This is the kind of language usage that made certain chreiai unforgettable.

But there is more. The last statement by the disciple is καὶ θάψαι τὸν πατέρα μου ("and to bury my father"), to which Jesus responds with καὶ ἄφες τοὺς νεκροὺς θάψαι τοὺς ἐαυτῶν νεκρούς ("and permit the dead to bury their own dead"). Jesus' response produces a perfectly balanced clause with θάψαι ("to bury") in the middle:

ἄφες τοὺς νεκροὺς	θάψαι	τοὺς ἐαυτῶν νεκρούς
("permit the dead")	("to bury")	("their own dead")

As the first clause in Jesus' response changed ἀπελθεῖν ("to go away") to ἀκολούθει ("follow"), so the second clause changes ἀπελθεῖν ("to go away") to ἄφες ("permit," or "let"). The disciple wanted permission (ἐπίστρεψον) to go away (ἀπελθεῖν) and bury his father, but Jesus directs him to permit (ἄφες) the dead to bury their own dead. Again, the use of sounds is especially clever as ἀπ(ε)- ("away") is changed into ἄφες ("permit"), and the sounds present in κυρ.ε ("lord"), . . . ωτον ("first"), and .ατερα ("father") are also present in τοὺς νεκρούς ("the dead") and ἐαυτῶν ("their own"). With these sounds, Jesus destroys the disciple's hopes of fulfilling both obligations one after the other. Any attempt to be loyal both to "lord" and "father" must be changed into "the dead" dealing with "their own dead." Is the disciple wily enough to leave his kin and live in a Cynic mode? Or has humiliation at the butt of a joke sent him back to kith and kin? About the disciple we do not know. But what a clever fellow Jesus is.

Although the response of Jesus leaves the disciple reeling, it is also so cryptic that interpreters disagree over its meaning. To the first part of the disciple's request about the burial, the rejoinder means either "let the real dead do it," "let the spiritually dead do it,"[6] or "let the gravediggers do it."[7] If the statement means "let the real dead do it," it probably is a paradoxical way of saying, "That business must look after itself."[8] If it

6. Hengel, *Nachfolge,* 8 and Marshall, *Gospel of Luke,* 411.
7. Schwarz, "Aphes tous nekrous," 272–76.
8. Manson, *Sayings of Jesus,* 73 and Klemm, "Das Wort," 73.

means "let the spiritually dead do it," it implies that those who do not follow Jesus have missed the life associated with the kingdom.[9] If it means "let the gravediggers do it," it implies that the obligation of following Jesus requires a person to leave tasks that would otherwise be his to fulfill. The last interpretation, that the burial is to be left to gravediggers, removes much of the scandal of Jesus' saying. It is, moreover, based on a reconstruction of the underlying Aramaic which has doubtful value for understanding the meaning of the saying in Matthew and Luke. Our present texts say that "the dead" (not "the gravediggers") are supposed to do the burying. The first part of the saying, therefore, either introduces a paradox or refers in a metaphorical manner to the spiritually dead.

If the first part of the saying is difficult, the last part is disturbing. Jesus tells the disciple that a dead father is not the possession of a person called to follow Jesus. No matter what particular nuance of meaning an interpreter gives this part of the saying, its implications are unsettling. The burial of one's father was a serious religious obligation for a Jew,[10] and this saying asks this disciple to disregard this duty. He must not go now, and it would be impossible to wait until later to bury his father. Jesus' statement opposes both the beginning and the end of the disciple's statement to Jesus, therefore, and it is likely that the implications were scandalous in Jewish society.[11]

There is, however, another dimension to the interchange. When we ask what the disciple should do, the answer is clear: he should follow Jesus without delay and without compromise. In contrast to the first unit, where Jesus changes "Teacher," which the scribe used to address him, to "Son of man," the second unit shows Jesus accepting "Lord" as his correct title of address. Jesus responds with the command "Follow me," like a lord commands a servant. This unit, therefore, does not leave the disciple motionless. It is directive, like deliberative speech (τὸ συμβουλευτικόν, Aristotle, *Rhet.* I.iii.7). When these two units follow one another in a sequence, the first unit stands as an initial exhibition of the authoritative ἦθος ("ethos") of Jesus in a pointed statement that destroys the presuppositions of the one who approaches him. The second unit contains a deliberative dimension (giving advice) along with the statement that destroys the disciple's presuppositions. Even though the disciple's basic hopes have been frustrated, Jesus has accepted the role of lord over his actions. Jesus gives the disciple direct advice, and he has to decide only if he will or will not act according to the injunction placed before him.

9. Marshall, *Gospel of Luke*, 411.

10. See, for example, the statement in Gen 50:5 and Tobith 4:3 and 6:15. See also the references collected in Strack and Billerbeck, *Kommentar*, I:487–89 and II,1:578–92.

11. Marshall, *Gospel of Luke*, 411.

On the basis of guidelines presented in the previous chapter, we have a new way to understand this sequence in Matthew. The internal logic of the sequence here opens with a narrator's positive comments about a person, then presents an example of the direct speech of the person, then reworks the speech of the person so that it presents a theme or thesis. The introductory sentence functions like a statement of praise which Hermogenes says a person should put at the beginning of an elaboration. With this sentence, Matthew asserts that Jesus is so popular that a great crowd of people throngs around him, and he embodies such authoritative qualities that he issues commands to people as a natural part of his activity. With his introductory comment, therefore, the narrator recommends Jesus to the audience on the basis of his popular appeal and his exercise of authority. After the introductory sentence, the narrator presents a chreia in which the authoritative character of the speaker is embodied in the first words he speaks. These words present a person who overturns the presuppositions of those who approach him and who refuses to offer images of solace and comfort either to them or to himself. After this chreia, a superbly well-constructed unit sets a deliberative thesis before the reader in the unforgettable form of "Follow me and leave the dead to bury their own dead." This sequence, then, has qualities of the first steps in a chreia elaboration. The arrangement of these abbreviated chreiai admirably set the stage for Jesus to deliver a deliberative thesis in a poignant, directive manner at the end of the unit. The authority of the advice at the end comes from the $\mathring{\eta}\theta o\varsigma$ ("ethos") of the speaker that both the narrator and the direct speech of Jesus have established. The sequence, then, has a rhetorical logic. The introductory comment and the first chreia establish an appropriate relationship between the speaker and the audience before the speaker launches his particular thesis about the demands of life and death.

2. Luke 9:51–62

Analysis of the parallel material in Luke 9:51–62 shows further development of the logic in the Matthean unit. In Luke 9:51–56, as in Matt 8:18, the introduction features the narrator telling the reader about Jesus. The introduction in Luke, however, is much longer, since it sets the stage not only for the chreiai which immediately follow but for Jesus' entire journey to Jerusalem.[12] The introductory unit summarizes events that characterize Jesus as a person who acts on the basis of controlled, reflective thoughts and disciples as people who respond on the basis of natural or traditional inclinations:

12. Marshall, *Gospel of Luke*, 403–4.

When the days drew near for him to be received up, he set his face to go to Jerusalem. And he sent messengers ahead of him, who went and entered a village of the Samaritans, to make ready for him; but the people would not receive him, because his face was set toward Jerusalem. And when his disciples James and John saw it, they said, "Lord, do you want us to bid fire come down from heaven and consume them?" But he turned and rebuked them. And they went on to another village. (Luke 9:51–56)

In this introduction, disciples speak to Jesus, but direct speech is not put on the lips of Jesus. Rather, the narrator tells the reader that Jesus set his face toward Jerusalem (9:51), sent two messengers ahead (9:51) who went into a Samaritan village and met rejection (9:52–53), rebuked James and John (9:55), and went into another village (9:56). The narrator has characterized the intentions, actions, speech, and relationships of Jesus and his disciples, skillfully preparing for direct speech by Jesus. We observed earlier how the introductory verse in Matt 8:18 began like a chreia but ended by describing Jesus' speech rather than letting Jesus exhibit his authority through direct speech. Luke's introduction maintains a similar approach to Jesus' speech. This kind of composition is appropriate for an introduction, since it creates anticipation within the reader for the direct statement of the theme (cf. Quintilian IV.i.5). The reader wants to hear direct speech by Jesus himself, and the reader hears it in the next units. Both the scribal tradition and scholarly interpretation reveal the manner in which these verses set the stage for direct speech by Jesus. Later scribes actually provided direct speech, some filling in Luke 9:55 simply with "You do not know to what kind of spirit you belong," and others adding to this the rationale "for the Son of man did not come to destroy human lives but to save them."[13] Also, Dibelius posited the existence of a tradition with a response by Jesus.[14] Probably the original verses in Luke, however, simply characterized the disciples' inclination to retaliate in the manner of a man of God (2 Kgs 1:10, 12) and Jesus' self-control as he followed a position of "no retaliation."[15]

The final verses, then, introduce alternative attributes of character for Jesus and for those who follow. James and John respond on the basis of traditional ideas of powerful messiahship associated with Elijah,[16] and Jesus responds with deliberate resolve based on a reformulation of past tradition. The direct speech of the two disciples influences the reader's attitude toward the people, in the subsequent units, who talk to Jesus about becoming his disciples. The unfulfilled chreia at the end of the introduction provides an excellent transition to the statement of the

---

13. For a full discussion of these verses, see Ross, "Rejected Words."
14. Dibelius, *From Tradition to Gospel*, 47–48.
15. Marshall, *Gospel of Luke*, 408.
16. Flender, *St. Luke*, 33–34.

theme in the next unit. This is precisely the kind of approach the rhetoricians recommended in an *exordium*.[17] The verses at the end of the unit build anticipation for direct speech by Jesus and create a point of view for the reader to evaluate the ensuing dialogue between Jesus and potential followers. This point of view guides the presentation and elaboration of the theme, and it establishes the overall framework for controlling the meaning of the chreiai in their new rhetorical setting.

After the introduction, a unit occurs in which Jesus comes to speech. But Jesus is not the first to speak. In the mode of the introduction, a person comes to Jesus and addresses him, and Jesus responds with aggressive, picturesque words:

> As they were going along the road, a man said to him, "I will follow you wherever you go." And Jesus said to him, "Foxes have holes and birds of the air have nests; but the Son of man has nowhere to lay his head." (Luke 9:57–58)

This unit, in contrast to the Matthean version (8:19), does not say that the person is a scribe and does not feature the person addressing Jesus as "Teacher." Rather, the introduction features James and John addressing Jesus as "Lord" ($\kappa \acute{\upsilon} \rho \iota \epsilon$, 9:54), and the person in this unit indicates by his willingness to follow Jesus "wherever he goes" that he also accepts Jesus as Lord. The absence of the use of the title "Lord" creates a sequence in which a form of $\mathring{\alpha} \kappa o \lambda o \upsilon \theta \epsilon \widehat{\iota} \nu$ ("to follow") is the first word of direct speech in three successive units (9:57, 59, 61) as "someone" ($\tau \iota s$, 9:57), "another" ($\acute{\epsilon} \tau \epsilon \rho o s$, 9:59), and "another" ($\acute{\epsilon} \tau \epsilon \rho o s$, 9:61) approach Jesus. The absense of the title of address, therefore, helps to highlight the theme of "following" that the unit elaborates.

After the introduction, the reader encounters three brief units rather than two as in Matthew. The first unit recaptures the determination of Jesus to go to Jerusalem by indicating that they were "on the road" ($\grave{\epsilon} \nu \tau \widehat{\eta} \; \grave{o} \delta \widehat{\omega}$, 9:57). Then the interlocutor introduces the central theme of the elaboration with the statement "I will follow you wherever you go." When Jesus thwarts the intentions of the one who approaches him, the reader knows that Jesus is thinking about the severe problems associated with going to Jerusalem. The people in Jerusalem will not accept him, even as the Samaritans, who do not accept Jerusalem, do not accept him. Also, the reader knows that the person who approached Jesus has spoken out of a naive, uninformed perception of Jesus' mission and its consequences. In the Lukan version, then, a specific framework of meaning guides the reader's interpretation of the Son of man's wandering around with no place to lay his head. If neither the Jews in Jerusalem nor the Samaritans will accept Jesus, where can he and his

---

17. See, for example, Quintilian, *Inst. Orat.* IV.i.26.

followers turn for relaxation, comfort, or basic needs? It is obvious that the person who approached Jesus has no understanding of the marginal relationship he will have to established society and its benefits if he becomes a follower of Jesus.

Whereas an established framework of understanding about Jesus and his disciples controls the meaning of the initial chreia, the next unit takes Jesus' speech even further into an organized system of religious thought. Jesus opens the unit with a command to a person to follow him. To this the person responds, "Let me first go and bury my father," and Jesus counters with, "Leave the dead to bury their own dead, but you go and proclaim the kingdom of God." In Luke, as in Matthew, this unit features deliberative speech. But now our author has formulated the unit even more like the elaboration of a chreia. With Jesus' initial statement, he makes the first person's offer to follow him the theme of his own speech. Then the question by the interlocutor allows Jesus to restate the theme in terms of going out and proclaiming the kingdom of God. A different ordering of the words supports the approach in Luke. Instead of ἐπίσρεψόν μοι πρῶτον ἀπελθεῖν καὶ θάψαι ("permit me first to go away and to bury," Matt 8:21), Luke 9:59 reads: ἐπίστρεψόν μοι ἀπελθόντι πρῶτον θάψαι ("let me go away first to bury"). The Lukan ordering of the words sets the stage for a double saying which makes a statement about burying in the first clause and about going away in the second clause:

> leave the dead to bury (θάψαι) their own dead,
> but you go away (ἀπελθών) and proclaim the kingdom of God.

Now the answer to the man's request has two parts, and the second part reiterates a form of ἀπέρχεσθαι ("to go away"). This results in a word-pattern whereby the threefold repetition of ἀκολουθεῖν ("to follow," 9:57, 59, 61) establishes a framework for elaborating the theme of following, and the threefold repetition of ἀπέρχεσθαι ("to go away," 9:57, 59, 60) provides an avenue for instruction about the kingdom of God. The second chreia, then, restates the first chreia in terms of two related themes: following and going away. An exhortation at the beginning by Jesus gives prominence to the theme of following in the sequence, and a statement at the end about going away fills the theme with didactic content about the kingdom of God. This arrangement domesticates the second chreia within a historical framework that presents Jesus on the road to Jerusalem and a didactic framework that presents instruction about the kingdom of God. The Matthean version, in contrast, leaves the abrupt saying, "Follow me and leave the dead to bury their own dead" at the very end of the unit. In Luke, the final comment is "you go and proclaim the kingdom of God." With the modifications in Luke, the aggressive chreia has become part of a program of instruction not only concerning Jesus' journey to Jerusalem (introduced in Luke 9:51) but also concerning proclamation of the kingdom of God, which is an explicit part of Jesus' activity in the Lukan account (4:43; 6:20; 8:1; 9:2,11).

In Luke, therefore, the first two chreiai introduce Jesus as an authoritative speaker, present the theme "Follow me," and restate the theme in terms of a set of actions associated with Jerusalem and the kingdom of God. But the sequence does not end here. An additional unit stands in Luke as follows:

> Another said, "I will follow you, Lord; but let me first say farewell to those at my home." And Jesus said to him, "No one who puts his hand to the plow and looks back is fit for the kingdom of God." (Luke 9:61–62)

This unit features "another" person repeating the first part of the person's statement in the first chreia ("I will follow you," 9:57) and the first part of the person's statement in the second chreia ("Lord, let me first . . .," 9:59). Then the person makes a request related to family attachments which is milder than the request in the second unit. The situation does not have the characteristics of a crisis, like the unit before it that features the death of the person's father. Rather, the situation is like Elisha's request to Elijah simply to bid his parents farewell before he leaves them (1 Kgs 19:20). These features suggest that Luke has carried the ἦθος ("ethos") of Jesus and the theme of following into even more domesticated and traditional settings.

The role of the final Lukan unit in an elaboration of the theme is evident from the repetition of the phrase "kingdom of God." But there is another rhetorical dimension at work in the unit. Jesus' response is a maxim. A maxim, according to Aristotle (*Rhet.* II.xxi.2), is a general statement about the objects of human actions and what should be chosen or avoided with reference to them. The statement "No one who puts his hand to the plow and looks back is fit for the kingdom of God" is a general statement about human action directed toward the kingdom of God. There are, of course, different kinds of maxims. This one is representative of the kind that "are clear to those who consider them" as soon as they are uttered (Aristotle, *Rhet.* II.xxi.5). In other words, Jesus' maxim is like the one cited by Aristotle (*Rhet.* II.xxi.5): οὐδεὶς ἐραυτὴς ὅς τις οὐκ ἀεὶ φιλεῖ ("He is no lover who does not love always."). The content of the saying itself is clear, with the result that its meaning is evident.

When the third unit in Luke ends with a maxim, an important rhetorical sequence has occurred. Maxims are important parts of rhetorical syllogisms (which Aristotle calls "enthymemes"). According to Aristotle (*Rhet.* II.xxi.2): "Maxims are the premises or conclusions of enthymemes without the syllogism." The meaning of Aristotle's assertion can easily be seen in the famous syllogism:

First premise: All men are mortal.
Second premise: Socrates is a man.
Conclusion: Therefore, Socrates is mortal.

The first premise of this syllogism is a maxim. The conclusion, which is specific, results from the application of the maxim ("All men are mortal.") to a specific premise ("Socrates is a man."). In a rhetorical setting, in contrast to a logical demonstration, the speaker regularly presents the maxim in the form of a rationale after the conclusion.[18] For example, a speaker could state the preceding logical syllogism as a rhetorical enthymeme: "Socrates is mortal, because all men are mortal." There is no need to state the second premise, since the hearers will presuppose that Socrates is a man. In a rhetorical setting, then, it is customary to introduce the conclusion first, to provide a rationale in a maxim which follows, and to omit the second premise.

In the sequence in Luke, the maxim in the third unit provides a general premise (a rationale) for the deliberative exhortations before it. It provides a reason why a disciple who follows Jesus must "leave the dead to bury their own dead and go, proclaim the kingdom of God," as well as why a disciple cannot return to say farewell to his family. Prior to the maxim, the only basis for the exhortation was Jesus' authoritative $\mathring{\eta}\theta os$ ("ethos"). The disciple should go because the authoritative personage whom he approached said that he should go. But the third unit introduces an argumentative reason why he should leave all attachments and go: "No one who puts his hand to the plow and looks back is fit for the kingdom of God." This rationale suggests that the disciple should act uncompromisingly because people who turn aside from a task that requires straightforward concentration are unfit for the task they began. With such a rationale, the unit has moved to another form of logic, namely, deductive logic. In contrast, the logic of $\mathring{\eta}\theta os$ ("ethos") is the logic of induction. Jesus is an authoritative person, because it is possible to tell about exemplary occasions in which various people recognized his authority. The logic of $\mathring{\eta}\theta os$ ("ethos") supports itself through examples that illustrate its truth. When Jesus' speech moves beyond the exhibition of $\mathring{\eta}\theta os$ ("ethos") in cleverness and exhortation to the exhibition of $\mathring{\eta}\theta os$ ("ethos") in a maxim, it has interwoven inductive and deductive reasoning.

The third unit in the Lukan version, therefore, introduces an underlying syllogism. When it is possible to reconstruct such a syllogism, deductive logic is present in the argumentation. The syllogism is as follows:

---

18. Aristotle makes this point in *Rhet.* II.xxi.2.

> First premise: No one who puts his hand to the plow and looks back is fit for the kingdom of God.
> Second premise: You wish to be fit for the kingdom of God.
> Conclusion: Therefore, leave the dead to bury the dead, and go, proclaim the kingdom of God.

The three units in Luke have successfully established a thesis with a rationale. This rhetorical move has set the stage for an elaboration that could present a complete argument. In this setting, however, we do not get a complete elaboration. We simply get the establishment of a deliberative thesis (a disciple should go uncompromisingly and proclaim the kingdom of God) supported by a rationale.

Before we leave the Lukan unit, we should notice two more characteristics of the maxim. First, the maxim provides a rationale which has strong support in Mediterranean tradition. The situation evoked by this maxim goes back as far as Hesiod's *Works and Days*, where the plowman is defined as:

> he who attends to his work and drives a straight furrow and no longer gapes after his comrades, but keeps his mind on his work. (l. 443)

A plowman must devote himself entirely to his work without allowing his interest in other people to interrupt him. Hesiod indicates that the sower (l. 445) and the one who covers the seed by harrowing ($\dot{\epsilon}\pi\iota$-$\sigma\kappa\alpha\phi\epsilon\dot{\upsilon}s$, l. 470) are most likely to cause the distraction. In an Egyptian plowing scene available to us,[19] a plowman has submitted to the temptation to stop, turn around, and converse with another man who is standing with his arms folded.[20] But this was not a desirable situation, since the plowing and planting needed to be completed within as short a period as possible, customarily ten days,[21] in order for the crop to receive proper moisture and be ready at the appropriate time for harvest. According to Homeric tradition, the press of time meant that the plowman had to keep going throughout the day without eating until nightfall, though he might get a drink at the end of the furrow (*Iliad* 18.544–47). Homer's *Odyssey* refers to the necessary commitment of the plowman and the plowman's eagerness for the day to end in a scene that is informative for the interpretation of Luke 9:62:

> But Odysseus would ever turn his head toward the blazing sun ($\pi o \lambda \lambda \grave{\alpha} \pi \rho \grave{o}s$ $\dot{\eta} \acute{\epsilon} \lambda \iota o \nu \kappa \epsilon \phi \alpha \lambda \grave{\eta} \tau \rho \acute{\epsilon} \pi \epsilon \pi \alpha \mu \phi \alpha \nu \acute{o} \omega \nu \tau \alpha$), eager to see it set, for verily he was eager to return home. And as a man longs for supper, for whom all day long a yoke of wine-dark oxen has drawn the jointed plow through fallow land, and

19. Wilkinson, *Popular Account*, ii.13.

20. West, *Hesiod*, 271, note 444.

21. For the details, see the "Instruction of Ninurta," 34–40 cited in West, *Hesiod*, 5 and 271, note 444.

gladly for him does the light of the sun sink, that he may busy him with his supper, and his knees grow weary as he goes; even so gladly for Odysseus did the light of the sun sink. (*Odyssey* 13.28–35)

Odysseus continually turned his head toward the sun as he longed for the sunset, but he did not turn his head and look back (βλέπων εἰς τὰ ὀπίσω, Luke 9:62). Clearly, a good plowman could turn his head momentarily to the side without ceasing his work or plowing unsatisfactorily. If, however, a person turned to look behind him, he had either stopped his plowing, as in the Egyptian scene, or he would have changed the angle of the plow so that the furrow would be shallow or crooked or both. The situation evoked in the rationale in Luke 9:62, then, is well known in Mediterranean tradition and would provide rich guidelines for understanding the ramifications of becoming a disciple and proclaiming the kingdom of God.

Second, this maxim moves the reader from the arena of wildlife in the initial chreia (foxes and birds of the air) to domestic life (plowing a furrow). The association of plowing with domestic life is obvious from the Homeric passage where Odysseus longs for the comfort of supper. Hesiod's discussion of the things needed in advance of the plowing, which include a house, a woman, and an ox,[22] also supports plowing's association with domestic life. Plowing is part of domestic living where a home offers the comforts of food and rest. The analogy of plowing, therefore, establishes contact with a different arena of life than the analogy with foxes and birds. Consequently, we have a sequence that domesticates the chreia both logically and metaphorically. The domestication occurs through repetition, restatement, ellipsis, and metaphor. Repetition of the themes of following, going away, and requesting permission establishes continuity. Restatement provides the setting for instruction to go out and proclaim the kingdom of God. Ellipsis provides efficient composition, especially in the last unit when Jesus' response omits exhortation and reversal of the person's statement in order to present a rationale for the exhortations. Metaphor provides the occasion for moving from a state of existence even more primitive than birds' and foxes' ("wandering around" without even their comforts) to a state of existence associated with the activities that produce food for a secure and comfortable life at home.

In the three units in Luke, we have the beginning steps of an elaboration containing an introduction, the statement of a theme, a restatement of the theme to associate it with the kingdom of God, and a rationale that grounds the theme in a well-known situation in domestic life. With this elaboration, the two abrupt chreiai from Q tradition that reflect a critical, untamed approach to society have located a home

22. *Works and Days*, 458–92.

within an account which portrays Jesus as a person who has quietly calculated the costs of his activity and has carefully reworked previous tradition to understand it. His responses, therefore, come out of an educational program designed to move people away from their natural or traditional inclinations into a system of understanding informed by the history of Jerusalem and Samaria, and the renewal of that history in the ministry of Jesus and the church. The elaboration of these chreiai has domesticated them within a didactic, historical framework that presents a series of events which led Jesus to Jerusalem and the church out of Jerusalem into the world. In this framework, untamed chreiai have become poignant, picturesque challenges to the person who is weighing the pros and cons of joining Christianity, which is now perceived as a movement that explains itself to others through an account of the events that led to its formation (Luke 1:1–4).

Before ending the analysis of these units, it will be instructive to return to the Matthean unit for an additional observation. There is, in fact, another unit in Matthew that is part of the rhetorical sequence elaborating the theme of following. The introductory verse (8:18) in which Jesus commands his disciples to go to the other side of the sea sets the stage not only for the two chreia-units but for an additional unit in which the disciples follow Jesus into a boat (8:23). The Matthean sequence, then, elaborates the theme of following in a way that is different from Luke. In the introductory verse, the narrator tells us that Jesus issued a command to go to the other side. In the first chreia-unit, a scribe tells Jesus he will follow him (8:19), in the next unit Jesus tells a disciple to follow him (8:22), and in the final unit the narrator tells us that Jesus' disciples followed him into a boat (8:23). Several scholars have explored the final unit well through modern methods of criticism.[23] The unit features the disciples during the time of the church with its eschatological tremors ($\sigma\epsilon\iota\sigma\mu oi$, 8:24; cf. 24:7; 27:51, 54; 28:2). When the disciples encounter difficulty, they cry out in a ritualistic manner, "Lord, save (us), we are perishing" (8:25). Jesus' response distinguishes between little faith and much faith, a distinction that is appropriate in a gathered community of faith rather than in a mission setting where initial belief is being sought. At the end, a congregation of "men" marvel that Jesus' power controls not only humans but also forces within the cosmos. The story, then, presents the church in the midst of its challenges in the world.

From the perspective of rhetorical criticism, the final Matthean unit presents a model of Jesus as lord over the church and the disciples as obedient but never sufficient believers in the church. In other words, the third unit elaborates the difficulties of following through argument from

23. Van Iersel and Linmans, "Storm on the Lake."

example. Here is a significant difference from the Lukan approach. In Luke, the introduction established the nature of the ἦθος ("ethos") of Jesus and the disciples. Then, the paradigmatic nature of the chreiai is presupposed as the narrator uses the thought and action in the chreiai to set forth a thesis about following and proclaiming the kingdom that is supported by a premise (i.e., a rationale) about plowing a furrow. This approach interweaves inductive and deductive logic, and it represents an embryonic stage of elaboration that could lead to a complete argument as exhibited by Hermogenes. Matthew's version, in contrast, remains in the realm of inductive argumentation. The chreiai present a scribe being told he will not be able to do what he thinks he can do (8:19–20), a disciple being told to respond uncompromisingly to a command to follow (8:21–22), and all of Jesus' disciples being insufficient for their task but appropriately petitioning the lord of the church (8:23–27). This sequence presents examples of appropriate and inappropriate approaches to discipleship. It does not satisfactorily set the stage for a complete elaboration as Hermogenes exhibited it, since it does not attempt to provide a rationale for the imperative or declarative statements in the units. Without a rationale, the argumentation remains inductive. It argues on the basis of ἦθος and example, but not on the basis of deductive logic. Only if inductive logic is interwoven with deductive logic will there be an opportunity to develop the unit into a complete argument.

3. Conclusion

Analysis of the development of the theme of following with two chreiai customarily attributed to Q tradition reveals different uses of these traditions in Matthew and Luke. Matthew stays in the realm of inductive logic, developing the theme through ἦθος and example in a setting of crossing the sea. Luke, in contrast, prefaces the chreiai with a unit that characterizes the intentions, actions, speech, and interrelations of Jesus and his disciples as Jesus sets his face toward Jerusalem. Then he composes the chreiai in a manner that introduces the theme of following and restates the theme before he presents a rationale at the end. The rationale introduces deductive logic into a rhetorical sequence based on inductive logic, grounding the assertions in a well-known situation in domestic life in Mediterranean society.

The difference between the presentation of the chreiai in Matthew and Luke is significant rhetorically. The issue is whether it is sufficient in the Christian community to ground certain assertions simply in the ἦθος ("ethos") of Jesus, or whether it is advantageous to provide one or more rationales from the arena of common experiences in life. When the reasoning establishes a basis for one or more assertions through a rationale that moves outside the arena of the ἦθος of Jesus, it moves into the realm of elaboration as discussed by Hermogenes. It is probably natural for any apophthegmatic tradition to contain the initial moves illustrated by these sections in Matthew and Luke. It remains to be seen, however, if parts of the synoptic tradition contain forms of elaboration beyond these initial stages.

FOUR

The Anointing of Jesus: Elaboration within a Chreia

Burton L. Mack

In the Gospel tradition there are four stories about a woman who anoints Jesus with perfumed oil (Mark 14:3–9; Matt 26:6–13; Luke 7:36–50; John 12:1–8). The stories are similar in that (1) the setting is a meal, except in Matthew where someone in the tradition has probably deleted the mention of a meal, (2) those present raise objections, and (3) Jesus responds to the objection, justifying the woman's action. But the differences are difficult to reconcile. The character of the woman ranges from "sinner" (Luke) to the exemplary Mary (John). The objections range from "waste" (Mark, Matthew), and failure to give alms instead (Mark, Matthew, John), to the fact that Jesus allowed it to happen (Luke). The geographical and historical placements do not agree, and the nature of Jesus' response differs markedly, especially when comparing Mark and Luke. And, finally, the literary place and purpose of the story in the four gospels is not the same.

Scholarship is therefore generally undecided about the relationships among the four stories. There appears to be some agreement, however, that Luke's story, though quite different than Mark's, contains at least some elements dependent upon Mark. There is also some agreement that John shows influence both of the Markan and Lukan stories, though John may have known the Markan form from oral tradition.[1] And scholarship regularly has understood Matthew as a slightly abbreviated reading of Mark. But beyond these general agreements, there is little clarity about how to understand the similarities and differences

---

1. Haenchen in *Weg Jesu* holds this latter position.

among the four accounts. Attention has focused primarily on the stories in Mark and Luke, however, because, both individually and as a set, they present interesting challenges to the form-critical approach to synoptic materials.

1. Problems for the Form-Critical Approach

Both Mark and Luke have resisted form-critical classification. This is because each contains a mixture of characteristics normally associated with one or another of the pure types of synoptic material. In the case of Mark's story, Bultmann settled for "biographical apophthegm,"[2] Dibelius saw it as a "paradigm,"[3] and Lohmeyer recognized elements in it that reminded him of the "controversy story."[4] Taylor called it a "story about Jesus which is on its way to become a pronouncement-story."[5] Recent scholars in the tradition of both form and redaction criticism have conceded that the Markan story is a "singularly mixed form"[6] with an "entangled history."[7]

The form-critical approach to this complexity has been to determine the stages in the growth of the tradition, accounting for the additions and changes that accrued at each point, in order to bracket them and arrive at the original form and setting. The earlier form critics tended to see the growth of the tradition as accrual to the story of sayings that could change its point by addition at the end. Schweizer still proceeds in this fashion, accepting Bultmann's opinion that the earliest form of the story concluded with verses 6 or 7 (Schweizer says verse 7), then accounting for verse 8a as a new explanation, verse 8b as a still later addition, and finally verse 9 as a Markan redaction.[8] But contemporary form critics have criticized the peel-back approach as too simple. They have been worried by the fact that the earliest form, reconstructed in this way, lacks sense. They have also struggled with the logic of the additions, which do not appear to follow from one another, nor harmonize as a whole. Both Schenke and Dormeyer agree, for instance, that verse 8 ("for burial") is needed in order to explicate the sense of verse 6 ("good work"), and that it (rather than verse 7) must have been the point of climax for the original story. They disagree, however, among other points, on when and why verse 7 was added (the poor "always," Jesus "not always"). Schenke thinks it was added prior to Mark to address community concerns about almsgiving, and embarrassment about the

2. *History of the Synoptic Tradition*, 37.
3. *From Tradition to Gospel*, 43.
4. *Markus*, 291.
5. *Gospel According to St. Mark*, 529.
6. Dormeyer, *Die Passion Jesu*, 81.
7. Schenke, *Studien zur Passionsgeschichte*, 89.
8. Schweizer, *Good News According to Mark*, 289–90.

apparent extravagance of the woman's deed.[9] Dormeyer sees verse 7 as Markan redaction in order, apparently, to introduce dialogue and align the story with the controversies of the passion week.[10] Thus the more recent form critics, preferring to separate layers of the tradition rather than to reduce by excluding tack-ons, agree that it is verse 8 which gives the story sense, but can't agree about much else.

Mark 14:8, it might be remembered, was precisely the point at which Bultmann found it necessary to draw the line. That was because it was verse 8 which linked the story expressly to the passion narrative, assumed a post-Easter christology, and attributed a symbolic meaning to the action that neither those present nor the woman herself could have understood. If verses 8 and 9 were excluded, Bultmann thought, the story could be seen as an early biographical apophthegm with some claim to historical plausibility. This he argued on the basis that the scene was not "idealized."[11] He did not say what the point of the story may have been. When, therefore, more recent attempts to make sense of the story find verse 8 to be crucial for its being told at all, a lovely embarrassment for liberal form critics results. The story only makes sense in its complex form, and it must relate to a subtle and advanced theological reflection on the passion. But then it is most difficult to explain the prehistory of the story, especially why it appears to build upon such an unlikely account as that of the curious action of a woman who could not have known the meaning of what she was doing.

Conservative scholars are far less troubled, of course. Both Pesch[12] and Gnilka,[13] for instance, follow Jeremias[14] in thinking that most of the account (with some reservations about Markan redaction here and there) is plausible as a passion week event. These scholars also note the difficulty of making sense of the line of thought in the story, a difficulty given with the multiple points which a surface reading encounters. But they overcome this difficulty by arguing on the one hand that Jesus was engaging in Rabbinic debate on the distinction between almsgiving and good works, and by accepting that Jesus was aware of his imminent death as saving event on the other. For these scholars the woman's deed was an act of devotion (though she may not have realized its full symbolic significance), the objection raised was reasonable (there is no irony in the story), and Jesus' response forthright (not "tendentious" in any way, as Gnilka says[15]).

Only Derrett, as far as I can see, has dared to look closely at the scene

---

9. Schenke, *Studien zur Passionsgeschichte*, 108–9.
10. Dormeyer, *Die Passion Jesu*, 77–81.
11. Bultmann, *History of the Synoptic Tradition*, 37.
12. "Die Salbung Jesu."
13. *Markus*.
14. "Die Salbungsgeschichte."
15. *Markus*, 226.

(verse 3) and ask why the woman's deed was objectionable in the first place.[16] He notes that the scenes are similar in Mark and Luke, but that the objections raised in each are different. Could it be, he wonders, that an early form of the story common to both was simply about a woman's deed, found objectionable to some, to which objection Jesus responded in some telling way? He considers this plausible, finds the Lukan scene to provide the clues as to what was objectionable about the woman's act, and theorizes that the fragmentation of the tradition may have resulted from diverse attempts to comment on Jesus' response.[17] He infers from Luke that the original story may have left the source of complaint "vague,"[18] but shows that it must have been some perception of the woman, her gesture with regard to Jesus, and the fact that he allowed it which challenged conventional mores. He marshals considerable evidence to argue that her circumstances reflect those of an "ex-prostitute," and that her behavior would readily have created an embarrassing position for Jesus.[19]

Derrett is undoubtedly right (although "prostitute" would be better than "ex-prostitute"; "hetare" would be better than "prostitute"; and there is no reason to think that her act was religious devotion). Most scholars have mentioned the untoward circumstances and the peculiar nature of the action that gets the story started. It matters little, from this perspective, whether the woman anointed Jesus' head (so Mark, Matthew) or his feet (Luke, John). That it was a woman, unannounced at a meal with guests, who voluntarily poured out an expensive, perfumed oil upon him would be noteworthy indeed, no matter what role or characterization we imagine for Jesus. Most scholars have seen this, and commented upon the possibility that the tradition could easily have misunderstood the woman's character and action. But none, except Derrett, has regarded the unseemliness of the scene itself to have defined that which was objectionable about it and chosen rather to start the investigation with the objections articulated by the opponents in the two accounts.

In Mark the objection is about the "waste," a marvelous tour de force that shifts attention onto an issue capable of elaboration, while allowing the flavor of unseemliness to stand. Traditional scholarship does not seem to see the humor in that at all, though Derrett sees the irony. In Luke the objection that the bystanders direct toward Jesus is not that he allows the woman to perform, but that he must not be a true prophet, or else he would know what kind of a woman she was. This is another very clever shift in naming the issue. But most scholars rush to Jesus' defense,

16. Derrett, "Anointing at Bethany."
17. Derrett, "Anointing at Bethany," 266.
18. Derrett, "Anointing at Bethany," 267.
19. Derrett, "Anointing at Bethany," 267.

thankful that Luke has preserved the story so well, and that Jesus' lesson to the Pharisees is so clear! Even Derrett disappoints us as he continues his investigation. He does see the artistry of Mark's story, the shrewdness of the woman's action, and the cleverness of Jesus' argumentation. But he reads it as history after all, assumes that the woman had been "released from a life of shame,"[20] and that "Jesus could be the soul of tact without compromising his mission as leader and teacher."[21]

So we are back at square one with the question of history and tradition. Bultmann was certainly right about the high christology reflected in the Markan story as it stands, and its implausibility as historical account. The same, of course, is true for Luke. But the story Bultmann offers as biographical apophthegm (14:3–6 or 7) does not make sense without verse 8, as recent studies have shown. This means that neither Mark nor Luke gives us the original story line. What has fallen out is Jesus' (plausibly clever) original rejoinder. The story originally must have told about some other appropriate objection and ended with some other (brief) response, exactly as Derrett has suspected. It must have been, that is, a Cynic chreia. Transmission in the early Christian communities would have changed it by supplying objections more to the point of the practical and theological issues facing those communities. This would account for the divergences between Mark and Luke, were we able to imagine a way with story material which could account for those changes in just the way they have occurred. This chapter will argue that such a way with stories can be shown. It is called elaboration. Our thesis will be that the original story was a chreia, that those who transmitted it expanded it in two different ways in the course of transmission, and that the expansions followed the pattern of chreia elaboration as learned in the Hellenistic school. In this case, the elaboration functions as a device for narrative expansion within the story itself. Jesus will propose a thesis about the significance of the enigmatic action, then go on to elaborate the point himself, ending with his own authoritative pronouncement on the situation. The notion of authority that allows this curiously self-referential mode of argumentation is unusual; but the pattern of elaboration employed is not unusual at all.

2. The Chreia and Its Narrative Elaboration

The major concern of this essay will be to demonstrate and explore the rhetorical pattern of elaboration in the composition of Mark 14:3–9 and Luke 7:36–50. But before moving to that exploration, some discussion about the four variants as narrative amplifications of a common

20. Derrett, "Anointing at Bethany," 268.
21. Derrett, "Anointing at Bethany," 278.

scene will be helpful. There are several observations to be made that relate to the question of a chreia as point of departure for a (narrative) elaboration, and the conditions under which the author could achieve such an elaboration.

We may begin by listing six formal characteristics that all of the four variants have in common: (1) the scene is similar, including meal, the presence of Jesus and other guests, entrance of a woman, and her action; (2) in each case some bystander raises an objection; (3) Jesus responds to the objection; (4) the response consists of making several statements or points, culminating in a strong pronouncement; (5) in each case we can identify specifics, peculiar to a particular gospel's version, that enable that version to contribute significantly to the thematic and narrative development of its larger gospel content; and (6) the characterization of Jesus that the elaboration assumes or develops is highly christological. Jesus is no mere prophet or teacher.

There is nothing in this list of observations with which traditional scholarship would take exception. Scholars have repeatedly emphasized item 5 in redaction-critical studies. They have frequently noted item 6, although they usually handle it obliquely in asides that reveal a scholar's position on the question of the historical Jesus and the Christ of faith. Item 4 is the rub. Here is where scholars have usually raised form- and tradition-critical questions. How, so the question goes in general, could a single narrative have given rise to such diverse dialogue? And, how can we understand the multiple points in the extended response to have come together as a unit? It is curious that scholars have not taken the compositional process called redaction as a model on which to build a theory of variants in pre-gospel strata of the synoptic tradition. Most scholars readily acknowledge that each evangelist has introduced specific changes into a received tradition for particular purposes. Some of these changes are quite drastic (cf. John). But there is noticeable caution, if not resistance, to the idea that the received tradition itself may be the product of similar authorial creativity. One reason for this caution is that the larger narrative context which allows and controls redaction-critical analyses is not at hand for smaller compositions. What we have lacked is a compositional model which can account both for the similarities and the differences of just such a set of stories as the four under discussion. Our suggestion will be that the rhetorical techniques of chreia elaboration provide us with such a model.

The major components of a chreia are given with the first three items above: scene, challenge, response. It is the similarity of the four descriptions of the scene that raises the question of a common story behind the four accounts. We would recognize any one account as a chreia, were it to end with a single, pointed rejoinder. Instead, each of the accounts contains a complex set of sayings at this point. And it does not appear that any one of these statements would do as a single-statement response to the situation. We cannot, therefore, reconstruct an original chreia from the material at hand. But it is not difficult to imagine such a story about Jesus, given others which do come to focus on a single pronouncement.

We can, however, take a closer look at the scene. Various authors apparently found it remarkable in and of itself, and capable of multiple readings. All variants retain the narration of the action of a woman. Commentators have noticed that her act is unmotivated, therefore surprising, and that it is uncommon given what we know of social mores in Palestine, thus enigmatic. This means that it is the action of the woman itself that not only sets the scene, but determines the scene as challenging. There are many examples of chreiai in Hellenistic literature in which someone's behavior other than that of the principal person sets the scene as challenging. We may conclude that Jesus' response will have to meet that challenge. But what was the challenge?

As the accounts now stand, a third party articulates the challenge that Jesus must address. This feature also is not uncommon in Hellenistic chreiai as a way to make precise the challenge, and set things up for the rejoinder. But here the variant traditions part ways. Mark's variant directs the objection at the woman's action (as wasteful); Luke directs the objection at Jesus himself (for allowing such a thing to happen). Both, however, can be readings of the same scene. This is especially so, since the woman's action directly involved Jesus, implicating him personally in both its surprising and embarrassing aspects. If it were a chreia, Jesus' response would have to meet a complex challenge, addressing both the woman's deed and his own acceptance of it. In both Mark and Luke Jesus' extended response actually does take up both of these aspects of the challenge, even though the articulated objection names but one of them. It is part of the artistry of each elaboration to interweave the unarticulated aspect of the challenge-response with the expressed aspect, and combine them constructively in a single conclusion.

We may question, however, whether either of the two articulated objections (Luke, Mark) are original, since both of them set things up precisely for the extended responses. And each of these responses assumes a high christological characterization for Jesus, worthy of receiving an act of devotion. Characterization is exactly what chreiai achieve, of course. But it would not be difficult to understand the original chreia scene as a challenge for someone other than a savior. It would, in fact, be much more appropriate and challenging for someone like a prophet or teacher, engaged in some kind of social critique and ethical discourse. It would also make a more interesting story. So, if there is an original chreia as the common source for Mark and Luke, it may have characterized Jesus quite differently. And it may have ended with a more aphoristic rejoinder. A shift in the characterization of Jesus, in keeping with the development of christologies in several Christian communities, would put tremendous pressure on such a chreia. The texts as we have them clearly show that the scene could continue to be suggestive. But these later communities would have to recast the point of the scene's challenge. Such a recasting could account for our stories, and the articulated objections in the mouth of third parties would have achieved it. That the objections in Mark and Luke appear not to encompass the full complexity of the challenge of the scene is therefore understandable. They shift the focus away from the challenge as embarrassment, rename it as an issue appropriate to Jesus as the Christ, and introduce another character to sustain the brunt of the response. Now it is the ones who object who carry the onus. They are ignorant of the meaning of the enigmatic action, and thus are potentially the real opponents. The storytellers have cleverly constructed each objection by naming the challenge in such a way that Jesus can counter it by evoking Christian values. And as he does so, his elaborate response takes up and resolves even those aspects of the chreia's challenge not acknowledged by the interlocutors: it justifies and praises the woman; it parries and "instructs" the objectors; and it portrays Jesus as the master teacher and the Christ.

We want now to look more closely at the texts as we have them, in order to trace these rhetorical achievements. We shall see that their outlines follow the pattern of elaboration, and that their modes of argumentation develop themes in much the same way as our example in Hermogenes does. If we follow our suggestion about an original chreia, then what we have before us are chreiai expanded into larger narrative units by a condensed elaboration taking place within the story itself. If we do not follow this suggestion, then what we have are two longer stories (Mark, Luke) featuring different elaborate responses to the same scene, both of which the authors constructed, formally, according to the same rhetorical pattern. Either way, the importance of a memorable scene and the significance of a learned pattern of persuasion are both in view.

3.   The Pattern of Elaboration in Mark and Luke

Our study will focus on the stories in Mark and Luke. Our purpose will be to trace out the pattern of elaboration in each story by identifying the rhetorical functions of each part or saying of the story. In order to enhance our thesis that these stories are expanded chreiai, we will also identify the major components of a chreia: setting, question, response. First, we shall give the text, the sections identified by (1) formal correlation to chreia components, (2) brief designations of the way in which the elaboration has amplified the chreia components, and (3) their rhetorical functions. Numbers in parentheses at the left will indicate items in the pattern of elaboration in Hermogenes (see chapter 2). Following the text we will give a brief analysis of its rhetorical logic.

3.1   The Pattern in Mark 14:3–9

Chreia Component: Setting
Amplification: Probably only slightly embellished
Rhetorical Function: *Narratio*

> And while he was at Bethany in the house of Simon the leper, as he sat at table, a woman came with an alabaster jar of ointment of pure nard, very costly, and she broke the jar and poured it over his head. (vs 3)

Chreia Component: Challenge, Question
Amplification: Hostile emotions emphasized; Objection specified and expressed
Rhetorical Function: *Quaestio*

> But there were some who said to themselves indignantly, "Why was the ointment thus wasted? For this ointment might have been sold for more than three hundred denarii, and given to the poor." And they reproached her. (vss 4–5)

Chreia Component: Response
Amplification: Extended response addressing the objectors
Rhetorical Function: Elaboration, *Argumentatio*

(2) *Response* (to redirect the question)

> But Jesus said, "Let her alone; why do you trouble *her*?" (vs 6a)

(3) *Rationale* (as thesis)

> She has done a *beautiful thing* to me. (vs 6b)

(4) *Contrary* (as contrast)

> "For you *always* have the poor with you . . .; but you will *not always* have me." (vs 7a, c)

(5) *Analogy* (implied)

> ". . . and whenever you will, you can *do good* to them"; (vs 7b)

(6) *Example*

> "She has done what she could; she has anointed my body beforehand for burying." (vs 8)

(7) *Judgment* (as encomiastic period)

> "And truly I say to you, wherever the gospel is preached in the whole world, what she has done will be told in memory of her." (vs 9)

Mark's story has the form of a slightly expanded chreia. It is brief, graphic in description, and swift in its movement toward a final pronouncement. Nevertheless, Jesus' response does contain all of the basic elements of a rhetorical elaboration. It does not, however, fully develop any of the elements. The result is a series of statements with interlocking themes, tropes, and rhetorical topics, all entangled. It assumes a rather specific knowledge of the intricacies of Jewish convention and law. And its rhetorical logic proceeds by allusion and suggestion, rather than by specifying relationships.

One might wonder whether such an "elaboration" could be convincing. The answer is certainly that readers who may have taken the objectors' criticism of the woman seriously would not have found it convincing. But the objection is a fictitious construction, in any case, designed to set the stage for what readers sympathetic to Jesus and the woman will hope to see as a brilliant rebuttal. It is this judicial aspect of the argumentation (was the woman's action wrong or right legally?) that is dense, entangled, and implausible as serious address to the objectors. Formally the rudiments of a case are there. But the case rides on a clever distinction derived midrashically (poor always/Jesus not always), a distinction that assumes a high christology in order to work. So the judicial argumentation is a rhetorical device to transform a Cynic chreia (containing challenge and objection) into a constructive paradigm. The judicial argumentation yields therefore by degrees to a deliberative thesis (the woman's action was "good") in order finally to conclude on an epideictic note (the woman's action was exemplary and "worthy of praise"). We can see here the process of domestication of Cynic type chreiai in the synoptic tradition. If it does not work too smoothly in the Markan story, we may be looking at an early attempt. As we shall see, Luke has fully domesticated the chreia in his elaboration.

Mark's elaboration gives the amplification of the objection more space than might seem necessary. This was probably due to the difficulty encountered in shifting the challenge away from the scene's obvious point, namely an embarrassing situation for a prophet or teacher. The setting itself does not appear to be greatly embellished. It probably reflects the description of the woman's action in the original chreia, although Mark probably added the localization in Bethany[22] in keeping with his geographical symbolism of the passion week (Bethany/Jerusalem). And the emphasis upon the costliness of the nard may also be an addition that anticipates and makes plausible the opening objection.

The objection is that the action was a "waste" ($\dot{a}\pi\omega\lambda\epsilon\iota a$) of the costly

---

22. See Schenke, *Studien zur Passionsgeschichte* for the full argument that Mark added the reference to Bethany in 14:3.

perfume. Someone carefully selected this objection as one that would allow for a clever argumentation, an argumentation which could (1) justify the woman's action, (2) get Jesus off the hook of having accepted an unseemly gesture (the real, but hidden issue), and (3) show Jesus to be master of the situation precisely because he is the Christ. But this objection is hardly one that would have occurred to the reader; it follows strangely on the description of the woman's action. To make it plausible, the author has done two things. First, he has emphasized the hostility of those who object by means of a twofold mention that frames their statement of objection (they expressed indignation; they reproached her). This characterization of the objectors momentarily shifts the focus from the stated objection itself to the motivation of the objectors. It allows the reader to reserve judgment on the reasonableness of the stated objection by suggesting that more may be at stake. At least one will have to take those objectors seriously.

The second device intended to make such a surprising issue plausible is the addition of a stated reason ("might have been sold, given to the poor"). This suggestion for an alternative use of the perfume does provide a standard against which one may judge the "waste." It also puts the objectors strongly on the side of piety and conventional ethics. And it begins to explain their indignation. With this suggestion they have proposed another course of action as better (a deliberative thesis), and it sets the stage nicely for Jesus' response as a rebuttal over a deliberative issue. Once the elaboration has achieved this, the reader is ready to go along with it and see what Jesus will say. But his response will also have to meet the implicit challenge to Jesus' character, given with the chreia scene. And the ironic potential of the woman's generous gesture toward Jesus as a "waste," though submerged for the time being by the serious considerations of piety, will certainly have to surface again.

Thus the objection is skillfully crafted. It specifies the challenge of the chreia in such a way as to invite just that kind of elaboration which the new christological characterization of Jesus requires. It has eased the situation of embarrassment for Jesus already, by allowing him to address a partial and contentious interpretation of it instead of having to confront the issue of his own integrity initially by insinuating that the motives of the objectors are dishonest. They, not he, can now come under fire.

Jesus' response consists of a very compact set of statements that proceed without interruption toward a climactic prophetic pronouncement. The objectors do not speak again. But the response continues to use the second person address to the end. It is a little speech, stilted in style, and dense, almost cryptic, in argumentation. It does remind one of a student's classroom exercise, except for its subtleties.

The first words (introduction) address the objectors and define the speech situation as debate between hostile parties. The imperative "Let her alone" immediately defines Jesus' position over against the objectors with respect to the woman's deed. It also subtly suggests that the event now also involves them as active participants. The question that follows is not mere narrative embellishment. The objectors had asked *why* the perfume had been wasted? Now they are being asked "*why* do you trouble *her*?" To question their motives tarnishes their stated objection as well. It also indicates one of the levels at which Jesus will re-define the issue at sake and make his argument. The issue is one of intentionality (*why*, indeed! *status qualitas* in technical terminology), and of definition (*what* exactly?—*status definitivus*).

The rationale is immediately given in the form of a thesis: "She did a good thing (καλὸν ἔργον) for me." The use of καλόν is rhetorically significant. It is the final category that defines the major objective of the epideictic speech. Teachers of rhetoric also understood the final categories as a set (see chapter 2) as particularly appropriate "arguments" in the development of theses. If Jesus can show that the action was καλόν, he will have succeeded in countering the objection ("wasteful").

That καλόν occurs as an adjective does not detract from its rhetorical significance. The rhetorical handbooks usually list the final categories as substantized adjectives, and they appear in declamations either in that form as predicates, or simply as adjectives modifying nouns. They are abstractions of cultural values, however, and require the consent of the audience as to what standards define them. Jesus' statement, therefore, confronts us with a most unusual situation. In order for Jesus' argument to be persuasive, the audience will have to agree on what constitutes a good work. The objectors have already expressed themselves on this matter, and it appears that their standard will be the conventions of Jewish piety. The term καλόν can work both ways, of course, evoking both Jewish and Christian values. So we shall have to wait and see how Jesus will define it, and whether his argument appears persuasive.

The argument from the contrary that follows is not clearly focused, but that may be by design. It is, instead, suggestive, collecting together a number of the comparisons and contrasts given with the situation, and playing them off against one another. The effect will be to subvert the proposal of the objectors by calling its clarity into question. Jesus' statement does this by suggesting that the situation is much more complex than they have assumed.

The statement itself is rather straightforward, to be sure: "You always have the poor . . . you will not always have me." On the surface of it, the assertion is both banal (if we do not read theological significance into Jesus' not always being present) and presumptuous (in its implicit claim for some exceptional status of Jesus over against the poor). But the

contrast between Jesus and the poor only makes explicit what the objectors have already implicitly introduced. Rhetorically, therefore, Jesus
has accepted their proposal of a difference between "wasting" the perfume on *him* versus giving the money to the *poor*. In the process of doing
that, however, he specifies the difference between himself and the poor
(poor *always* present; Jesus *not always* present). The objectors will have
to consider this point seriously, because it is derived shrewdly as a point
of midrash. The verse in question is Deut 15:11: "The poor will always be
with you in the land." No one will have missed the appeal to an
acknowledged code (Torah). They will have to agree that the law says
that about the poor (among other things). And they will hardly be able
to disagree about the point Jesus makes from it (poor *always*; I *not*
always). But if they allow this distinction to determine the comparison/
contrast between Jesus and the poor, they may already have conceded
too much, since considering presence and (imminent) absence to be the
major difference between the poor and Jesus implicitly acknowledges
some similarity between them and makes differences in other respects
ambiguous. Insofar as this is so, it calls into question the basis for
denying that the woman's expenditure upon Jesus was a good work.

The analogy that emerges from the comparison of Jesus and the poor
is "doing good works." Ordinarily, one would expect an explicit illustra-
tion ($\pi\alpha\rho\alpha\beta o\lambda\acute{\eta}$) to make the argument from analogy (e.g., "just as with
those who do good deeds, so . . ."). In this case, however, the analogy is
introduced only in passing, keeping the reader's attention focused on
the immediate scene, and leaving the precise definition of doing good
works open to further specification. But as a shared conception about a
general pattern of ethical behavior, doing a good deed easily falls within
the provenance of the rhetorical analogy. And the way in which the
elaboration introduces it into the argumentation shows that it refers to
some general practice. The analogy occurs between the two statements
of the contrast. Since the poor are always there, Jesus says, "you can do
good ($\epsilon\mathring{v}$ $\pi o\iota\widehat{\eta}\sigma\alpha\iota$) to them whenever you will." This statement throws
the spotlight upon the objectors and, linked as the analogy is to the
contrast between Jesus and the poor, it opens up yet another contrastive
perspective on the chreia situation. What the objectors are *able* to do any
time may be compared with what the woman *did* in an opportune time.
By association it is possible now to think that her action also was a good
deed.

Clearly, the combination of the analogy and the contrary has seriously eroded the objectors' premises. The basic contrast (always/not
always) has given rise to a series of comparisons (Jesus—poor;
objectors—woman; alms—good deeds). But the comparisons are not
contrastive in all respects. It becomes more and more difficult to keep in
mind exactly what it was that made giving alms to the poor "good," and

presenting Jesus with a gift "bad." Nothing has been resolved yet. But because things are no longer as simple as they once seemed, it is now difficult to resist the thought that "she did a good thing for me."

The argumentation comes to a climax in verse 8: "She did what she could (ὃ ἔσχεν ἐποίησεν). She was ahead of time in anointing my body for burial." These are startling statements, given the issue that has been under consideration. Suddenly the christological intention of the elaboration surfaces in a most unusual notion that stuns the modern imagination. Because this interpretation of the woman's deed is so strange, it immediately raises a set of new questions about its meaning. It is difficult to determine how many of the questions raised for modern scholars would have occurred to first-century readers. They have to do with the curious complex of christological ideas relating "body," "burial," "anointing," and a passion week setting for a symbolic anointing in "anticipation" of Jesus' death. They also have to do with questions about the woman's gestures, intentions, and knowledge of the significance of her action. These questions may or may not be important for reconstructing early Christian interpretations of the death of Jesus, for assessing the persuasiveness of the story for early Christians, or for determining its redaction-critical setting. But they should not detract us from noticing the way in which the statements function rhetorically in the development of Jesus' elaboration.

With respect to the preceding argumentation, the two statements provide a brilliant conclusion. Jesus had said that the objectors could (δύνασθαι) do good whenever they wished. There may be a bit of sarcasm in this statement, for it sets up a contrastive comparison between their ability to perform and the woman's actual performance. The statement that "she did what she could" now picks up this contrast. And it subtly suggests a line of thought that could prove to be quite embarrassing for the objectors: they could (δύνασθαι) do good (but have they done so?). The woman did accomplish (ἔργασθαι) a good deed (but how "could" she?). The peculiar terminology and syntax of the statement (ὃ ἔσχεν ἐποίησεν) makes it probable that we are not reading too much into the statement. The desire to distinguish between "what lay in her power" and "what lay in the objectors' power" might account for such peculiar terms and syntax. Derrett sees this as the main point in fact. He suggests that the story may still understand the woman even at this stage of the tradition as an ex-prostitute. If so, money or goods earned from her profession would not be acceptable for alms or offerings. She would not be *able* to do what the objectors had advised.[23] But even if this is not the point, what was available to her was an opportunity not always present, in distinction to an opportunity always present for the objectors. Jere-

23. Derrett, "Anointing at Bethany," 268.

mias and others have argued that this distinction is quite important for the argument.[24] They understand Jesus to be distinguishing between almsgiving and doing good works. According to Jewish convention, one could give alms to the poor at any time; but one did good works as occasion arose, and for anyone. That "she did what she had in her power to do" must then be a consideration with some judicial significance. Derrett and Jeremias, as mentioned above, have proposed plausible references to Jewish legal distinctions that could (partially) justify or explain the act as a good work. In terms of Hellenistic rhetoric the issue would be one of the quality of the action. And Jesus would be saying that it was the action available to her, i.e., "possible" (δυνατόν), if not "necessary" (ἀναγκαῖον), either of which would justify her action.

That she "anointed *for burial*" is the final judicial consideration. Jeremias has shown that the burial of the dead occurs regularly in lists of good works to be performed in times of specific need. He has argued that such good works took obligatory precedence over giving alms. He concluded, therefore, that the argumentation in our story clinches its point with the designation of the deed as an anointing for burial.[25] If that is what it was, there can be no question about its being a good deed. In terms of Hellenistic rhetoric this association would serve well as a concluding argument, showing that the deed was "legal" or "right" (δίκαιον).

But all of that is possible only if the chreia deed can be thought of in some way as an anointing for burial. Jesus has prepared for this by drawing the contrast between the poor and himself in terms of always/ not always. It was a clever move, enabling the comparisons and contrasts to work advantageously, in order, finally, to make plausible the specific good deed as an anointing for burial in anticipation of his not always being there. It also makes possible one final argument that can round out the consideration on the deed as good. Jeremias's point about the definition of a good deed as a timely response to occasional situations of need is apropos here. That she did what she could at a time opportune to her, in anticipation of Jesus' need, fits Jeremias's definition of a good deed. It also illustrates what the Greeks called "the expedient" or "the advantageous" (τὸ συμφέρον). So this elaboration has shown the woman's deed to be "expedient," "legal," "possible," and "necessary," as well as "good" (καλόν). That's quite an argumentation.

With that established, the epideictic mode of argumentation can surface. Mark 14:8 already is a kind of example-in-the-making. It uses the conclusion of the argument to point back to the chreia scene itself and claim it as an actual instance of doing a good deed. But now the end

24. See, for example, Jeremias, "Die Salbungsgeschichte," 110.
25. Jeremias, "Die Salbungsgeschichte."

of the elaboration links the good deed to the characterization of Jesus as the Christ and to the kerygma of his saving death. That understanding, of course, was at work all along, and the fact that the argumentation has left the objectors behind will not have bothered Christian readers. The point was not to convince the objectors anyway, but to celebrate the victory over them that the new christology made possible. And with that verse 9 can follow.

The judgment links the story as a memorial of the woman's deed with the gospel. The saying is a combination of prophetic and celebrative assertion. As such, it raises a number of theological and conceptual problems for modern scholars, because it is not clear how the memorial of the woman enhances the gospel, nor how early Christians could have transmitted it without knowing her name. These questions we will have to overlook. Rhetorically, however, the move is appropriately conclusive to the set of issues that the chreia raised, and to the several modes of argumentation that the elaboration engaged. The challenge that the chreia presented was twofold: the unseemliness of the woman's action and what that might imply about Jesus. Both challenges have been met. The woman's action turns out to have been a good deed; and Jesus turns out to be the Christ in anticipation of his death. Both themes converge in the interpretation of the deed as an "anointing for burial" (hardly a "waste"). This means that the conclusion contains both a laudation of the woman and a gospel of the Christ. The author does not shy away from attributing this saying to Jesus. The use of the amen formula indicates, in fact, that it serves rhetorically as the citation from an authority. That Jesus proclaims himself by means of this laudation of the woman apparently was not a conceptual problem. It follows from the way in which the early Christian communities appropriated the techniques of chreia analysis and elaboration. The decision to recast a simple chreia as a serious debate against objectors meant that Jesus would have to be the author of the elaboration. The loss of the pointed saying in the original chreia found compensation in the appropriate slot of the elaboration. Jesus' judgment is the new memorable rejoinder.

3.2   The Pattern of Elaboration in Luke 7:36–50

Chreia Component: Setting
Amplification: Description of Scene, Characters, Event
Rhetorical Function: *Narratio*

> One of the Pharisees asked him to eat with him, and he went into the Pharisee's house, and sat at table. And behold, a woman of the city, who was a sinner, when she learned that he was sitting at table in the Pharisee's house, brought an alabaster flask of ointment, and standing behind him at his feet, weeping, she began to wet his feet with her tears, and wiped them with the hair of her head, and kissed his feet, and anointed them with the ointment. (vss 36–38)

Chreia Component: Challenge, Question
Amplification: Question specified, but not expressed
Rhetorical Function: *Quaestio*

> Now when the Pharisee who had invited him saw it, he said to himself, "If this man were a prophet, he would have known who and what sort of woman this is who is touching him, for she is a sinner." (vs 39)

Chreia Component: Response
Amplification: A Dialogue ensues about the matter
Rhetorical Function: Elaboration; *Argumentatio*

(1)   *Introduction* (Ethos of Speech-Situation established)

> And Jesus answering said to him, "Simon, I have something to say to you." And he answered, "What is it, Teacher?" (vs 40)

(5)   *Analogy* (Contains comparison by working with the topic "greater/lesser")

> "A certain creditor had two debtors, one owed five hundred denarii, and the other fifty. When they could not pay, he forgave them both. Now which of them will love him more?" Simon answered, "The one, I suppose, to whom he forgave more." And he said to him, "You have judged rightly." (vss 41–43)

(6)   *Example* (Developed through contrast)

> Then turning toward the woman he said to Simon, "Do you see this woman? I entered your house, you gave me no water for my feet, but she has wet my feet with her tears and wiped them with her hair. You gave me no kiss, but from the time I came in she has not ceased to kiss my feet. You did not anoint my head with oil, but she has anointed my feet with ointment." (vss 44–46)

(3,4)   *Rationale* and *Contrary*

> "Therefore I tell you, her sins, which are many, are forgiven, for she loved much; but he who is forgiven little, loves little." (vs 47)

(8)   *Conclusion*

> And he said to her, "Your sins are forgiven." (vs 48)

Chreia Component: Challenge, Question
Amplification: The question rephrased
Rhetorical Function: Rebuttal; Redefinition of *Quaestio*

> Then those who were at table with him began to say among themselves, "Who is this, who even forgives sins?" (vs 49)

(7)   *Judgment*

> And he said to the woman, "Your faith has saved you; go in peace." (vs 50)

Luke's story is a chreia, amplified narratively by using the standard arguments in the pattern of elaboration. It has expanded the scene in order to introduce characterization appropriate to the issue that will be determined. The question of the Pharisee specifies, but does not articulate, the issue. The question implicitly objects to the action of the woman, but directs that objection toward Jesus, thus catching up the two aspects of the challenging situation. Since the Pharisee does not express the question, however, it presents an additional challenge: will Jesus even discern the objection (that the woman is a sinner; that as a prophet he should know that and should not have allowed the action to happen). The challenge to Jesus' discernment allows Luke to develop Jesus' superiority not only in terms of his rhetorical skills, but also in terms of his special status as savior. Luke can now expand Jesus' response into a dialogue that will defend the woman (judicial issue), instruct the Pharisee (deliberative issue), and establish his own status as one who forgives sinners (epideictic issue). The latter point is the one Luke wishes to emphasize. He does this by re-introducing the challenge at the end, rephrasing it in such a way as to allow Jesus to address it explicitly.

The argumentation does not follow the sequence of the elaboration pattern. Luke develops the argumentation inductively, beginning with a parable, the analogical function of which will only become clear when the argumentation gives the rationale. A parable (*analogy*) is appropriate rhetorically for the introduction of an inductive line of argumentation. It is also appropriate narratively, as an oblique entrée into a situation of unarticulated challenge. The choice of this particular parable is clever, for it gives the theme of the elaboration (forgiveness), as well as the major rhetorical topic (comparison). The general topic of comparison will allow for the development of a contrast in the example, as well as an opposition in the rationale. The conclusion also uses this topic (comparison), although not expressly. But the reader will know that the argumentation as a whole has shown the woman to be "forgiven," not (any longer?) a "sinner." A skillful use of the topic of comparison links the several parts of the elaboration rhetorically and aligns the judicial, deliberative, and epideictic issues to be resolved.

An explication of the situation in light of the analogy creates the example. It develops by contrast and results in both a positive and a (relatively) negative example of behavior motivated by love.

The rationale for the woman's action now appears. It is a conclusion to the inductive argumentation: "Much forgiven," "*for* she loved much." But it functions also as the rationale for the chreia: the woman acted that way *because* "her many sins are forgiven." The statement of the contrary clarifies the point: "The one who is forgiven little, loves little."

Since the argumentation has won the rationale by induction, it may now (re)state the rationale in a simple form as the conclusion: Her character is not that of a "sinner," as the objector had assumed; she is "forgiven." This means that the Pharisee was wrong and that Jesus has succeeded in countering one aspect of the challenge (that the woman was a sinner). He succeeded because the Pharisee had agreed to the validity of the point made by the analogy (a Socratic play, cf. Quintilian V. xi.3). He has also succeeded in demonstrating that he was a "prophet," thus countering the additional challenge of discernment presented by the Pharisee's doubt and silence.

But Jesus is not merely a prophet, so the argumentation has not fully met the second aspect of the challenge presented by the implicating action of the chreia. Luke shrewdly lets the other guests raise this challenge. They can raise it because Jesus has stated the conclusion in the form of an address to the woman: "Your sins are forgiven." The rhetorical ambivalence of this statement (conclusion/judgment) allows the guests to take it as an action of Jesus (Luke does not mind): "Who is this, who even forgives sins?" The "even" tips us off that the guests have accepted the demonstration of the prophetic character of Jesus. Now the issue has to do with the fact that the woman expressed her action of love (which demonstrated that she was forgiven) *toward* Jesus himself. Luke does not let this get out of hand. But he leaves the reader with the strong suggestion that Jesus has met the challenge of the chreia in respect to his character, if he is the one who forgives sins. And that is a judgment that Jesus cannot make for the reader. So the self-defense reaches a certain self-referential limit at this point. Luke ends the story, therefore, with a reference to the woman's *faith* as the cause or basis for her salvation. But this reference occurs in another very strong pronouncement by Jesus that functions in the elaboration as the citation of an authority. To manipulate the elaboration sequence in such a way as to conclude with a statement of Jesus as the statement from an authority is Luke's carefully devised achievement: "Your faith has saved you; go in peace." The thinly veiled liturgical nuance of dismissal, and the pronouncement of peace as the last word of a verbal battle, are touches that allow the authoritative judgment to come in last place. Traditionally, the appeal to emotions (argument by pathos) occupied the end of the rhetorical speech.

We might see this final judgment as curiously enigmatic, i.e., a kind of saying appropriate as a chreia response. If we follow our earlier suggestion that Luke's story is an expanded recasting of an originally brief chreia, we might imagine the process as follows: Luke deleted the original (brief) response. In its place he gives the extended elaboration. But this also ends climactically in a poignant, chreia-like statement. The new pronouncement is acceptable, however, precisely because of the new characterization of Jesus. We could argue, therefore, that Luke has expanded the chreia internally in order to achieve this new characterization. Luke's skill in the rhetorical analysis and elaboration of chreiai can be seen in this clever shift in characterization. But Luke has not elaborated the chreia on the model of a Hermogenes or a Plutarch. He has chosen to let Jesus speak for himself (by ἠθοποιΐα). The curious result is that Jesus, not Luke, appears as the master of rhetoric, elaborating his own chreia.

4. Astonishments

We have analyzed the stories in Mark and Luke with the elaboration pattern in mind. Attention to the rhetorical functions of the sequences of sayings material has exposed a rather comprehensive and coherent argumentation in each case. This discovery comes as something of a surprise and challenge.

The surprise is not that Hellenistic patterns of thought may have been at work in early Christianity. That we have known. It is rather that these thought patterns may have been essentially rhetorical, concerned more with cultural values and the logic of persuasion than with conceptual issues and the logic of philosophical investigation. The stories we have analyzed, for instance, merely assumed the new convictions about Jesus, ethics, authority, and so on. The argumentation was not concerned to demonstrate how one came to those convictions, or how one could ground or justify them philosophically. The aim was to demonstrate that an action which might appear questionable from one set of conventions could be seen as justified from the perspective of the new set of convictions.

For such a purpose it would appear that the Hellenistic pattern of elaboration would not be helpful. Its rhetorical effectiveness was dependent upon a generally shared set of cultural conventions, values, and traditions. And, as we saw in chapter two, the elaboration pattern seemed to lend itself best to the supporting argumentation of ethical maxims and clear theses. Neither of these conditions pertains in the case of the anointing stories. Here we see a chreia scene of the Cynic type raising the issue of unconventionality. The debate that ensues is precisely about that issue, and the argumentation purportedly persuades the objectors that they are wrong. This is strange, both because the argumentation assumes a set of convictions not shared by the objectors, and because the debate peters out, in any case, and ends with a pronouncement just as enigmatic at the level of the characterization of Jesus as the Christ, as the original scene was ethically ambiguous at the level of culturally conditioned human behavior. One has the impression of viewing a graphic by Escher in which geese become fish as one traces out the line pattern in layers against the changing intensity of a shaded background. One is not sure exactly when the transformation took place.

Neither is one sure exactly what the purpose of rhetorical persuasion is in our stories. The arguments are clearly insufficient for the persuasion of the objectors. And Christian readers, apparently, were already convinced. Perhaps we are to understand it as the quest of a new movement for its own appropriate topics. The pattern of elaboration is used. But the traditional values and canons of both its Jewish past and its Hellenistic environment are no longer adequate. By searching through its own emerging stock of convictions, memories, and narrative lore, the new movement must craft its own proofs for its own new system of values.

If we compare these stories with the elaboration exercise in Hermogenes (see chapter 2), several unusual features emerge. The synoptic stories have used the pattern to domesticate an objectionable chreia. They have achieved this transformation by turning the response into a rebuttal. The peculiar mixture of rhetorical modes of argumentation is necessary, therefore, if the final purpose is to make a positive point about the chreia (as paradigmatic). Since the chreia is understood to be open to mis-interpretation, it is possible to rearrange the sequence of the elaboration pattern, allowing the point of the argumentation (rationale, thesis) to emerge fully only at the end. The process of the domestication of Jesus chreiai by means of internal rhetorical elaboration means that Jesus becomes his own advocate and authority. The reticence of Mark and Luke to position themselves as interpreters and defenders of traditional Jesus chreiai, as, for instance, Hermogenes does with Isocrates' saying, has the effect of attributing total authority to Jesus. This, too, may be an indication of the extreme pressure upon the early movement to create self-definitional categories where there were none.

The movement will have to create examples. Analogies may have to contain an aspect of the unusual (cf. Luke's "certain creditor"), or the contingent ("who ever . . ."). The contrary may deal less in dialectical inversions, more in contrastive comparison. Judgments will be difficult to manage, unless the movement can claim scripture without harming itself, or can press a saying of Jesus into service.

But these are considerations for which we are not yet ready. First we must show that the pattern is at work elsewhere in the gospels, providing for the organization of aphoristic and narrative materials according to the principles of rhetorical persuasion. If we can demonstrate that, we may be able to say more about the function of the unit types and the process of composition in the synoptic tradition. It is already clear, in any case, that the elaboration pattern provides a way of analyzing the rhetorical design of clusters and blocks of sayings-material. This puts pressure upon form- and redaction-critical assumptions about "collections," "additions," "insertions," "layers," and so forth. Redactional and tradition-critical questions are still fully in order. But our studies have already shown that, by detecting the pattern in these stories, they do make sense as we have them. This means that we can use the elaboration pattern to explore logical relationships among small units of speech material otherwise appearing as innocently or curiously juxtaposed. If, as in the case of our two stories, a collection of sayings turns out to be a coherent argumentation, the burden of proof will have to rest with those who wish to dismantle it in the interest of the history of isolated sayings.

The only "seam" of major significance that we have discovered in this exercise is that which exists between the scene itself and the two distinctive elaborations of it. This finding gives considerable pause to one trained in the tradition of Bultmann. The assumption has been that the sayings attracted scenes in the course of the growth of the synoptic tradition. But in the case of these stories, it appears to have worked the other way around. The importance of a remarkable or typical scene for the kind of characterization the chreia makes possible appears to be assured. If early Jesus traditions took the form of chreiai, we may need to take the typical chreia scenes in the synoptic tradition more seriously than we have.

FIVE

Plucking Grain on the Sabbath

Vernon K. Robbins

In a previous chapter, we saw how rhetorical induction in the Matthean sayings about foxes and birds and leaving the dead was reformulated into an argument containing both inductive and deductive reasoning in Luke. In the present chapter, we will explore the characteristics of judicial rhetoric in the pericopes about the Plucking of Grain on the Sabbath.

The type of interaction that occurs in the story where Jesus' disciples pluck grain on the sabbath led Dibelius to include it among paradigms,[1] Bultmann among apophthegms,[2] and Vincent Taylor among pronouncement stories.[3] When Pharisees observe the action of the disciples on the sabbath, they assert that the disciples are engaged in unlawful activity. As Jesus begins a defense of the action of his disciples, he presents a precedent from the action of David. This approach features Jesus in a role similar to a defense attorney representing one or more clients who have had a charge launched against them. After the precedent, Jesus presents a rationale for the action of his disciples in the lordship of the Son of man. This personal grounding of the argument, which is unusual for judicial rhetoric, brings the story to an end, and, unlike a courtroom setting, there is no jury that pronounces a verdict of guilt or innocence. The story, therefore, uses judicial rhetoric in a particular way to meet the goals of the narrator. In the Markan and Lukan

1. *From Tradition to Gospel*, 43.
2. *History of the Synoptic Tradition*, 16–17.
3. *Formation of the Gospel Tradition*, 65.

107

versions of the story, the presentation of the personal rationale for the action of the disciples absorbs the issue of guilt or innocence. The Matthean version, in contrast, confronts the judicial issue directly and shows Jesus arguing that the disciples are guiltless of any wrongdoing. Our analysis, then, must probe not only the particular use of judicial rhetoric in the story but also the variations in rhetorical strategy among the different versions in the synoptic gospels.

A rhetorical approach to the three extant versions of the story arouses special interest in the nature of judicial rhetoric in Mediterranean culture. This type of rhetoric envisions a setting in which someone has accused someone else of doing something illegal. The official public setting for judicial rhetoric is the courtroom. This kind of rhetoric has alternatively been called forensic, dikanic (from the Greek δικανικός), legal, or judicial in English terminology. Following the lead of George A. Kennedy,[4] we will call it judicial. The essential acts surrounding judicial rhetoric include a statement of the case, arguments, counterarguments, and a verdict. These acts create a setting where people need to speak skillfully to influence a judge and/or jury. Rhetoricians discussed at length the nature of judicial speeches, working from the components they considered essential for speechmakers, be they prosecutors or defenders. The goal of the rhetoric was to uphold truth and justice by determining if a particular person or persons, in a particular instance, were speaking truthfully or falsely and had acted within the law or in violation of it. The means toward these ends were accusation and defense, and those who listened had the responsibility to decide, on the basis of the evidence and arguments, if the person or persons were guilty or innocent.

In accord with their knowledge of the courtroom, rhetoricians determined that there were essential parts to a judicial speech, and they discussed these under the topic of "arrangement" or *dispositio*.[5] It was not unusual for rhetoricians to divide the speech into an introduction, statement of the case, division, proof, refutation, and conclusion.[6] Aristotle, however, argued that a speech contains two essential parts: statement and proof. The speaker must, of course, begin a speech and end it. Therefore, a speech regularly has four parts: introduction, statement, proof, and conclusion. The introduction should compel the attention of the auditors, explain the subject of the speech, stress the importance of the subject to the auditors' personal interests, and arouse or dispel prejudice.[7] The statement should present the facts of the case in a manner that establishes the favorable character of the speaker and the unfavorable character of the opponent(s), describe the actors in various

4. *New Testament Interpretation*, 19–20.
5. Cf. *Rhet. ad Her.* III.ix–x.
6. *Rhet. ad Her.* III.ix.
7. Aristotle, *Rhet.* III.xiv.

states of feeling, and exhibit the moral character of the persons through detail that shows them acting from conscious choice either for good or bad.[8] The proof will demonstrate the issue of the case (customarily called *stasis*) by concentrating on fact, definition, quality, jurisdiction, or legal question. In other words, the proof will support the statement of the case through argument as follows:

> The issue is one of fact if the central question is whether something was done at all, or was done by a specific person at a specific time: "Did Jesus heal on the Sabbath?" involves stasis of fact. The question is one of definition if the facts are admitted, but there is disagreement about the definition of the terms: "What constitutes healing?" or "Who is my neighbor?" (Luke 10:29–37). The question is one of quality if facts and definitions are admitted by all parties, but the action is justified on other grounds: "Is it right to break the law in order to heal on the Sabbath?" In stasis of jurisdiction a speaker rejects the right of a tribunal to make a judgment, which is perhaps implied in Stephen's speech to the Council in Acts 7. In a legal question there is an expressed doubt about a law itself, for example about the difference between its wording and intent. The law might prohibit a variety of activities on the Sabbath but not specifically mention healing: "Was it the intent of the law to prevent healing?"[9]

Refutation uses the same means as the constructive proof, so it is not given a separate place in the judicial speech by Aristotle. It is customary, Aristotle says, for constructive argument to come first, then refutation, but "if the adversary's proofs have been overwhelming, then the obstacles to the auditors' accepting our proofs must be removed by refuting first."[10] After the proof, the conclusion will reinforce a favorable attitude to the speaker and an unfavorable one to the opponents, amplify the significance of the facts that are favorable to the speaker, reinforce states of feeling favorable to the speaker's case, and recapitulate the arguments.

When judicial rhetoric occurs in a pronouncement story instead of a speech, the introduction and the statement regularly emerge in narrative clauses and speech that establish the setting, and the proof and conclusion occur in response to the setting.[11] We will begin by looking at the rhetorical dimensions common to all the versions in the synoptic tradition. The interest at this point will be to uncover the features that have persisted through all the synoptic performances of the story. Care will be taken not to impose any feature from "one particular version" on this common tradition. The implication is that something may be learned about storytelling in the sphere of Christianity called "the synoptic

---

8. Aristotle, *Rhet.* III.xvi.

9. Kennedy, *New Testament Interpretation*, 18–19.

10. Hill, "Rhetoric of Aristotle," 68.

11. See Tannehill, "Introduction: The Pronouncement Story," 1 and "Types and Functions of Apophthegms," 1795.

tradition" if we look at the features common to all the stories. Second, we will analyze the rhetorical dimensions of various reconstructed versions that interpreters posit to be earlier forms of the story. Third, we will analyze the rhetorical characteristics of the Markan, Lukan, and Matthean versions individually.

1. The Common Synoptic Story

Where a story exists in triple tradition, it is good to analyze those components that have persisted throughout the three performances. This approach produces a "truly synoptic version" that, as a more neutral "common" version, can aid the interpreter in arbitrating between various "earlier" versions posited by source, form, and redaction critics and the versions that exist in Matthew, Mark, and Luke.[12] If a person constructs a "synoptic" version out of the common items in Matthew, Mark, and Luke, a basic story emerges that pictures Pharisees confronting Jesus and his disciples while they are going through grainfields on the sabbath. When we divide the story according to the parts of the judicial speech, it appears as follows:

(1) *Introduction*

He was going through grainfields on the sabbath, and his disciples were plucking heads of grain.

(2) *Statement of the Case*

And Pharisees said, "[You/they] are doing what is not lawful on the Sabbath."

(3) *Refutation (Example as Precedent)*

And he said to them, "Have you not read what David did, when he was hungry, and those with him: how he entered the house of God and [he/they] ate the bread of the Presence, which it is not lawful except for the priests to eat?"

(4) *Conclusion (Judgment as Rationale)*

"The Son of man is lord of the Sabbath."[13]

---

12. Cf. Hooker, *Son of Man*, 94–95 and 98.

13. The Greek text of the common version is as follows. The square brackets ([. . .]) indicate variation in person and number in a verb that all three synoptic versions use.

Introduction:

πορευ[3d sg.] διὰ σπορίμων σαββα[dative]
καὶ/δὲ οἱ μαθηταὶ αὐτοῦ τιλλ[] στάχυας

Statement:

καὶ/δὲ Φαρισαι[plural] εἶπαν/ἔλεγον,

The major challenges for an interpreter of this story lie in its abbreviated form, a feature characteristic of chreia composition. Presuppositions and nuances of meaning reside in compact statements that require active involvement by the auditor to understand the implications. Each part of the story, therefore, calls for special comment.

Every version of the opening statement refers to Jesus and "his disciples." This means, as Daube skillfully has shown, that the relationships between a Master and his disciples establish the social framework for the story.[14] A person who is a disciple has accepted a social position of subordinance for the purpose of learning through imitation and instruction. It is the responsibility of the Master to teach and encourage good actions and thoughts and to correct and discourage bad actions and thoughts.[15] The introduction identifies the topic of the story (plucking of grain on the sabbath) and compels the interest of the auditor by exhibiting a difference between the action of the Master and the action of his disciples: only the disciples pluck grain. The auditor awaits the action of the Master. Will Jesus reprimand his disciples for engaging in this kind of action on the Sabbath, or will he use this occasion to teach them something distinctive about his way of life?

The next part of the story introduces Pharisees, role opposites of Jesus, who make a statement that refers to the disciples' activity as unlawful. The entrance of the Pharisees at this point in the story is likely to place them in an unfavorable position. As mentioned above, Jesus has not plucked any grain. An auditor regularly begins with a favorable disposition toward a leader who has responsibility for a group of subordinates, and Jesus has done nothing to call such a disposition into question. Therefore, the auditor is likely to begin with a positive attitude toward Jesus. Also, since Jesus has not plucked any grain but the dis-

---

ποιε[plural referring to or addressing the disciples]
ὃ οὐκ ἔξεστιν σαββα[dative]

Refutation:

καὶ/δὲ λέγει/εἶπεν αὐτοῖς/πρὸς
αὐτούς, οὐκ/οὐδὲ/οὐδέποτε ἀνέγνωτε
τί/ὃ ἐποίησεν Δαυίδ, ὅτε/ὁπότε ἐπείνασεν
καὶ οἱ μετ᾽ αὐτοῦ; πῶς/ὡς εἰσῆλθεν εἰς τὸν
οἶκον τοῦ θεοῦ καὶ τοὺς ἄρτους τῆς προθέσεως
ἔφαγον/ἔφαγεν ὃ/οὓς οὐκ
ἔξον/ἔξεστιν φαγεῖν εἰ μὴ τοὺς
ἱερεῖς/τοῖς ἱερεῦσιν

Conclusion:

κύριός ἐστιν τοῦ σαββάτου ὁ υἱὸς τοῦ ἀνθρώπου

14. Daube, "Responsibilities."
15. Robbins, *Jesus the Teacher*, 63–65.

ciples have, the auditor is awaiting Jesus' statement to the disciples on this day that is guided by special obligations in Jewish society. When Pharisees evaluate the actions of Jesus' disciples, they are likely to be interfering with the auditor's expectations that Jesus will speak next. Instead, the Pharisees intrude on the domain of the Master like an outsider may intrude on a parent's interaction with a son or daughter.[16] Moreover, when the Pharisees focus their attention on the activity of Jesus' disciples, the auditor may view them as people who concern themselves with subordinates of another adult rather than dealing directly with the actions of adults of equal standing. The presence or absence of these dimensions will depend to a great extent on the tone with which the story is narrated. But the entrance of the Pharisees is likely to arouse prejudice against them because they enter a setting where their equal has not engaged in anything questionable, they make a statement that may be considered an intrusion on the Master's inter-action with his disciples, and they involve themselves with the actions of inferiors rather than equals.

As Daube has observed, the mutual responsibilities a Master and his disciples impose on one another are somewhat different from the obligations third parties in the outside world impose on them.[17] When third parties intervene, both the Master and the disciples have to decide to what degree they will be accountable for the other's actions. The Pharisees' statement against Jesus' disciples turns the attention toward the accountability of Jesus for the action of his disciples. In rhetorical terms, this shifts a potential deliberative situation between Jesus and his disciples to a judicial situation where a third party launches an accusation. When the Pharisees speak, their interpretation of the plucking of grain requires a response. It would be inconclusive for the disciples to respond, since they are simply in a learning role. Rather, the Master himself must respond. As the Pharisees speak, they exhibit a set of assumptions in a stereotypical manner characteristic of sophists and other role opposites of Socrates in Plato's *Dialogues* (e.g., The Sophist, Gorgias, Protagoras). The statement concerning "lawfulness" ($\xi\xi\epsilon\sigma\tau\iota\nu$) presupposes a set of Sabbath laws either based on or deduced from Jewish Scripture. Their criticism must be met, even if they have entered the scene in a disadvantageous manner.

As the story continues in the abbreviated style characteristic of chreia composition, all the synoptic versions feature no proof by the Pharisees who state the case against Jesus' disciples. The narrator presupposes that the auditor will hear the statement as a serious charge

16. Daube, "Responsibilities," 3.
17. Daube, "Responsibilities," 1–4.

backed by Jewish tradition. But the absence of proof by the Pharisees leaves them in an extremely vulnerable position. As Aristotle says:

> He who speaks first should state his own proofs and afterwards meet the arguments of the opponent, refuting them or pulling them to pieces beforehand.[18]

The narrator, however, has the Pharisees state a case without even producing the law on which the case is based, let alone applying the law to the case. Once they have stated their case, the Pharisees leave their proof unstated and allow Jesus to take the lead in the argument. When Jesus begins, then, it is not necessary for him to "first state the arguments against the opponent's speech, refuting and answering it by syllogisms . . ."[19] Rather, all he needs to do is "destroy *the impression* made by the adversary . . . then substantiate [his] own case."[20] The single impression left by the Pharisees is that a law exists somewhere that makes the disciples' action unlawful. The law that lies behind this charge would not be universal, but would be a particular law from "those established by each people in reference to themselves, which again are divided into written and unwritten."[21] It is, in fact, not entirely clear what the Pharisees would say. Deut 23:25 specifically allows a person to pluck some of a neighbor's grain: "When you go into your neighbor's grain, you may pluck the heads with your hand, but you shall not put a sickle to your neighbor's standing grain." If the concern is harvesting on the sabbath, they may quote Exod 34:21: "Six days you shall work, but on the seventh you shall rest; in plowing time and in harvest you shall rest." Reaping is the third prohibition in the Mishnah among the thirty-nine main categories of work forbidden on the sabbath,[22] and interpreters regularly presuppose this to be the violation even though neither the Pharisees nor Jesus specifically say so.[23] Jesus' refutation presupposes that the Pharisees would produce, if asked, some quotation or deduction from scripture. When Jesus refers to "reading" about what David did, he attacks the impression left by the Pharisees that scripture unambiguously forbids the act performed by the disciples. The response has the following effect: if lawfulness is determined by scripture, then one must read the story about David when he and his companions ate the shewbread from the altar. But the response is not simply stated in a declara-

---

18. Aristotle, *Rhet.* III.xvii.14.
19. Aristotle, *Rhet.* III.xvii.15.
20. Aristotle, *Rhet.* III.xvii.15.
21. Aristotle, *Rhet.* I.xiii.1.
22. See, for example, M. Shab. VII.2 and TJ Shab. VII.2, 9c.
23. See, for example, Lohse, σάββατον, 20–24; Cohen, "Rabbinic Law," 91–92; and Kimbrough, "Concept of Sabbath at Qumran," 483–502.

tive manner. In all three versions it occurs as a question: "Have you not read what David did, when he was hungry, and those with him . . .?" This form of response signals Jesus' establishment of stasis, a "complete stop" or stand-off:[24]

> a stasis or issue, whenever, and however it occurs, takes the form of a question which focuses the contrary views of proponents and opponents. Those presenting the better answer to the question succeed in breaking down the stasiastic impasse in their favor, and the stasis disappears.[25]

Jesus' question establishes stasis, the "point in the proceedings at which the contesting parties [meet] 'head-on' by taking opposing positions on a question at hand."[26] Stasis occurs, because Jesus confronts the Pharisees with a precedent that counters the thesis that scripture is entirely on their side: scripture contains an episode where David and his companions ate bread that was unlawful for anyone but the priests to eat. How could Pharisees, who read the scriptures so carefully, have missed this story? Jesus has scored rhetorically in three ways: (1) he has cited a passage from written authority; (2) he has presented a precedent from the life of an exemplary person in Jewish heritage; and (3) he has responded in an interrogative, periodic construction that balances "*is not lawful* on the Sabbath" with a statement that David and his companions ate what "*is not lawful* except for the priests to eat."[27]

But what kind of response is this? If the stasis or issue were one of fact, the argument may have been that the disciples looked like they were plucking heads of grain but were simply touching them. But Jesus does not dispute that they were plucking grain, nor does he dispute that it is the sabbath. If the issue were definition, the argument may have been that the plucking did not constitute work (harvesting), since they were not using a sickle. But Jesus does not address the Pharisees' presupposition that the plucking is a kind of work on the sabbath. Does the issue concern the quality of the action: that the action was allowable in a special circumstance? Is the issue jurisdiction, so that Jesus' response is a way of telling the Pharisees they have no right to make a judgment because the disciples are not their responsibility? Or is the issue a legal question: whether sabbath laws were meant to restrict certain basic activities within life? The last three possibilities must be probed as we analyze the different versions of the story.

The refutation constructed from the ingredients common to all the synoptic versions appears to address the quality of the act. But Jesus' response is not entirely straightforward. His account of the incident

24. See Nadeau, "Hermogenes' *On Stases*," 388.
25. Nadeau, "Hermogenes' *On Stases*," 375.
26. Nadeau, "Hermogenes' *On Stases*," 376.
27. Cf. Lane, *Gospel According to Mark*, 117.

destroys the impression that scripture is solely on the side of the Pharisees, but it addresses the issue with innuendo and rebuttal characteristic
of epideictic rather than judicial rhetoric.[28] Interpreters have noticed that
the Davidic incident is not a decisive precedent, since the companions of
David did not procure the shewbread analogous to the disciples' plucking of grain. Moreover, the Hebrew Bible does not state that the event
occurred on a sabbath, though some rabbinic traditions understood it
so.[29] The Davidic argument is a subversion of the statement of the
Pharisees rather than a decisive refutation. This is, of course, the stuff of
which chreiai are made. For this reason it is important to look more
closely at the argumentative use of the Davidic example. Daube has
observed that the story in 1 Samuel 21 features David alone. From this
observation, he suggests that the original version of the Davidic argument lacked the references to David's companions in vss 25–26.[30] But
this approach can lead the interpreter away from the argumentative use
of the example. In the Old Testament story, David goes alone to priest
Ahimelech (LXX: Abimelech) and requests five loaves, or whatever is
there, for young men whom he will meet to carry out the special charge
with which the king has sent him to Nob (vss 1–3). The priest informs
David that he has no common bread but only holy bread, and he is
concerned to know if the young men have abstained from women (vs 4).
David assures the priest that women are kept from all of them even
when he goes on an ordinary journey, and how much more is this true
on this expedition initiated by the king (vs 5). As a result of this conversation, the priest gives David the shewbread (vs 6). Daube's point is that
David was alone, and this is a correct observation. The complete truth is
that David never meets any young men, and he never intended to meet
any. In other words, David's discussion of the young men is a ruse to get
the bread. In essence, David tricked Ahimelech. But, as Bultmann has
insisted, one must read the story according to principles at work in the
use of scriptural passages during the first century.[31] It appears, however,
that Bultmann did not ask a fundamental question that must be asked,
namely: What principle or pattern is operative in the application of the
Davidic incident to the plucking incident? As James Raymond has said,
"examples are, at some level, enthymemes, . . . examples are patterns
inferred from one set of circumstances and applied to others."[32] In other
words, there is an assumption or premise underlying the use of an

28. Aristotle (*Rhet.* I.iii.4) mentions epideictic rhetoric in a setting of judicial
rhetoric and a well-known example is Demosthenes' *On the Crown*. See Nadeau,
"Hermogenes' *On Stases*," 376–77.

29. See, for example, BMenahoth 95B and Yalqut Shim'oni (130) to 1 Sam 21:5.

30. Daube, "Responsibilities," 4–7. And cf. Suhl, *Die Funktion*, 85.

31. Bultmann, *History of the Synoptic Tradition*, 16.

32. Raymond, "Enthymemes, Examples, and Rhetorical Method," 147.

example, and the premise that underlies the application of the David story appears to be this: the priest accepted the principle that it is appropriate for a leader whom the king has sent on a special task to insist that regular procedures be bypassed in order to provide food for the men for whom he has responsibility.[33] The priest accepted this principle when David used it with him, so the Pharisees should now accept the principle.

Identifying the principle operative in the application of the Davidic example takes the interpreter a step closer to the stasis or issue of the case. In the common synoptic version, the issue is, as mentioned above, not fact or definition, but quality. Since the stasis of quality in the common version concerns an act rather than a written law, the stasis occurs at a rational ($\lambda o \gamma \iota \kappa \acute{\eta}$) rather than legal ($\nu o \mu \iota \kappa \acute{\eta}$) level.[34] In other words, since the Pharisees have not cited a specific law, and Jesus does not respond to a law upon which he presupposes they have based their charge, the issue is not the intent or letter of a certain law but some matter of logic (rational stasis) concerning the act. Within this rational realm, Jesus responds with a counterproposition ($\dot{\alpha} \nu \tau \acute{\iota} \theta \epsilon \sigma \iota s$) which admits that the act was unlawful.[35] Jesus admits the unlawfulness when he emphasizes that David and his companions ate what was unlawful for anyone but the priests to eat. When, however, a defendant admits the unlawfulness of the act, it is natural to shift the blame on something or someone else ($\mu \epsilon \tau \acute{\alpha} \sigma \tau \alpha \sigma \iota s$).[36] Instead, Jesus draws attention to his own presence through an inference ($\sigma \upsilon \lambda \lambda o \gamma \iota \sigma \mu \acute{o} s$) from the "concept of the equal" ($\dot{\alpha} \pi \grave{o}$ $\tau o \hat{\upsilon}$ $\check{\iota} \sigma o \upsilon$).[37] Herein lies the feature which gives Jesus' response the rhetorical quality so well exemplified in chreiai. The response is based on an inference that the Pharisees did not register firmly enough in their minds that Jesus was there with the disciples. The response, then, is not only, "Have you never read what David did," but it implies: "Hey, you must not have seen *me* here with them." The Pharisees have presented the case that the disciples have plucked grain contrary to the law. Jesus' rebuttal implies that the situation in which the disciples acted is equal to the situation David and his companions faced. Since the priest permitted David and his companions to have the bread, the action of the disciples is also permitted, even if by definition it is

33. Cf. Lane, *Gospel According to Mark*, 117.

34. See Hermogenes 37,20 and the English translation in Nadeau, "Hermogenes' *On Stases*," 393.

35. See Hermogenes 38,16–18 and the English translation in Nadeau, "Hermogenes' *On Stases*, 394.

36. See Hermogenes 39,6–9 and the English translation in Nadeau, "Hermogenes' *On Stases*, 394.

37. See Hermogenes 89,16 and the English translation in Nadeau, "Hermogenes' *On Stases*, 418.

illegal. This is the standard function of inference as explained by Hermogenes: inference (συλλογισμός) opposes definition (ὅρος) by suggesting that the act is different from that which is not permitted by law.[38] Inference distinguishes, then, between "that which is illegal" and "that which is not permitted."[39] The disciples' act may be illegal, but, as can be seen from the Davidic incident, it is not among those items which are never permitted.

This approach to the story opens another issue. Each synoptic version concludes the story with the saying: "the Son of man is lord of the Sabbath." Why? Our analysis suggests that this saying takes the rational stasis one step further by having Jesus shift the blame[40] (μετάστασις) explicitly to himself. Prior to the occurrence of the saying, a shift of blame is perhaps implicit, but the argument is that the plucking situation is equal to the Davidic situation. When the saying is present, Jesus explicitly shifts the blame from the disciples to himself, and the implication is that the blame has shifted to someone who has appropriate attributes to take the blame. In this stage of the tradition, "the Son of man" would be a third person circumlocution for a first person reference. Jesus would use the phrase "the Son of man" out of a "desire to express himself equivocally," exhibiting a conventional form of humility in a statement filled with certitude that he has the right to do what he is doing.[41] The use of both the Davidic precedent and the saying that the Son of man is lord of the sabbath presupposes that a person who has special responsibilities has the right to act in special ways for his own sake and the sake of his companions.

In a number of ways, the features of the common synoptic version reflect dynamics of the Q material. The appeal to David functions as an analogy much as the appeal to Noah (Matt 24:37–39/Luke 17:26–27), Jonah (Matt 12:41/Luke 11:32), and Solomon (Matt 12:42/Luke 11:31) in Q. In addition, the use of the term κύριος is noticeable (Matt 7:21/Luke 6:46; Matt 8:8/Luke 7:6; Matt 8:21/[Luke 9:59]), and the saying that the Son of man is κύριος of the Sabbath has a tone similar to "leave the dead to bury the dead" (Matt 8:22/Luke 9:60), especially after those who have addressed him have called him κύριος. What is lacking in Q is sabbath controversy and reference to David. Solomon, the model of wisdom, attracts the attention in the Q tradition (Matt 12:42/Luke 11:31; Matt 6:29/Luke 12:27), rather than his father David who was known for his

38. See Hermogenes 60,10–12 and the English translation in Nadeau, "Hermogenes' *On Stases*, 404.

39. See Hermogenes 88,17–18 and the English translation in Nadeau, "Hermogenes' *On Stases*, 417.

40. See Hermogenes 39,6–9 and the English translation in Nadeau, "Hermogenes' *On Stases*, 394.

41. See Vermes, "Appendix E," 324.

military strength. Also, the Q material, at least in its "minimal" version, contains no units featuring accusation that Jesus or his disciples engage in unlawful activity on the sabbath.[42]

It is informative to ask if there could have been a Q version of the story of the plucking of grain. There are six features shared by Matthew and Luke against Mark: (1) a statement in the initial verse that the disciples were "eating" the grain that they plucked; (2) εἶπαν ("they said") as the verb introducing the statement of the Pharisees; (3) emphatic reference to "sabbath" at the end of the Pharisees' statement; (4) εἶπεν ("he said") introducing the speech of Jesus; (5) emphatic assertion that the shewbread was for the priests "only"; and (6) word order in the final verse that places ὁ υἱὸς τοῦ ἀνθρώπου ("the Son of man") in emphatic final position. These features would bring the disciples' action one step closer to the Davidic example (they were eating the grain they plucked), emphasize "sabbath" as the issue (emphatic position in the speech of the Pharisees and Jesus), and highlight the right of David and those with him to eat something for the priests *only*. This could mean that the sabbath was the central issue rather than the Son of man. In other words, the story would take its place alongside other traditions which exhibit Jesus' authority over funerals ("leave the dead to bury the dead") and over illness ("Lord, . . . say the word and my servant will be healed": Matt 8:8/Luke 7:6–7). Along with this, the activity of the disciples will support the view that a disciple will not be above his teacher, but he will be like him (Matt 10:24–25/Luke 6:40). The conclusion of the story with the reference to the Son of man will suggest that Jesus is greater not only than Jonah (Matt 12:41/Luke 11:32) and Solomon (Matt 12:42/Luke 11:31) but also is greater than David. The Davidic incident might also suggest that just as David was freed from "holiness" restrictions when he was wandering without a home with his associates, so Jesus is free from sabbath restrictions as he travels around as "the Son of man who has nowhere to lay his head" (Matt 8:20/Luke 9:58). The Son of man and his disciples, then, lack not only the comforts available to foxes and birds, but they also lack some of the restrictions of domesticated life.

Even though it seems likely that the story existed in a Q form, it is impossible to know if it ever existed in its "common synoptic" form. At the stage in which the Son of man saying stands as a conclusion to the Davidic example the story has the nature of a controversy story that functions with christological dynamics consonant with the Q tradition.

42. Edwards, *A Theology of Q*, presents a "minimal" version of the Q material in this pericope. For those unwilling to talk about Q material, they should nevertheless explore the christological dimensions in the material that shows minor agreements between Matthew and Luke against Mark. If an interpreter discusses this material as representative of a certain "edition" of the synoptic material, he or she may still see its significance in the development of synoptic tradition.

It appears that the story with the six features shared by Matthew and Luke against Mark was present in a late edition of the Q material. If Mark did not have access to a version of the Q material, his source for the story (perhaps Mark 2:1–3:6)[43] evidently adapted it from an edition of Q which contained the Son of man saying.

In summary, the constituents in the "common synoptic" version point to a story that features Jesus' defense of the disciples with an incident during David's flight from Saul. The priest of the sanctuary at Nob consented to bypass the prescriptions for the shewbread when David forced his hand with a pretension that he was under a special charge from the king and that he had a group of men under his command. In this setting, David put the kind of leverage on the priest that Jesus is putting on the Pharisees. As David used an aggressive argument to justify a variation from established prescriptions, so Jesus uses an aggressive argument that implies that the plucking occasion is equal to the Davidic occasion, that the Pharisees evidently have never read the Davidic story, and that they have misjudged the importance of Jesus' presence with the disciples. His argument is a tour de force analogous to David's encounter with the priest. This kind of audacity the conclusion makes explicit: "the Son of man is lord of the sabbath." When this saying is present as a conclusion, the story contains a range of dynamics similar to units in Q tradition. From the minor agreements of Matthew and Luke against Mark, it appears that a version of the story existed in a later edition of Q material. If Mark did not get the story from an edition of Q, he evidently found it in a "controversy story" source that had adapted the story from a version of Q.

2. The Search for the Original Form

Our analysis thus far could suggest that the most original version simply featured the disciples' plucking of grain on the sabbath, a statement by Pharisees that the act was unlawful, and a response by Jesus with the analogy of David's procuring of the shewbread. This form of the story would have a chreia-like quality that would support its preservation and bring it into circles of the Jesus movement associated with the Q tradition. Without the Son of man saying as a conclusion, the stasis of the story would reside in the periodic formulation that ended with "not lawful except for the priests to eat." Roloff considers the form with the Davidic argument to be the most original form. He stresses the veiled allusion to David/Jesus typology and an inference *a minori ad maius*.[44] Without the Son of man saying, however, it would be wrong to

43. See Kuhn, *Ältere Sammlungen*, 53–98.
44. Roloff, *Das Kerygma*, 52–62.

claim that the argument is that Jesus is "greater than David." Rather, the argument would be that he is "equal to David." Only with the presence of the Son of man saying would the argument become lesser to greater, as do the comparisons with Jonah (Matt 12:41/Luke 11:32) and Solomon (Matt 12:42/Luke 11:31) in Q.

In 1832 H. A. W. Meyer observed that David's example does not explicitly refer to the sabbath. He suggested, therefore, that Jesus had responded to the Pharisees in two steps: first answering the issue about the law (Mark 2:25–26); then addressing the issue about the sabbath (Mark 2:27–28).[45] Boismard has suggested that the original story did not presuppose that the disciples plucked the grain *on the sabbath*, since Jesus' response with the Davidic example did not address the topic of the sabbath. The Pharisees, therefore, reproached the disciples simply for plucking someone else's grain, and Jesus defended their action with the Davidic example. This would mean that the Pharisees are viewed as more restrictive than the Deuteronomic prescription, and Jesus illustrated his magnanimity against the Pharisees' restrictiveness.[46] Suhl proposes the more likely thesis that the earliest form of the story was a sabbath controversy and Jesus' response with the Davidic example expanded the issue beyond the sabbath to the law itself.[47]

From a rhetorical perspective, interpreters who consider the Davidic example to have been an integral part of the early form of the story see some principle of analogy at work in the earliest form of the tradition. The analogy would lie between the Davidic situation and the situation in which Jesus' disciples pluck grain. Since analogy is a form of induction, these interpreters are emphasizing an inductive form of reasoning in the earliest form that uses an example to refute the accusation by the Pharisees. Another group of interpreters reconstructs the earliest form by removing the Davidic example and accepting the unique Markan saying to arrive at an argument which contains deductive reasoning. In other words, when E. Klostermann first proposed that Mark 2:23, 24, and 27 were the original framework of the story,[48] he set the implication in motion that the earliest form of the tradition contained a logic based on deduction rather than induction. In rhetorical terms, the proposal suggests that the earliest form had the nature of an "enthymematic chreia."[49] An enthymematic chreia produces a rhetorical syllogism and has the force of a logical syllogism. In this instance the syllogism would be:

45. Meyer, *Markus.*
46. Boismard, *Synopse des quatre evangiles,* 116–17.
47. Suhl, *Die Funktion,* 86.
48. Klostermann, *Das Markusevangelium,* 29.
49. See Theon 208,4–10.

General premise: The sabbath was made [by God] for the sake [needs] of man, not man for the sabbath.

Concrete premise: The disciples plucked grain out of need [hunger].

Presupposed Conclusion: Therefore, the disciples did not violate God's purpose for the sabbath.

Here, the rationale for the action of the disciples is a deduction based on the sequence of creation and the hierarchies established with that sequence. The implication of this version is that if Jesus' view was radical for his day, at least it contained decisive logic. Bultmann takes this "enthymematic approach" one step further by proposing that Mark 2:27 was an "independently circulating saying."[50] In this form, it was free to function as the premise both for a situation where the disciples plucked grain on the sabbath and for a conclusion in an enthymematic couplet in which "Son of man" meant "man." This could mean, then, that Mark 2:27–28 would have the force of a rhetorical syllogism in which the general premise is so obvious that it would never be stated:

Presupposed General premise: That for which something was made is master over that which was made for it.

Concrete premise: The sabbath was made for man, not man for the sabbath.

Conclusion: Therefore, man is master of the sabbath.

Going yet one step further, Bultmann suggested that early Christians used the Davidic incident apart from its present context in controversies of the early church. With this approach, all the units of the composite story have emerged enthymematically. Either, as Bultmann says, vs 27 was the original answer to vss 23–24 (in our terms forming an enthymematic chreia with an underlying syllogism according to the first example above) and vs 28 was a natural continuation of vs 27 (expanding the enthymematic premise into an enthymematic couplet at the end, with the Son of man meaning "man," as in the second example above), or vss 27–28 already existed as an enthymematic couplet prior to their introduction into the Markan context (as in the second example above). At a later stage, kerygmatic impulses brought the enthymematic units together in a composite setting created by the community.[51]

This approach to the reconstruction of the tradition presupposes that "enthymematic" (deductive) reasoning will be earlier and more original, and "analogical" (inductive) reasoning will emerge as early Christians preach "Jesus" rather than "Jesus' message." But there are many difficulties with such an approach. Bultmann's analysis begins with an

---

50. Bultmann, *History of the Synoptic Tradition*, 16.
51. Bultmann, *History of the Synoptic Tradition*, 16–17.

observation that the Pharisees object to the actions of Jesus' disciples rather than Jesus himself. This feature is a clue, from his perspective, that the situation was created by early Christians. To be sure, early Christians are narrating all of these situations, but there is no substantial reason to doubt that Jesus regularly was attended by disciple-companions, and there could have been an occasion when someone raised a question about the actions of those around him. Second, there is no special reason to suggest that Jesus' response to a question about the activity of his disciple-companions would satisfy the requirements for a decisive rabbinic argument. Our best evidence suggests that Jesus came from a region of Galilee known for Jewish figures like Honi the Circle-Drawer and Hanina ben Dosa whose traditions suggest idiosyncratic activities and statements rather than decisive halakhic arguments, and there is no evidence that Jesus sought the kind of training available in a setting like the Houses of Hillel or Shammai in Jerusalem, or that settings like these were available in Galilee.[52] Third, it is probably fortuitous, though natural because of the lack of "logical fit," to argue that the Davidic example was initially associated with a different setting and transported to the setting of the Plucking of the Grain.[53] The kind of tour de force that results from the use of the Davidic example is not unusual in chreiai outside New Testament tradition,[54] and it is not uncommon in other gospel traditions to depict Jesus responding with aggressive, but less than decisive, remarks.[55] Fourth, the presence of the Davidic example in every performance of the story available to us suggests that it contained dynamics that gave it good rhetorical strength as a response to the charge against the disciples. Fifth, it would be wrong to suggest that the situation was created for the Davidic example or the sabbath or Son of man sayings, because none of them contains a reference that implies the special circumstances of the plucking situation. Sixth, argumentative use of stories and sayings regularly moves them toward a more enthymematic, deductive form, since this form, as Aristotle observed, is more decisive. To be sure, Aristotle says that the most suitable form of judicial argument is the enthymeme, since demonstration is possible for past fact.[56] Therefore, it would be better for Jesus to respond with an enthymeme than an example. But just because it would be better does not necessarily make it the key for reconstructing the earliest form of the

52. See, for example, Vermes, *Jesus the Jew*, 69–82 and Vermes, *Jesus and the World of Judaism*, 1–14.

53. See Bultmann, *History of the Synoptic Tradition*, 16 and Taylor, *Formation of the Gospel Tradition*, 81.

54. See, for example, Robbins, "Pronouncement Stories," 56–58.

55. For examples, see Silbermann, "Schoolboys and Storytellers," 110–15 and Carson, "Jesus and the Sabbath," 62.

56. Aristotle, *Rhet.* III.xvii-xviii.

tradition. In essence, Bultmann was functioning as his own Aristotle when he accepted the separation of the Davidic example from the plucking situation and reconstructed the history of transmission so that the earliest units were enthymematic in form.

In summary, it is a highly suspect procedure to reconstruct the history of the tradition so that units and forms containing deductive logic, which may depend on features unique to one gospel, are asserted to be earlier, and by this means to argue that a chreia-like situation and response in the unit are "composite" in nature. Rather, the earlier stages of tradition may be expected to reflect "tacit assumption," "unstated premise," and tour de force which are bolstered by various forms of rationale and argumentative stategies in later stages. The earliest form of the tradition, therefore, is likely to be found in the plucking situation, the statement of the Pharisees, and Jesus' response with the Davidic example. At a later stage, the Son of man saying functioned as a conclusion, and various forms of rationale and argumentation were added.

3. The Version in Mark 2:23–28

The Markan version of the story has four distinctive characteristics. First, the opening comment asserts that Jesus was $\pi\alpha\rho\alpha\pi\sigma\rho\epsilon\acute{u}\epsilon\sigma\theta\alpha\iota$ $\delta\iota\grave{a}$ $\tau\hat{\omega}\nu$ $\sigma\pi\sigma\rho\acute{\iota}\mu\omega\nu$ ("passing *alongside* through the grainfields") and that his disciples began $\acute{o}\delta\grave{o}\nu$ $\pi\sigma\iota\epsilon\hat{\iota}\nu$ $\tau\acute{\iota}\lambda\lambda\sigma\nu\tau\epsilon s$ $\tau\sigma\grave{u}s$ $\sigma\tau\acute{a}\chi\nu\alpha s$ ("to make a path [or road] plucking the heads"). In the midst of these comments, there is no statement that the disciples were hungry or were eating the grain. Second, the Pharisees put their statement in the form of a question to Jesus: "Look, why are they doing on the sabbath what is not lawful?" Third, the Davidic example contains the statement that David did this "when he was in need," and it ends with the comment that "he gave also to those who were with him." Fourth, among Jesus' statements to the Pharisees is a saying found nowhere else in the New Testament: "The sabbath was made for the sake of man, not man for the sake of the sabbath" (Mark 2:27).

Scholars have said much about the disciples' "making a path." After the initial attention to the clause by Meyer, B. Murmelstein supported the appropriateness of Jesus' use of the Davidic example not only through rabbinic traditions that presupposed the occurrence of David's action on the sabbath but also through a tradition where the king is allowed to make a road and none may protest against him.[57] In rhetorical terms, then, the "situation" in the Markan version may be significantly different from the other synoptic versions. In Mark, according to Murmelstein, the disciples may be making a road for the king on the

---

57. See, for example, BSanh II.4 as discussed in Murmelstein, "Jesu Gang."

sabbath. Thus, the selection of a Davidic example is especially apposite. When David had a special need during the time he was establishing himself as king, the priest at Nob gave him holy food on the sabbath even though the prescriptions for the use of the bread forbade its consumption by anyone but the priests. When Jesus (the provisional messianic king) has a special need on the sabbath, his disciples make a path for him. As long as they do not use a sickle, they are not violating Deut 23:25, and as long as they are serving the needs of Jesus, their action is supported by 1 Samuel 21.

Recently, Derrett has revised Murmelstein's analysis by giving attention to the verb "to pass alongside." For Derrett, this verb refers to "bypassing" a town in order not to violate the quadrilateral sabbath limits. A person would bypass on footpaths that had been sown over during planting but ones that the public had to reopen if they were to remain as paths. The disciples were stripping the heads with their fingers (τίλλειν) as they walked along the path, opening it for themselves and Jesus, and they undoubtedly ate some of the grain and even gave Jesus some of it to eat. The Pharisees object, according to Derrett, for three reasons: (a) the disciples' making of a path undoubtedly flattened furrows, which was forbidden on the sabbath, and the Pharisees may even have objected to the principle of "bypassing"; (b) the disciples were simply "wasting" the grain; and (c) the action of the disciples was analogous to threshing.[58]

It is difficult to know what to do with this line of interpretation. On the one hand, the comments in the opening of the Markan story seem to reflect nuances that the interpreter should attempt to uncover. On the other hand, the conclusions of Murmelstein and Derrett leave the impression of "over-interpretation," though they are pursuing an important direction of thought. A suggestion will be made for a possible resolution at the end of this section.

In Mark, the Pharisees state their case against the disciples' action in the form of a question to Jesus: "Look, why are they doing what is not lawful on the sabbath?" This gives the story the nature of a pre-trial inquiry or an initial interrogation, which would be consistent with the legal requirement of M. Sanhedrin VII.8 that a warning be given prior to prosecution for a sabbath violation.[59] The person who begins an interrogation should ask a question that is advantageous to himself.[60] This question is advantageous to the Pharisees only if a person has a positive disposition toward them as interpreters of scripture. This is not a

---

58. Derrett, "Judaica in St. Mark," 6–8.
59. Cf. Lane, *Gospel According to Mark*, 115.
60. Quintilian gives this advice in *Inst. Orat.* V.vii.16.

"gentle" question, but an aggressive question that asserts that the disciples' action is unlawful and demands a rationale.

When Jesus provides a rationale, he emphasizes at the beginning that David did this "when he was in need and he himself was hungry and those with him." Then at the end of the story Jesus emphasizes that David did not only eat the shewbread himself, but "gave some also to those with him." These emphases are surely the clue to the argumentative use of the example in Mark.[61] Interpreters rather uniformly feel that the emphasis upon David's eating of the bread in the example has been the occasion for developing the eating features. What the interpreter must do in addition, however, is pursue the significance of these emphases within the narrative purpose of the Gospel of Mark.[62] These emphases must be kept in mind, therefore, as we move to the remaining parts of the Markan version.

The Markan version ends with an enthymematic couplet in syllogistic form:

Premise: The sabbath was made for man, not man for the sabbath.

Conclusion: Therefore ($\omega\sigma\tau\epsilon$) lord is the Son of man even of the sabbath.[63]

These sayings provide a new turn in the story, and the introduction of them with $\kappa\alpha\grave{\iota} \ \acute{\epsilon}\lambda\epsilon\gamma\epsilon\nu \ \alpha\grave{\upsilon}\tauo\hat{\iota}\varsigma$ ("and he said to them") indicates the narrator's awareness of this. The shift results from focussing attention upon God's institution of the sabbath and making the Son of man's authority derivative in some way of God's purpose for the sabbath. The question

61. Cf. Lane, *Gospel According to Mark*, 116–17.

62. Interpretation of the Davidic example in Mark regularly focusses attention on the inaccurate reference to Abiathar as highpriest. Wenham ("Mark 2,26," 156) has suggested the statement functions like $\grave{\epsilon}\pi\grave{\iota} \ \tauo\hat{\upsilon} \ \beta\acute{\alpha}\tauo\upsilon$ ("in the passage about the bush") in Mark 12:26 and refers to the passage concerning the burning bush. In accord with this, $\grave{\epsilon}\pi\grave{\iota} \ \text{'}A\beta\iota\alpha\theta\acute{\alpha}\rho$ would refer to the section of Samuel dealing with Abiathar's loyalty to David (1 Sam 21:20) that led to his appointment as highpriest by David. Derrett ("Judaica in St. Mark," 9), however, suggests that the statement means "in front of Abiathar" and emphasizes that the crucial person at Nob was Abiathar, the son of Ahimelech, because he saw David do this and never suggested that it was wrong by some later requirement of recompense after David appointed him highpriest. A third possibility could move in a similar direction. The earliest form of the tradition, emerging in oral tradition either with Jesus or some early Christians, or with Mark, simply associated Abiathar with this instance, since he was the famous priest from Nob who became David's highpriest.

63. Roloff (*Das Kerygma*, 58–62) has argued that vs 27 is the premise for vs 28, whereas Schweizer (*Good News According to Mark*, 39–40) has argued that vs 28 originally formed the premise for vs 27. D. Nineham (*Saint Mark*, 116, n. 1) suggests that Mark 2:27 makes explicit the principle implied in the action of David. Suhl (*Die Funktion*, 86) proposes that Mark inserted 2:27, which weakened the sabbath commandment to situations in which people are in need.

then is: How is the Son of man's lordship over the sabbath derivative of God's institution of it for man? Following Roloff's interpretation,[64] a person might suggest that the Davidic story provides the middle premise in the following way:

(a) The sabbath was made for man, not man for the sabbath.
(b) David was lord over the sabbath and gave to those with him [the right to eat the bread].
(c) Thus, how much more is the Son of man lord of the sabbath [and gave to those with him the right to pluck the grain].

The weakness of this suggestion lies in the lack of assertion that David got the bread on a sabbath. The strength of the suggestion lies in the special Markan emphasis that David gave "also to those with him" (Mark 2:26), which is balanced by the assertion that the Son of man is lord "also of the sabbath" (Mark 2:28). The special role of "the Son of man," then, would be to *transfer to those over whom he has authority rights that belong especially to him*. In this way, the disciple would become like his teacher.

If one pays closer attention to the special emphases in the Markan recitation of the Davidic example, however, a slightly different understanding emerges. The stasis in Mark may be slightly different from what it is in the reconstructed synoptic version or the posited earlier versions when Jesus asserts that David "was in need" (Mark 2:25). This remark may indicate that Jesus is introducing a counterplea (ἀντίστασις) that argues that the disciples' act produced a benefit.[65] The benefit arises because there was a need and the disciples' action met that need. If the counterplea is being pursued in the enthymematic couplet at the end, the underlying syllogism would be something like this:

General Premise: The sabbath was made by God for man.

Presupposed Concrete Premise: The Son of man came with God's authority to serve man with that which God created for man.

Therefore, the Son of man is lord even of the sabbath [so that he has the authority to use it to serve the needs of man].

The missing premise, then, would be amazingly close to Mark 10:45: "For the Son of man came not to be served but to serve. . . ." If the interpreter wishes to pursue this further in the opening verse of the story, he or she may suggest that the disciples' "making a path" produces a benefit for Jesus, because he is able to walk along the path they make. If one pursues this angle, the action of the disciples prior to the triumphal entry

64. *Das Kerygma*, 52–62.
65. See Hermogenes 38,21–39 and the English translation in Nadeau, "Hermogenes' *On Stases*," 394.

is an interesting parallel, since Jesus tells them that when they are asked, "Why are you doing this" (Mark 11:3: τί ποιεῖτε τοῦτο; cf. Mark 2:24), they should respond, "His lord has need of it" (ὁ κύριος αὐτοῦ χρείαν ἔχει: Mark 11:3; cf. Mark 2:25, 28). In addition, the scene concerning the disciples' action with the colt brings forth not only reference to the title κύριος (Mark 11:3 and "Blessed is he who comes in the name of κυρίου: Mark 11:9) but also reference to David ("Blessed is the coming kingdom of our father David": Mark 11:10). Also, the Markan Jesus asserts in his discussion of the scribes' understanding of the Messiah that "David himself calls him lord" (κύριος). If the interpreter looks for premises and conclusions asserted in other parts of the Markan narrative to under- stand what is presupposed in the middle premise, then, it is possible to suggest that the constellation of references to "David," "having need," "the Son of man," and "lord" may reflect a pattern of thought that is part of Mark's understanding of the Son of man as one who serves, who teaches his disciples to respond to needs, and who has authority grounded in expectations and assertions associated with David.[66]

In relation to this analysis, Lane's emphasis on Mark 2:28 as the conclusion to the preceding action and speech in the Plucking Story is highly suggestive. His final comments on the pericope suggest an under- lying syllogism as follows:

> General Premise: "God instituted the Sabbath for the sake of man."

> Concrete Premise: "Jesus' act and word established the true intention of the Sabbath and expressed the weakness of a human system of fencing the Law with restrictions."

> Conclusion: "So then the Son of man is Lord of the Sabbath."[67]

The effect of Lane's proposal is to suggest that there is a gain in the middle premise that comes from reflection on the effect of Jesus' action and speech. This is important for two reasons. First, our probe of under- lying syllogisms is not an attempt to reduce the stories and sayings to syllogistic logic and reasoning. Rather, it is an attempt to position the statements so that a person can define more sharply their argumentative force. The base of a syllogism is, after all, tautological. In contrast, moral,

---

66. I do not agree, then, with interpreters who suggest that Mark considered beliefs associated with David to be "false christology." Rather, Mark supports his point of view through careful use of Davidic example (Mark 2:25–26), through application of the title "Son of David" to Jesus (Mark 10:47, 48), through reference to David's kingdom (Mark 11:10), and through explicit citation of David's speech with interpretation (Mark 12:36–37). It is quite wrong for an interpreter to assert a meaning for the last two clauses in Mark 12:37 which overlooks the premise presupposed by the narrator that "David himself called the Messiah Lord." For further support of this position, see Robbins, "Healing of Blind Bartimaeus."

67. Lane, *Gospel According to Mark*, 120.

ethical, and religious reasoning regularly shows a "gain" between the initial premise and the conclusion.[68] These "gains" often have been implied by the square brackets and the added phrases that keep the reconstructed forms from being reductions to formal logic. Second, Lane's comments exhibit the creative tension between the rhetoric "in" the story and the rhetoric "of" the story in the Markan narrative.[69]

For the most part, we have attempted to probe the rhetoric "in" the story of the Plucking of the Grain. At the point where we discussed the function of the form "in a Q environment," we probed the possible rhetoric "of" the story in a setting where references to Jesus as "Son of man" and "lord" and sayings about "foxes and birds," "leaving the dead," and "healing by your word" were known and used. At the present point in our analysis, we have moved to the rhetoric "of" the story in the Gospel of Mark. This is also the move Lane has made when he says that "the Son of man" in Mark 2:28 should be interpreted by analogy to Mark 2:10, where the Son of man has authority to forgive sins on earth.[70] Lane's comments should call to mind that the rhetoric "of" the story occurs in a domain where Jesus has healed a leper and told him to offer for his cleansing "what Moses commanded" (Mark 1:44), a context which establishes a certain credibility ($\mathring{\eta}\theta os$) for Jesus in the realm of Mosaic legislation. Then Jesus has engaged in what might be called "law reform." After forgiving a paralytic's sins and healing him (Mark 2:1–12), and defending his eating with tax collectors and sinners (Mark 2:13–18), he justifies the disciples' failure to fast with an argument that "new wine is for new wineskins" (Mark 2:22; cf. "new" teaching in Mark 1:27). The next story is the account of the Plucking of the Grain, in which, Lane suggests, Jesus' act and word "established the true intention of the Sabbath and exposed the weakness of a human system of fencing the Law with restrictions."[71] In rhetorical terms, Lane is suggesting that the stasis "of" the story in its narrative setting is "legal question."[72] In other words, the reader of the Markan sequence would grasp that laws are being reformed. In the Plucking Story, then, the "letter" of the law about "reaping" on the sabbath has been reformed according to the "intent" of the law. The basic stasis of the overall story, then, occurs when Jesus asserts that God never meant to deprive people in need when he insti-

---

68. I am grateful to my graduate assistant Russell Sisson for emphasizing this in our discussions. See Holmer, *Grammar of Faith*, 44–80, 136–58 as well as his *Making Christian Sense*, 98–118.

69. I am indebted to Thomas M. Conley, a specialist in ancient and modern rhetoric in the Department of Speech Communication at the University of Illinois, for this distinction.

70. Lane, *Gospel According to Mark*, 120.

71. Lane, *Gospel According to Mark*, 120.

72. See Kennedy, *New Testament Interpretation*, 19.

tuted the sabbath. This view is surely correct. There is an additional feature, however, that emerges from the saying about the Son of man. After the "intent" of the law has been established through the saying that God instituted the sabbath "for man," the Son of man saying appears to take the stasis yet one step further to "jurisdiction":[73] the Pharisees are out of their domain when they attempt to make a judgment in the arena where the Son of man is in charge. In the domain of Jesus' activity, the Pharisees lose their competence to apply scripture appropriately, because their frame of reference does not move beyond the halakhic interpretation of scripture, that amounts to an interpretation of the letter rather than the intent of God's laws in his created order.

The overall rhetoric of the story, then, redefines sabbath law and takes it out of the jurisdiction of Pharisees. This redefinition may serve a deliberative function in early Christianity, guiding people's action in the future, or it may serve a judicial function, guiding people's judgments of actions that other people have performed. Since the action of the disciples is grounded in the purpose for which God instituted the sabbath, there is a broad foundation for deliberation about action on the sabbath in the future. Since a specific judgment is made about a specific action, this story may function as a precedent by which to judge other actions. It is not accidental, then, that this story receives close attention in discussions that use Jesus' view of the sabbath to establish guidelines for advising about appropriate sabbath activity and for judging certain activities to be inappropriate.[74]

4. The Version in Luke 6:1–6

In contrast to the Markan version, the Lukan version does not develop the rhetoric "in" the story with special rhetorical figures. Rather, Luke tells the story with "special touches" in a style characteristic of abbreviated composition in chreiai. At the beginning of the story, Luke makes it clear that the disciples were plucking and eating the heads of grain, and he ends the sentence with an assertion that they were doing this by rubbing the heads "in their hands." The statement about the plucking and eating indicates that the disciples were not wasting the grain, and the emphatic placement of "in their hands" suggests that the narrator is aware of the special provision in Deut 23:25 (LXX: Deut 24:1) for a person to gather ἐν ταῖς χερσί σου στάχυς, "a head in your hands." The composition of this verse, then, emphasizes that the primary issue is sabbath work, that the disciples were not needlessly wasting the grain, and that their action was permitted by law on any day other than the

73. See Kennedy, *New Testament Interpretation*, 19.
74. Cf. Carson, "Jesus and the Sabbath."

sabbath. In accord with this approach to the story, the narrator emphasizes that the issue is sabbath activity by placing "on a sabbath" in an
emphatic initial position after ἐγένετο δέ ("and it happened") in the
opening verse (Luke 6:1) and "on the sabbath" in an emphatic final
position in the Pharisees' question (Luke 6:2). The response to the sabbath issue, then, is skillfully met in the final verse as "of the sabbath"
stands between "lord is" and "the Son of man." Only the Lukan version
arranges all of these features in this manner. The result is a neatly
constructed progression that emphasizes the occurrence of the incident
on the sabbath and its justification through the lordship of the Son of
man.

Jesus' recitation of the Davidic incident in Luke occurs in response to
the Pharisees' query of the disciples rather than Jesus. This is a nice
compositional touch, found only in Luke, that emphasizes that the
Pharisees hold Jesus responsible for the actions of the disciples in this
situation, and not the disciples themselves. When Jesus speaks in defense of his disciples, his opening comment is especially strong when,
after the Pharisees have asked the disciples, "Why are you doing . . .?",
Jesus intervenes with "*This*, have you not read, which *David did* . . .?" As
Jesus recites the Davidic incident he states that David "took," "ate," and
"gave" the loaves to his companions. Again this is a special touch,
emphasizing that David "took" the loaves, rather than being given them,
but "having taken them," he gave them to his disciples in a manner that
evokes eucharistic imagery which reappears in the feeding of the five
thousand (Luke 9:16–17) and the Last Supper (Luke 22:19). Then the
recitation of the Davidic incident ends with an emphasis that the loaves
were not lawful for anyone to eat "except *only* the priests." This feature,
found also in Matthew, emphasizes that a person must realize the
weightiness of what David did: David indeed took something that was
meant "only" for the priests. The final saying then comes as a quick
conclusion: And he said to them, "Lord of the sabbath is the Son of
man."

The Lukan version, then, is an excellent example of decisive chreia
composition in abbreviated style. The narrator has no interest in elaborating any of the internal features of the story. Rather, the story is to
function as a παράδειγμα ("example") that exhibits Jesus' lordship over
the sabbath. Any skillful reader will see the care with which the disciples enacted a more humane version of the halakhic law that pro-
hibited reaping on the sabbath. Also, he or she will see how Jesus
defended a more humane version of the law with a story in which David
used items from the temple for the benefit both of himself and others,
rather than allowing them to serve the needs of the priests only. This
approach to the story may remind a Hellenistic reader of reforms of

sanctuaries and rituals like those attributed to Apollonius of Tyana.[75] It also reminds a person of the use of παραδείγματα ("examples") in biographical literature of the first and second centuries C.E. This approach is characterized by an interest in the rhetoric "of" the story as a paradigm of a person's activity rather than internal elaboration of the story. Once the author has carefully established the ethos of the person in whom he is interested through the standard τόποι ("topics") surrounding his birth, youth, and young adulthood (Luke 1–4:13),[76] the purpose of the person's activity is set forth in a scene that inaugurates his adult career (Luke 4:16–30),[77] then large units of material featuring παραδείγματα ("examples"), ἀπομνημονεύματα ("reminiscences"), and speeches gradually extend and elaborate the issues as the author carries out the overall goals for the account. For Luke, the Plucking of the Grain is next to last in a series of stories leading up to Jesus' appointment of twelve disciples (Luke 6:12–16) and his Sermon on the Plain (Luke 6:20–49). In this position, it helps to provide the narrative context in which Jesus can conclude a speech to "a great crowd of his disciples and a great multitude" (Luke 6:17) with an appeal which asks: "Why do you call me 'Lord, Lord,' and do not do what I tell you? . . ." (Luke 6:46).

These observations support the general consensus that Luke's version of the story is especially "christological," with its quick movement to the final saying that the Son of man is lord of the sabbath.[78] The emphasis on the authoritative nature of Jesus' activity makes it difficult to say if the final saying is something the reader should deduce from the story as a conclusion,[79] or whether the christological assertion is really a premise that allows the narrator to tell the story in such an abbreviated style. If the final saying functions as a premise, the underlying reasoning is something like this:

General Premise: The Son of man is lord of the sabbath.

Presupposed Concrete Premise: The disciples have done what the Son of man permits them to do.

Conclusion: Therefore, the disciples have not violated the sabbath.

The rhetorical function of παραδείγματα ("examples") of this length, however, usually is to restate a premise in the same context in which

75. See Philostratus, *Life of Apollonius* IV.21–30.

76. See Talbert, "Prophecies of Future Greatness."

77. Cf. Plutarch, *Alexander* 14.1–9.

78. Neirynck, "Jesus and the Sabbath," 230; Banks, *Jesus and the Law*, 116; and Carson, "Jesus and the Sabbath," 68.

79. Banks, *Jesus and the Law*, 121; Grundmann, *Das Evangelium nach Lukas*, 135–36; Schmid, *Das Evangelium nach Markus*, 127 and Doeve, *Jewish Hermeneutics*, 165.

they support the premise inductively. Since the internal argumentation is so succinct, the story confirms beliefs that are already held more than it provides a base for specific decisions about future action. The rhetoric "of" the Lukan version, therefore, is noticeably epideictic. By showing that activity associated with Jesus must be accompanied by a new approach to sabbath laws, it confirms the first part of the final comment in the preceding story that "new wine must be put into new wineskins." Also, by showing the Pharisees, who know the old laws, possessing no desire for new laws, it supports the final part of the comment that "no one after drinking old wine desires new; for he says, 'The old is good.'" The contribution of the story, then, is to strengthen views about Jesus, the sabbath, Pharisees, and disciples that have been emerging in the narrative at least since the programmatic opening of Jesus' adult career in the synagogue at Nazareth on a sabbath day (Luke 4:16–30). Its deliberative or judicial qualities are therefore derivative of its epideictic qualities.

5. The Version in Matt 12:1–8

The Matthean version, in contrast to the Lukan version, exhibits extensive internal elaboration. The goal of the elaboration is to destroy any impression that the disciples engaged in, or that Jesus condoned, unlawful activity. The narrator, then, is concerned with the rhetoric "in" the story itself, and he elaborates it so that an almost "complete" argument demonstrates his point of view. The elaborated form in Matthew exhibits a significant number of rhetorical steps that appear neither in Mark nor Luke. A display of these steps looks like the following:

(1) *Introduction*

At that time Jesus went through the grainfields on the sabbath; his disciples were hungry, and they began to pluck heads of grain and to eat.

(2) *Statement of the Case*

But when the Pharisees saw it, they said to him, "Look, your disciples are doing what is not lawful to do on the sabbath."

(3) *Argument from Example (ἐκ παραδείγματος) in Written Testimony*

He said to them, "Have you not read what David did, when he was hungry, and those who were with him: how he entered the house of God and ate the bread of the Presence, which it was not lawful for him to eat nor for those who were with him, but only for the priests?"

(4) *Argument from Analogy (ἐκ παραβολῆς) in the Law*

Or have you not read in the law how on the sabbath the priests in the temple profane the sabbath, and are *guiltless*?

(5) *Argument from Comparison (πρός τι): Lesser to Greater*

I tell you, something greater than the temple is here.

(6) *Argument from Judgment (ἐκ κρίσεως) in Syllogistic Form*

And if you had known what this means, "I desire mercy, and not sacrifice," you would not have condemned the *guiltless*.

(8) *Rationale as Conclusion*

For lord of the sabbath is the Son of man.

When comparing the Matthean version with the Markan and Lukan versions, the well-constructed segmentation of the story becomes obvious. The primary device which establishes the segments is the conjunction δέ ("and"). In a sequence, δέ ("and") is used to introduce the action of the disciples (οἱ δὲ μαθηταὶ αὐτοῦ: 12:1), the speech of the Pharisees (οἱ δὲ Φαρισαῖοι: 12:2), the opening response of Jesus (οἱ δὲ εἶπεν: 12:3), the beginning of the final argument (λέγω δὲ ὑμῖν: 12:6), and the syllogism within the final argument (εἰ δὲ ἐγνώκειτε: 12:7). This segmentation signals a conscious elaboration of the argument in steps that build upon one another to a conclusion that has great significance to the narrator.

The beginning segments exhibit in stereotypical fashion the procedures associated with chreia composition. In contrast to the other versions, the opening verse of the Matthean version explicitly introduces ὁ Ἰησοῦς ("Jesus") as the πρόσωπον ("character") who is the center of attention. When the Pharisees respond to the action of the disciples, the clause begins in stereotypical chreia style: οἱ δὲ Φαρισαῖοι ἰδόντες εἶπαν αὐτῷ ("and having seen, the Pharisees said to him"; 12:2). Then, Jesus' response to the Pharisees is introduced according to the simple procedures associated with chreia composition: ὁ δὲ εἶπεν αὐτοῖς ("and he said to them"; 12:3). Through this approach, the story does not become a narrative (διήγημα or διήγησις) but maintains the sharp qualities of a chreia that features the decisive speech and action of a specific person.

When the narrator introduces the disciples (12:1), he explains not only their actions ("they began to pluck heads and to eat"), but also the reason for the action ("they were hungry"). This feature is present only in Matthew, and it is an excellent rhetorical procedure, showing a legitimate motivation for the action that can be a foundation upon which to build an argument.[80] The Matthean version introduces the reason first,

---

80. This feature fulfills Aristotle's advice in *Rhet.* I.x.14–18 to exhibit the good motivations behind the activity of the ones whom the speaker will defend in the speech. It also accords with the practice of introducing "reasons" at the very beginning with the thesis, before expanding the reasons at a later stage. See, for example, *Rhet. ad Her.* IV.xliii.56–57.

so that the sequence is: "his disciples were hungry and began to pluck heads and to eat" (12:1).

In turn, the Pharisees state a case of unlawful activity to Jesus. In contrast to the other versions again, Matthew has them state the case as a declarative accusation rather than an inquiry, and the seriousness of the action: "Behold, your disciples *are doing* what is not lawful *to do* on the sabbath." In Matthew, then, the story comes closer than in the other versions to legal rhetoric in a trial setting. The accusation by the Pharisees functions as a legal charge against the disciples. This calls forth a response from Jesus that has more ingredients of a legal defense than any of the other versions. The implication is that the defense is successful, because it contains the components of a complete rhetorical argument.

Jesus begins his argument against the Pharisees' charge with an authoritative example from scripture. In Hermogenes' terms, this would be the argument ἐκ παραδείγματος ("from example"). In the Matthean version, Jesus responds to the Pharisees in terms that balance the explanation in the introduction. The balancing establishes a correspondence between the narration and defense of the act that suggests integrity (ἦθος) within the person stating the defense. Just as the disciples "were hungry, plucked, and ate," so David "was hungry, entered God's house, and ate."[81] Then this step in the argument ends with a *partitio* (or *divisio*)[82] that divides the topics into: "it was not lawful (a) for him (David) to eat, (b) nor for those with him, (c) except the priests only." This division establishes the basis for the move to the next step in the argument.

The Matthean argument develops its steps out of the topic of "the house of God" (i.e., the Temple), which was introduced as the locale from which David took the loaves, and "the priests," who are the final group mentioned at the end of the Davidic example. The first step is an argument from analogy (ἐκ παραβολῆς) based on sabbath activity of priests in the Temple. This analogy could be found in various portions of scripture, but the argument here is that it is found "in the law." Just as Matthew has carefully worded the argument from the Davidic example to balance the action of the disciples, so the argument from the analogy of the priests' activity counterbalances the statement of the case by the Pharisees. In the Pharisees' statement, repetition of "doing" moved toward an emphasis on "sabbath" at the end:

81. There is a textual uncertainty concerning whether "he" or "they" ate. See Metzger, *A Textual Commentary*, 31.

82. See Kennedy, *New Testament Interpretation*, 24, 88.

Behold your disciples *are doing*
what it is not lawful *to do*
> *on a sabbath.*

Repeating the opening words used to introduce the Davidic example
"Have you not read" (οὐκ ἀνέγνωτε), the narrator resumes attention to
written authority and produces an analogy from "the law" to supplement the Davidic example that is insufficient by rabbinic standards to
refute the accusation by the Pharisees.[83] As a counterbalance, the argument from analogy features repetition of "sabbath" that moves toward
an emphasis at the end on the priests' "being guiltless":

on the sabbath *the priests* in the temple
the sabbath desecrate,
> and *they are guiltless.*

This new argument replaces the Pharisees' verb "to perform an act"
(ποιεῖν) with "to desecrate" (βεβηλόω: "to perform an act that violates the
sanctity of a custom or place"). This new verb occurs in a setting that
places "the priests in the Temple" between two occurrences of "sabbath,"
and the statement ends with an assertion that the priests have not
violated any law through this activity. This argument has moved
through the division at the end of the counterproposition (ἀντίθεσις) to a
strained definition (βίαιος ὅρος)[84] based on a commonplace (τοπική),
which is a well-known topic or situation.[85] The straining of (or "violence
to": βίαιος) the definition is obvious in the reference to the priests'
activity as "desecration." The strength of the argument comes from its
foundation on the common sabbath activity of priests in the Temple.
Referring to this activity, the Matthean Jesus argues that the priests are
given the right (indeed the duty) to "desecrate" the sabbath (by sabbath
work) and *they are guiltless.*

The nature of this step is to move beyond the initial argument from
example, which appeared to admit the unlawfulness of the act, to an
argument that moves away from an acceptance of guilt to a plea-of-
justification (ἀντίληψις) that asserts that the disciples are innocent of
any wrongdoing. The key to the argument, from a rhetorician's standpoint, is its foundation on the "commonplace" of priestly activity on the

---

83. See Daube, *New Testament and Rabbinic Judaism,* 76–78.
84. See Hermogenes 74,2–4 and the English translation in Nadeau, "Hermogenes'
On Stases," 410.
85. Often a defendant responds with a countercharge (ἀντέγκλημα) that claims
that the one who suffered deserved to suffer, and it is supported with a commonplace, as Hermogenes 73,2–5 indicates. See Nadeau, "Hermogenes' *On Stases,* 410 for
an English translation. Matthew omits a countercharge since it is inappropriate and
the strained definition contains the commonplace.

sabbath in Jewish heritage. This commonplace could be found in virtually any portion of the Bible, but the argument is given decisiveness by pointing to its presence "in the law." With this move, the argument produces a principle deduced from the Torah that would be a significant rabbinic argument.[86] It is a powerful argument from analogy, based on continuity with the argument from example ("Have you not read . . . the house of God . . . except the priests only; or have you not read . . . the priests in the temple . . . and are guiltless), citation of a commonplace (sabbath activity of priest in the Temple), location in the law (the basis for halakha), hyperbolic description of the priests' activity as "desecration" ($\beta\epsilon\beta\eta\lambda\acute{o}\omega$), and argument that the priests are blameless (something every person would grant). This step moves through the counter-proposition ($\dot{a}\nu\tau\acute{\iota}\theta\epsilon\sigma\iota s$), which implies that the act was "permissible though unlawful," toward a plea-of-justification that is strong enough to imply that the Pharisees committed a base act of injustice when they brought an accusation of guilt upon innocent people. The argument from analogy, then, supports a strained definition, showing that the law provides for deeds that look like a desecration of the sabbath but are performed every sabbath without guilt.

The remaining steps must secure this turn of affairs, and the Matthean Jesus secures it with a sequence of steps within a final argument introduced with $\lambda\acute{\epsilon}\gamma\omega$ $\delta\grave{\epsilon}$ $\acute{v}\mu\hat{\iota}\nu$, ("I say to you"). The first rhetorical move is to argue that "greater than the Temple is here." The topic of the Temple provides the continuity, and the topic "lesser/greater" introduces a crucial transition from the disciples' act to Jesus' presence with the disciples. The issue remains whether the benefit provided by the disciples' act was greater than their wrong, since it is obvious that the priests provide a significant benefit to God's people by their sabbath work. Hermogenes suggests that the defendant's argument from comparison ($\pi\rho\acute{o}s$ $\tau\iota$) is concerned to show that the service performed by the deed was greater than the wrong.[87] In this instance, the comparison shifts the attention from the disciples themselves to Jesus, a shifting of blame ($\mu\epsilon\tau\acute{a}\sigma\tau\alpha\sigma\iota s$) in a setting where there is no admission of wrongdoing and where it is obvious that Jesus has found strong support for the disciples' act in the law. This argument provides the link with the next statement.

After shifting the attention to "something greater than the Temple," the Matthean Jesus introduces a judgment cited from a written authority in the form of a syllogism:[88]

---

86. See Daube, *New Testament and Rabbinic Judaism*, 76–79.
87. See Hermogenes 73,14–15 and the English translation in Nadeau, "Hermogenes' *On Stases*," 410.
88. See Theon 208,1–4.

"If you had known what this means, 'I desire mercy and not sacrifice,'
You would not have condemned the guiltless."

This is the thesis that follows the strained definition and comparison.[89]
The thesis stands in a contrary-to-fact form that fulfills Hermogenes'
recommendation of an argument from the contrary (ἐκ τοῦ ἐναντίου): "If
you had known . . . you would not have condemned." An argument
from the contrary regularly clarifies the positive thesis. In this instance it
implies it. In other words, when Jesus argues "If you had known 'I desire
mercy . . .,' you would not have condemned the guiltless," he is implying:
"Knowing 'I desire mercy,' I had the responsibility to let my disciples
pluck grain and eat it."[90] The argument in Matthew is similar to the
example Hermogenes gives:

> The thesis then follows in natural order to the effect that the general must act
> in the best interests of the state in every way possible, even if the citizens
> sometimes oppose a policy because of ignorance of their best interests, and
> that he must do a little damage for the sake of the greater good.[91]

In the Matthean argument, the thesis is grounded in a judgment cited
from an ancient authority (ἐκ κρίσεως in Hermogenes), namely Hosea
6:6. The quotation is, moreover, a word of the Lord to Israel (Hosea 4:1).
Jesus has enacted "mercy" according to the desire of God himself. This
principle would have been the basis on which the loaves of presence (a
sacrifice to God) were lawful for David to take and give to his companions, and it is the principle that functioned in Jesus' granting of
permission to the disciples to pluck grain. With this statement the proofs
have been found and the speaker is ready to deliver the final plea-of-
justification.

The final statement is a conclusion in the form of a rationale: "For
lord of the sabbath is the Son of man." In this position it functions as a
plea-of justification (ἀντίληψις) in a form like Hermogenes' example: "I
was general and the act was undoubtedly lawful."[92] At this point, the
speaker's defense lies fully in his justification of himself. In Matthew,
the narrator has moved the auditor from the rhetoric "in" the story to the
rhetoric "of" the story. The previous passage (Matt 11:25–30) ends with
the assertion that Jesus brings an "easier yoke" and "lighter burden"
(Matt 11:30). This easing of the burden is part of the knowledge the

89. See Hermogenes 74,4–9 and the English translation in Nadeau, "Hermogenes'
On Stases," 410.
90. Cf. Carson, "Jesus and the Sabbath," 67.
91. See Hermogenes 74,4–9 and the English translation in Nadeau, "Hermogenes'
On Stases," 410.
92. See Hermogenes 74,11–12 and the English translation in Nadeau, "Hermogenes' *On Stases*," 410.

Father has revealed to the Son (Matt 11:25–27). The story of the Plucking of the Grain is linked specifically to this pericope through its occurrence "at that time" (Matt 12:1).[93] While the rhetoric "in" the Plucking story exonerates the disciples of any wrongdoing, the rhetoric "of" the story exhibits Jesus' ability to guide and exonerate according to God's guidance (Hosea 6:6). Indeed, Jesus' citation of Hosea 6:6 in Matt 9:13 as well as Matt 12:7 shows that it provides a foundational principle for the activity of the Matthean Jesus. The Plucking of the Grain on the Sabbath is followed by Jesus' healing of a man with a withered hand (Matt 12:9–14), and in this setting Jesus asserts that "it is lawful on the sabbath to do well (do acts which produce benefit)" (Matt 12:12). This leads, then, to the lengthy quotation of Isa 42:1–4 that argues that Jesus fulfills the expectations for a chosen servant (Matt 12:18) who is a source of hope for the Gentiles (Matt 12:21).

Appeal to written authority plays a role in three steps in the argument: from example, from analogy, and from judgment. The Davidic example stood in the tradition and Matthew only slightly retouches it for his purposes. The argument from analogy in the law, however, is unique to Matthew. For the judgment, Matthew has found an authoritative saying in scripture and couched it in a contrary to fact construction that explores an argument from its contraries. This argument stands in the place of the Markan saying: "The sabbath was made for man, not man for the sabbath."[94] In contrast to the Markan saying, the Matthean citation from Hosea achieves two things. First, it brings the authority of explicit words from scripture into the setting. This is preferable to a proverbial saying that has no scriptural status. Second, the saying is placed in a setting of conditional contrary-to-fact logic: "And if you had known what this means . . ., you would not have condemned the guiltless." This negative form is superb in the setting of a counterattack where a person wishes to introduce a contrary thesis.

In summary, the Matthean version of the story elaborates the rhetoric "in" the story so that it approximates a complete argument against the charge of the Pharisees. Once the Davidic example is introduced, the topics of "the Temple" and "the priests" are the means for developing the arguments. Thus, the Matthean version elaborates the argument from the Davidic incident. Providing the reason for the disciples' action in the introduction (they were hungry, so they plucked and ate), the Davidic incident is a counterproposition in the form of an argument from example. The argument moves to a strained definition based on analogy followed by a comparison from lesser to greater that shifts the attention from the disciples to Jesus. After this, the Matthean Jesus introduces a

93. See Banks, *Jesus and the Law*, 113.
94. See Banks, *Jesus and the Law*, 120.

thesis in the form of a judgment embedded in an argument from contraries. Then the story ends with a plea-of-justification in the form of a
rationale.

Whatever the relationship between Matthew and Mark, Matthew
was not satisfied with an argument from one or more sayings in the
tradition that left an implication of wrongdoing on the disciples. If he
knew the Markan tradition with the saying "the sabbath was made for
man," he recognized that it was not decisive in Jewish circles.[95] He had to
develop a complete argument against the accusation. If Mark knew the
Matthean version, he considered the detailed exoneration of the disciples to be beside the point (I consider this order to be much harder to
envision) and preferred to leave an implication that the disciples had
performed an action considered unlawful by Pharisees and ground a
defense in a gnomic saying about God's institution of the sabbath. Since
Mark's argument admitted that the act violated the law, it stayed in the
arena of a counterproposition and counterplea that admitted guilt. Matthew wanted to turn back the implication of guilt. Therefore, he used a
strained definition to present a thesis based upon the law and explicit
citation of scripture (Hosea 6:6). Then, he could complete the argument
with a plea-of-justification grounded in the authority and knowledge of
the speaker.

6. Conclusion

No matter how the different versions of the Plucking of the Grain
develop the judicial rhetoric, each version contains the basic ingredients
of a "synopticized" chreia. The beginning of every version is an implication that Jesus' situation with his disciples is equal to David's situation
with his companions.

The common synoptic form of the story adds to the argument from
Davidic example a conclusion stating that the Son of man is lord of the
sabbath. The story with this conclusion contains dimensions that are
highly consonant with sayings in the Q tradition. Indeed, minor agreements between Matthew and Luke raise the possibility that a Q version
of this story did, in fact, exist. In this form, Jesus admits the unlawful
nature of the disciples' activity but introduces a counterproposition that
implies that, although the act was unlawful, it was nevertheless permissible.

Efforts to reconstruct the history of the tradition exhibit a separation

95. If the rabbinic parallel "The sabbath is delivered unto you, but you are not
delivered unto the sabbath" existed during the first century (see Mekilta Shabbata 1
to Exod 31:14, attributed to R. Simeon ben Menasya; cf. BYoma 85B where it is
attributed to Jonathan ben Joseph), Matthew will have known it was an argument
secondary to scripture itself.

between those interpreters who consider the Davidic argument to be part of the earliest form and those who consider the saying about the institution of the sabbath (that is unique to Mark) to have stood in place of the Davidic argument. From a rhetorical perspective, the attempt to reconstruct the earliest form on the basis of the sabbath saying looks suspicious, since it bypasses a chreia-like form on its way toward a proposal that the earliest stages were enthymematic in form. Chreia transmission outside the New Testament as well as in the gospel tradition suggests that the earliest stages regularly do not have an enthymematic core, but the use of chreiai in argumentative settings often moves them toward a more enthymematic form.

The Markan form of the story shows a development of an enthymematic argument in the final sayings. It is possible that this argument relates to presuppositions held elsewhere in Mark that the Son of man came to serve. For this reason, the reference to David's "having need" (unique to Mark) may indicate the presence of a counterplea based on Jesus' granting of permission to the disciples for the purpose of serving the needs of perhaps both themselves and Jesus.

The Lukan version of the story shows less interest in the rhetoric "in" the story than the rhetoric "of" the story. Thus, the story moves quickly, with special touches, from the inquiry of the Pharisees to the statement that the Son of man is lord of the sabbath. This compositional strategy provides an additional $\pi\alpha\rho\acute{\alpha}\delta\epsilon\iota\gamma\mu\alpha$ ("example") in a series that leads up to the selection of twelve disciples and the preaching of the Sermon on the Plain. In Luke, then, the narrator achieves his goals through epideictic rhetoric that is primarily interested in the power of the story when it is recited in an abbreviated form.

The Matthean version of the story is concerned to exonerate the disciples of any wrongdoing and to clarify that Jesus enacted a principle from God himself when the disciples plucked the grain on the sabbath. In this version, then, the narrator is highly interested in the rhetoric "in" the story, and he develops that rhetoric into an argument containing most of the rhetorical figures discussed by Hermogenes: argument from example, from analogy, from explicit citation, and from contraries. In the setting of the judicial rhetoric created by the plucking of grain, these rhetorical figures function as a counterproposition, a strained definition, a thesis, and a final plea-of-justification.

Every extant version of the story, therefore, contains the argument from Davidic example. Although some have considered this argument inappropriate, since Jesus' disciples rather than Jesus himself (by analogy to David) pluck the grain, it does exhibit characteristic features of a chreia-like tradition that probably existed at the earliest stage of the form. As we encounter the story in the synoptic gospels, we can see how it could be written in an abbreviated or elaborated form to serve the argumentative strategies of an individual writer. Since the story contained an argument from example, it contained a potential for elaboration (ἐργασία) using a rhetorical syllogism that grounded the serving of needs in God's institution of the sabbath (Mark) or using a sequence of arguments from analogy, comparison, explicit citation, and contraries to exonerate the disciples and Jesus of any wrongdoing (Matthew). Alternatively, Luke could compose the story in an abbreviated form to serve basic epideictic strategies in his narrative. In Mark and Matthew, elaboration signals a complex relation between the rhetoric "in" the story and the rhetoric "of" the story, since the rhetoric in the story has considerable complexity and richness within itself. In Luke, in contrast, the lack of elaboration signals a primary interest in the rhetoric "of" the story, and the reader sees that the story confirmed basic beliefs and attitudes which Luke espoused without a need to reorient or bolster the rhetoric in the basic components of the story.

SIX

Teaching in Parables: Elaboration in Mark 4:1–34

Burton L. Mack

1. A Curious Collection of Parables

In the fourth chapter of his gospel, Mark describes a scene by the sea in which Jesus teaches a large crowd "in parables." The literary unit (4:1–34) is packed with exegetical problems, as all New Testament scholars know. The scene changes at vs 10 where Jesus is alone with the disciples and "those about him," and it is not clear whether the crowds are in view again in vss 33–34, or whether the material makes a further distinction there between "those about him" and "his own disciples." The discussion in vss 10–11 is about parables (plural), but so far in Mark, Jesus has given only one parable (the Sower, vss 3–8). In vs 13 it is "this parable" that Jesus takes up for special consideration and interpretation. The interpretation is an "allegorical" reading of the parable that supplies terms of reference for several of the images in the parable. Apparently this rereading of a parable, a unique phenomenon in the synoptic tradition, answers to the "secret of the kingdom of God" that only those "inside" are granted. But it is not clear whether it is the content or the method of the allegory that does the trick for the disciples. Nor is it clear why Jesus' teaching begins with parables in the first place. The citation of Isa 6:9–10 just at this point ("lest they should turn again") sharpens the issue considerably. Are the parables intended, or are they not intended, to be understood? Jesus continues, in any case, to "teach" by using more of them. He employs an image of a lamp, an aphoristic saying (the Measure), and two additional seed-stories (Seed Growing Secretly; Mustard Seed) without further interpretation. In vs 34 the author tells us that

Jesus explained everything privately to his disciples, of course, but as the gospel proceeds it becomes clear that even that didn't help much. So, where are we?

It is clear that Mark intends 4:1–34 to be taken as a unit, given the period which vss 33–34 make. These verses pick up both on the description of the scene in vss 1–2, as well as on the discussion in vss 10–13. But what kind of unit is it? Three of the parables do tell about what happens to seeds, suggesting that a theme, or at least a principle of association, may have determined the collection. This has frequently been noted by scholars, and has been investigated thoroughly by Kuhn.[1] Kuhn begins with the observation of the similarity among the three parables, submits them to a rigorous form-critical analysis, and concludes that the three parables plus the allegory of the Sower formed a pre-Markan collection. This collection, according to Kuhn, intended to instruct Christians about the eventual success of the Christian mission, present appearances to the contrary. Kuhn is probably right about many of his form- and redaction-critical judgments, and his analysis of the similarity of the points scored by the individual parables in their reconstructed pre-Markan contexts is quite helpful. He is less helpful, however, when discussing such matters as the overall form of the collection, the sequential order of the parables, and the significance of the collection as a unit. And, because he is concerned primarily with the pre-Markan history of the parables, he intends his redaction-critical analyses mainly to separate the earlier layers of the tradition from Markan additions and reinterpretations. We are left, then, only with the notion of a "collection," in which Mark has inserted a bit of material containing the themes of secrecy and misunderstanding.

Most scholars working with the parables of the synoptic tradition apparently share this view of the collection of materials in Mark 4. The normal approach to the parables in general is to isolate and reconstruct an individual parable through redaction- and form-critical analyses. Interpretation may require recontexting by placement in the general setting of Jesus and his teaching, or the early church and its teaching. Or it may require classification of the parable to form a set with others of similar or contrasting types. But usually scholars handle their discussions on a parable-by-parable basis even when, eventually, they engage again the question of a parable's place, function, and reinterpretation in its gospel setting. In the case of the parables in Mark 4, most interpreters have apparently regarded the notion of a collection as sufficient to account for the literary unit. This is so in spite of the fact that innumerable exegetical investigations have taken as their subject the curious

---

1. See Kuhn, *Ältere Sammlungen.*

relationship of the parable of the Sower to its interpretation, a rather surprising sequence for a collection. The usual explanation of this phenomenon has been first to see it as evidence for allegorization, as the way in which early Christian communities domesticated parables, and second to note that Mark thought the distinction between encoded and decoded logos helpful for the development of his narrative themes of secrecy and misunderstanding. But neither explanation has forced further inquiry about the integration of the Sower parable and its interpretation into the larger literary unit.

It is the larger literary unit with which we are concerned in this essay. We assume a pre-Markan history of individual units, sub-sets, and of other ways of reading the material. Neverthless, we shall regard the literary unit as it stands in Mark's gospel as a Markan composition. Our thesis will be that Mark has organized the collection on the pattern of a chreia elaboration, i.e., it forms a little speech that develops its themes through a sequence of arguments in support and explication of the original saying. In our case the chreia is the parable of the Sower. Because other parables will elaborate this one, we have a particularly interesting case on our hands. Almost every argument (or component of the elaboration sequence) will be figural, derived by illustrative comparison (παραβολή). This being the case, we need to discuss briefly the notion of παραβολή in the rhetorical tradition before tracing out the elaboration pattern.

2. Parable and Παραβολή

New Testament scholars are accustomed to the definition of a parable as a literary form (narrative) with a specific semiotic function (metaphor). It is the metaphoric aspect of parables that has made possible a range of hermeneutical theories drawn from the New Criticism (literature as "aesthetic object"; meaning as "imagination"). The narrative aspect has, on the other hand, made it possible to analyze the parables in terms of structuralist theories of myth and (folk) narrative. Approaching the synoptic materials with this definition in mind, it has been possible to collect a sizable number of parables for study. Invariably, however, the process of classification has occasioned considerable fretting at the upper and lower limits of the definitional range. At the lower limit parables become quite brief, tend to lose their narrativity, and run into aphoristic and illustrative images (cf. the German *Gleichnis*). At the upper limit one encounters the problem of distinguishing parable from example story (less metaphor) and allegory (less reliance on imagination, more on referential decoding). This problem of definition and classification becomes even more complex when one observes that the synoptic tradition does not reserve the term παραβολή for the designation of parables. Our sources use it indiscriminately in reference to a wide range of images, sayings, and stories that have some kind of comparative function.

Making this observation does not deny the amazing advance in synoptic studies that contemporary parable research has achieved. Because of this research it is now clear that many of the narrative parables in the synoptic tradition are compositions that manifest singular poetic achievement, deeply human sensibilities, and great imaginative creativity and appeal. We must certainly include the parable of the Sower among these skillfully crafted stories, as the works of Crossan, Weeden, and others have shown.[2] But is it that kind of poetic achievement that the synoptic term παραβολή intends? If we understand παραβολή in its Greek sense, considerations of style, poetics, and effect upon the imagination would be in order, of course. But it is highly questionable whether genre-specific concerns are foremost in the designation of certain types of speech material as παραβολαί. We shall return to this point below.

If, on the other hand, we understand παραβολή in the sense of the Hebraic *mashal*—a possibility given with the Palestinian provenance of the origins of the Jesus traditions, and the Septuagintal evidence for translating *mashal* as παραβολή—we find ourselves venturing into an even less precisely defined arena of discourse. Interpreters have frequently appealed to the fact that the designation *mashal* includes aphoristic, enigmatic, and riddle-like sayings. Such an observation may indeed be helpful as we seek to understand the aphoristic quality and function of synoptic materials, including parables. But we cannot use it to justify limitation of the term παραβολή to that narrative form we have come to call parable.

The existence of such a genre as scholars now intend by the term parable is not therefore to be denied. Recent scholarship has frequently made reference to the existence of parables in this sense in the Old Testament, Rabbinic literature, and Apocalyptic, as well as in the writings of modern authors such as Kafka and Borges. And we are waiting eagerly for the publication of extrabiblical, ancient parables for comparison that James Breech has been collecting. The issue is not whether parables as a genre exist. The issue is whether Mark's statement that Jesus taught ἐν παραβολαῖς refers to parables as modern scholars define them, or to parables and other imagistic sayings in their rhetorical function as comparisons.

Our thesis will be that the term παραβολή in Mark 4 is best understood against the background of its technical significance in the Greek

---

2. See Weeden, "Recovering the Parabolic Intent" and Crossan, *In Parables*.

rhetorical tradition. McCall has provided us with a thorough philological investigation of παραβολή and related terms (εἰκών, ὁμοίωσις, εἰκασία, *simile, similitudo, comparatio*) in the Greco-Roman literatures of rhetoric and criticism.[3] The term refers in general to an "illustrative comparison" or "analogy." These literatures discuss it both under the rubric of style or poetics on the one hand, and under the rubric of proof or argumentation on the other. Stylistic observations recognize (1) that παραβολαί may range from metaphors, through what we would call similes, to non-figural comparisons between similar things. One also finds discussions of (2) the length appropriate to various literary contexts, (3) degree of detail in the explication of points of comparison, and (4) what difference it makes whether the two things compared are basically the same, similar but from different orders of reality, or different in all respects (i.e., contrastive). Appropriateness to the speech situation is always in view in these discussions which, for example, identify heightened and poetic forms of comparison thought to be distracting in judicial and deliberative situations. So, aesthetic and literary-critical observations are common in discussions of παραβολή; but nowhere is there evidence of what we would consider a genre-critical definition. Instead, comparisons could be made by using any of several forms and styles of speech. Considerations of form and style were important for questions of ornamentation versus argumentation, embellishment as helpful or distracting, and of the effectiveness of persuasive speech in general. But, by definition, the ancient literatures of rhetoric and criticism understood παραβολή more as a matter of content.

We have encountered παραβολή as an argument in the elaboration pattern. In that context we used the term analogy as a translation in order to capture the nuance of (rhetorical) logic that belongs to its technical definition. McCall suggests comparison as the broader term, but even this may be misleading. In English, comparison tends to suggest that the *tertium comparationis* is a matter of similarity. We now need to understand that a παραβολή could point out dissimilarities and contrasts as well as points of similarity between the two objects under comparison. One could make a point by means of a contrastive comparison. The purpose of comparison was understood to be instructive—to clarify, illustrate, or demonstrate some aspect of the subject under investigation. It was, in fact, this function of παραβολή that determined its prominent place in the theory and practice of rhetorical argumentation.

From Aristotle on, the rhetorical tradition regularly paired παραβολή with παράδειγμα in discussions of the topics, or sources from which orators could take their rhetorical arguments. Both were important ways for exploring and addressing the world of human affairs where prin-

3. See McCall, *Ancient Rhetorical Theories.*

ciples of order and arrangement were not always obvious, and logic had to be content with establishing probabilities through inductive reasoning. Both offered ways of pointing to incidents, events, and describable phenomena that could provide at least one case for the rhetor's contention about "the way things go." Brought to bear upon the subject under discussion, παράδειγμα and παραβολή furnished either a primary or a supporting argument, depending on their place in the development of the argumentation. The degree to which, as comparisons, they were appropriate to the point under consideration, and could be seen as an (other) incidence of that point, determined their effectiveness.

The παραβολή differed from the παράδειγμα, not in respect to its logical function in argumentation, but in respect to its content. The source of the παράδειγμα was history (and thus it depended upon a certain literacy for its effectiveness). The ancients understood it as fact, i.e., a specific (and precedent) case in actuality. The source of the παραβολή, however, was the generally available world of human observation and experience. They understood it as fiction, i.e., invented by the rhetor to illustrate the point to be made. It did not point to a specific and actual case, but generalized by casting its subjects as abstractions (e.g., "nature"), classes (e.g., "farmers"), or indefinite subjects (e.g., "a certain one"). As illustrative comparison, an orator could use a παραβολή to sharpen a (definitional) trait of the subject under consideration. As *primary* analogy in a process of inductive reasoning, a παραβολή *plus* rationale could establish a general thesis about the way things go. As a *supporting* argument, a παραβολή could expand the evidence for making the claim that one's definition of, or thesis about, the subject under consideration was plausible.

If we understood Mark's statement that Jesus "taught with παραβολαί" as a rhetorical observation, several important considerations immediately follow. One is that Mark had given some thought to the nature of Jesus' discourse as it was available to him in the traditions of his community. To characterize this discourse as primarily παραβολαί might be to distinguish it from other ways in which ancient communities understood "teachers" to speak, i.e., by using philosophical *dogmata*, proposing ethical *maxims*, or starting with traditional (e.g., scriptural) precedents of legal, ethical, or *paradigmatic* significance (cf. "not as the scribes," 1:22). Jesus would be seen, rather, as one who addressed the (or a) contemporary situation by inventing παραβολαί from the realm of generally observable human experience.

But what, then, would be the subject under consideration? By definition, παραβολή compares (or contrasts) two things. The answer that immediately comes to mind is the "kingdom of God." That the parables of Jesus are of the kingdom of God is, of course, a commonplace in New Testament scholarship. But, as is well known, the term kingdom of God itself is curiously problematic in its reference, whether to a notion, symbol, or social reality. This is so even if we grant the usual assumption about its pre-Jesus provenance in Jewish apocalyptic. The usual approach at this point is to acknowledge that Jesus' intention in the use of the term kingdom of God was to empty it of its older notions while evoking an as-yet-to-be-actualized new reality. On the other hand, however, scholars continue to use kingdom of God as an understandable term, referring to the "message" or the (existential, imaginative) "effect" of his teaching. But if kingdom of God is a notion (or experience) in-the-making, the rhetorical equation that παραβολή assumes (i.e., "parable *of* the kingdom") is under great pressure.

What if Mark's statement that Jesus "taught with παραβολαί" is an observation of, and reflection upon the strangeness of a "teaching" that offers analogies to a phenomenon yet-to-be-named or in-the-making? That would be an astute observation indeed. It would not mean that Mark was unclear about his own resolution of the problem, his own understanding of the significance of kingdom of God. It would mean that he had noticed the enigmatic rhetoricity characteristic of the preponderance of Jesus-materials available to him. It would mean that he had explored the question of the persuasiveness of a "new teaching" that consisted of παραβολαί to an as-yet-to-be-actualized social or apocalyptic phenomenon.

3. *Paideia* and the Kingdom of God

A rather advanced reflection upon the relation of rhetoric to culture may inform Mark's interest in the question of how a rhetoric of παραβολή could be effective for a "new" teaching. We saw in chapter 2 that the principles and practices of rhetoric assumed common cultural conventions and values in order to work out patterns of argumentation that would be persuasive. Issues under discussion would have to be matters of differing but possible perspectives on a situation. Constructive resolutions would require plausible alignment of the situation with commonly acceptable values. In the case of Cynic chreiai, we encounter an analytical and "deconstructive" rhetoric. But even in this case, the silence effected was not a result of absurdity, but of the acknowledgement of real incongruities among the several systems of social value and behavior in play. In the case of the elaboration of Isocrates' saying about *paideia*, on the other hand, the rhetoric of argumentation was actually tautological, so enculturated was the proposition to begin with.

Mark's choice of a seeds-παραβολή to sum up Jesus' teaching, is therefore extremely suggestive, since the image of agricultural endeavor, especially that of sowing seed, was the standard analogy for paideia (i.e., teaching and culture) during this period. In the scholarly discussions of the parable of the Sower, one does find reference to some of the parallels in Greco-Roman literature. But these discussions usually turn their attention quickly away from these parables, and toward Old Testament, Rabbinic, and Apocalyptic texts.[4] That has been unfortunate. One need not deny Mark's readership in the scriptures, and his participation in proto-rabbinic discourse, in order to investigate his acquaintance with common and readily-available stock-images of Hellenistic culture. If Mark has reflected about Jesus' teaching in παραβολαί with reference to the kingdom of God, his choice of just that παραβολή which for Hellenistic ears would evoke comparison with paideia (as teaching and culture) must be noteworthy. This essay cannot be the place to demonstrate the prevalence of the seed comparison to paideia, nor the extent to which Mark's parable (plus interpretation) agrees with the way in which it was used in Greco-Roman literature to illustrate the process of teaching-learning as enculturation.[5] The point is that such a parable would be extremely appropriate to such an investigation as we theorize for Mark. And it would be very clever, setting up the problem in terms of the comparison's uncertain referent (kingdom of God), while suggesting that the referent may bear some relation (by "comparison and contrast") to paideia as teaching and culture.

This, in any case, is what the elaboration of the parable will achieve. It will be about a logos and the modes of its "reception." And it will be about a kingdom and its mysterious ways. It will not explicate the logos of this kingdom in any way other than analogically. That will be the continuing frustration for Greek ears such as ours. But the pattern of elaboration may help us see the points at which this new kingdom does compare and contrast with conventional notions of culture, both Jewish and Hellenistic. If it can achieve that, it will be enough for Mark's purposes.

4. Tracing the Pattern of Elaboration

We seek now to identify the components of a rhetorical elaboration in Mark 4:1–34. Using Hermogenes' elaboration of a chreia as model, we shall begin by identifying the parable of the Sower as the chreia to be elaborated. We have already noticed that Mark announces it as a παραβολή, but that it does not contain any reference to the subject of comparison. If our thesis about παραβολή as comparison is correct, the elaboration will have to tackle that problem, whatever else Mark intends for the course of thematic and argumentational development. Even if

4. See, for example, Klauck, *Allegorie und Allegorese*, 192–96.
5. We will, however, shortly give four citations (one each from Hippocrates, Antiphon, Seneca, and Quintilian) in order to document the Hellenistic usage.

Mark intends to let the problem of a teaching that provides only one half of a comparison stand, he can hardly develop an elaboration of such a reading of the parable without alerting the reader to the way in which he or she is to take the παραβολή. The most appropriate place to do this would be in the rationale. But the danger will be not to lose the creative tension of teaching in "comparisons-without-reference" by supplying an unambiguous reference. Mark has handled this problem by having the disciples raise the question about what the parable could possibly mean. The phrase "secret of the kingdom of God" gives the answer. Kingdom of God provides the necessary reference for the comparison; "secret" assures that the reference term retains its essential ambiguity. The question will be whether the explanation Jesus gives about the logos of the παραβολή resolves or heightens that ambiguity.

We can compare this literary construction with Hermogenes' elaboration of Isocrates' saying (see chapter 2). In that case the saying itself gives the two terms of the comparison (paideia; cultivation). The elaboration, then, at the point of the argument from analogy, merely explicated the agricultural process ("As with farmers . . ."), and made more precise the process of paideia ("so with working with words . . ."). That could happen because the chreia itself was "approved," the metaphor apt, and the elaboration thoroughly constructive and supportive. But Mark chose to cast Jesus' teaching as an *enigmatic* chreia, and that means that it will require some decoding in the rationale.

The enigmatic character of Jesus' παραβολή reminds us of the Cynic chreia, rather than of the domesticated type. In the Cynic chreiai, however, the question preceded the saying, which then occurred as a response to the situation ("Once . . . upon being asked . . . NN said . . ."). Mark inverted the sequence of question-saying. Now it appears that Jesus' teaching itself is the occasion for the question or challenge to which Jesus must reply. And Mark can strive for that as an elaboration that explains the chreia, but also answers the objections or questions that the initiating chreia raised. This is formally similar to the way in which Mark elaborated the anointing story, and to the way in which Mark structured most of the pronouncement and controversy stories. It appears to be a major device for domesticating earlier Jesus anecdotes that may have consisted mainly of Cynic rejoinders to situations of social convention.

In addition to these general observations about the possibility of regarding the parable of the Sower as a chreia, and the subsequent material as elaboration, there are two literary observations that can serve as clues for the analysis. The first is the use of periodization throughout to mark off sections, provide transitions, and unite the elaboration as a whole. Verses 1–2a form a little period. Two statements that emphasize the need to "listen" and "hear" (vss 2b–9) form the chreia. The repetition of the call "to hear" in vs 23 sums up the issue that vss 10–25 have investigated. And verses 33–34 make of the whole a period by referring back to the introduction, and by summing up the theme of the entire elaboration ("hearing" the "word").

The second observation is the repeated use of καὶ ἔλεγεν ("and he said") and καὶ λέγει ("and he says") to introduce a section of material. This formula occurs eight times. With one exception (vs 9), the material that it introduces corresponds exactly to a specific function in the pattern of elaboration.

We can now give the text with its parts identified according to the components of the elaboration pattern. Afterward we shall discuss briefly each component as an argument, and make some observations on the argumentation as a whole.

5. The Pattern of Elaboration in Mark 4:1–34

(1) *Introduction*

Again he began to teach beside the sea. And a very large crowd gathered about him, so that he got into a boat and sat in it on the sea; and the whole crowd was beside the sea on the land. And he taught them many things in parables. (4:1–2a)

(2) *Chreia*

And in his teaching he said to them: "Listen!

A sower went out to sow. And as he sowed, some seed fell along the path, and the birds came and devoured it. Other seed fell on rocky ground, where it had not much soil, and immediately it sprang up, since it had no depth of soil; and when the sun rose it was scorched, and since it had no root it withered away. Other seed fell among thorns and the thorns grew up and choked it, and yielded no grain. And other seeds fell into good soil and brought forth grain, growing up and increasing and yielding thirtyfold and sixtyfold and a hundredfold."

And he said, "He who has ears to hear, let him hear." (4:2b–9)

(3) *Rationale*

(*Request for Rationale*)

And when he was alone, those who were about him with the twelve asked him concerning the parables. (4:10)

(*Rationale Given as Direct Statement*)

And he said to them, "To you has been given the secret of the kingdom of God. But for those outside everything is in parables; so that they may indeed see but not perceive, and may indeed hear but not understand; lest they should turn again, and be forgiven." (4:11–12)

(Rationale Given as Paraphrase of the Parable)

And he said to them, "Do you not understand this parable? How then will you understand all the parables?

The sower sows the word. And these are the ones along the path, where the word is sown; when they hear, Satan immediately comes and takes away the word which is sown in them. And these in like manner are the ones sown upon rocky ground, who, when they hear the word, immediately receive it with joy; and they have no root in themselves, but endure for a while; then, when tribulation or persecution arises on account of the word, immediately they fall away. And others are the ones sown among thorns; they are those who hear the word, but the cares of the world, and the delight in riches, and the desire for other things, enter in and choke the word, and it proves unfruitful. But those that were sown upon the good soil are the ones who hear the word and accept it and bear fruit, thirtyfold and sixtyfold and a hundredfold." (4:13–20)

(4) *Contrary*

And he said to them, "Is a lamp brought in to be put under a bushel, or under a bed, and not on a stand?

For there is nothing hid, except to be made manifest; nor is anything secret, except to come to light.

If anyone has ears to hear, let him hear." (4:21–23)

(7) *Judgment*

And he said to them. "Take heed what you hear. The measure you give will be the measure you get, and still more will be given you.

For to him who has will more be given; and from him who has not, even what he has will be taken away." (4:24–25)

(6) *Example*

And he said, "The kingdom of God is as if a man should scatter seed upon the ground, and should sleep and rise night and day, and the seed should sprout and grow, he knows not how. The earth produces of itself, first the blade, then the ear, then the full grain in the ear. But when the grain is ripe, at once he puts in the sickle, because the harvest has come." (4:26–29)

(5) *Analogy*

And he said, "With what can we compare the kingdom of God, or what parable shall we use for it? It is like a grain of mustard seed, which, when sown upon the ground, is the smallest of all the seeds on earth; yet when it is sown it grows up and becomes the greatest of all shrubs, and puts forth large branches, so that the birds of the air can make nests in its shade." (4:30–32)

(8) *Conclusion*

With many such parables he spoke the word to them, as they were

> able to hear it; he did not speak to them without a parable, but privately
> to his own disciples he explained everything. (4:33–34)

The introduction (1) establishes a setting appropriate to an extended discourse and prepares the reader for it by announcing that "he taught them many things by analogies." This announcement also serves as a characterization of Jesus (a teacher, of that sort), which adds an encomiastic touch with the observation about the "very large crowd" that gathered to hear him. This brief narrative account of a speech situation thus contains all of the functions relevant to the establishment of a proper $\mathring{\eta}\theta o\varsigma$ in the introduction of a speech. It corresponds to Hermogenes' brief "word of praise" that introduces the speaker of the chreia to be elaborated. The difference between Hermogenes' elaboration of Isocrates' saying and our text is just that Mark has used narrative description to turn the chreia-occasion into a full speech-situation so that Jesus can elaborate his own chreia.

The chreia (2) follows. Mark presents it as a $\pi \alpha \rho \alpha \beta o \lambda \mathring{\eta}$ that requires close attention. It is the example chosen to illustrate what Jesus' teaching was like, and the author expressly invites attention to it by the imperatives to listen (4:2b) and hear (4:9) that frame it. Paying close attention, however, to the $\pi \alpha \rho \alpha \beta o \lambda \mathring{\eta}$ leads the reader-listener not at first to insight, but to questions. One expects a $\pi \alpha \rho \alpha \beta o \lambda \mathring{\eta}$ to mention the object of reference. The $\pi \alpha \rho \alpha \beta o \lambda \mathring{\eta}$ does not. Such an omission is unnerving, in spite of the fact that the stock imagery used in the parable immediately brings to mind the process of education for Hellenistic ears, and the process of cultural history for Jewish ears. To evoke just these sets of notions is, of course, what Mark intended the $\pi \alpha \rho \alpha \beta o \lambda \mathring{\eta}$ to do. But the question now is twofold: What *is* the referent, and why does the $\pi \alpha \rho \alpha \beta o \lambda \mathring{\eta}$ not give it?

This enigmatic character of the $\pi \alpha \rho \alpha \beta o \lambda \mathring{\eta}$-without-reference is what makes it a chreia in need of elaboration. Since the introduction has announced a speech-situation, the chreia directs the questions that arise for the reader to the discourse that follows. In the tradition of rhetoric, an orator or author could use an analogy to establish a thesis inductively, as long as a rationale ($\alpha \mathring{\iota} \tau \acute{\iota} \alpha$) accompanied it. And in order to elaborate a chreia, the first thing to do was to propose a rationale. Perhaps, then, the rationale will provide the reader with the answers to the questions raised by the $\pi \alpha \rho \alpha \beta o \lambda \mathring{\eta}$.

The rationale (3) addresses precisely these questions that the curious chreia has raised. It consists of three parts. The first part makes clear that the questions that the $\pi \alpha \rho \alpha \beta o \lambda \mathring{\eta}$ has raised are to be understood as legitimate, arising from those who have listened intently and have tried to make sense of the teaching. They are those who are "inside" the teacher-listener circle of discourse, even though they have not "understood" the import of the parable. The plot thickens and, with the withdrawal of this inner circle from the public scene, the elaboration to follow may be expected to address both their questions about the chreia as well as their situation as those who should not have to ask but do. Part one does not provide any rationale per se. But it does situate the request for a rationale narratively. This move forms a bridge from the chreia situation to the setting for the elaboration, linking the two together.

Part two of the rationale provides the answer to the question about the missing referent. The parable is about the kingdom of God. This is immediately understandable if we see that the kingdom of God stands to Mark's Christian community as paideia-culture does to the Greeks. The similarity of these two notions in fact made it possible to use a stock analogy for paideia as the παραβολή of the kingdom. But this stock analogy also indicates a difference. The kingdom of God is a "secret," "given" only to those who are on the inside of its discourse. That is why, from the outside, the teaching of this kingdom appears as parable, i.e., παραβολή-without-referent.

At this point we might think that if the kingdom of God of the Jesus people is not like Greek paideia, it might be like Jewish notions of Israel. That, of course, would be no surprise, given the emergence of early Christian communities from within the matrices of first-century Judaism. But Mark's next move checks that misconception. He gives a citation from the Jewish scriptures to support the parable theory just given. On the outside one might "hear," of course, but one can not "understand." The citation serves simple rhetorical functions. It supports the distinction just made between "insiders" and "outsiders" by finding an appropriate aphorism within the traditional literature of the outsiders about "hearing" but not "understanding." It also makes it clear that the reference of the term kingdom of God is to be distinguished from Jewish as well as Greek culture. That the lack of understanding is not intended in any predestinarian sense is obvious from the very next statement. Neither do those on the inside understand. We need now to see why that is so.

The third part to the rationale is the so-called allegory of the Sower (4:13–20). It is, however, not an allegory at all, because it merely spells out the analogy that has been implicit all along. For Hellenistic ears, as we have said, the first thought will be that the story of the Sower is about paideia. Not only is cultivation the foundational analogy for culture in general, school children will have learned about the many ways in which one could use that general analogy to illustrate the process of enculturation through teaching and learning with words:

> The views of our teachers are as it were the seeds. Learning from childhood is analogous to the seeds falling betimes upon the prepared ground. (Hippocrates, III)

> As is the seed that is ploughed into the ground, so must one expect the harvest to be, and similarly when good education is ploughed into young persons, its effect lives and burgeons throughout their lives, and neither rain nor drought can destroy it. (Antiphon, fr. 60)

> Words should be scattered like seed; no matter how small the seed may be, if it once has found favorable ground, it unfolds its strength and from an insignificant thing spreads to its greatest growth. (Seneca, *Ep*. 38:2)

> If you wish to argue that the mind requires cultivation, you would use a comparison drawn from the soil, which if neglected produces thorns and thickets, but if cultivated will bear fruit. (Quintilian, V.xi.24)

So the "sower" is a stock analogy for the "teacher," "sowing" for "teaching," "seed" for "words," and "soils" for "students." There is nothing peculiar, nothing with which the Hellenistic listener would not have been familiar in the story of the sower announced as a παραβολή, then paraphrased in keeping with its usual reference to paideia. Why, then, has Mark cast the παραβολή as an enigmatic chreia, and the paraphrase as an esoteric interpretation?

The first thing to be said is that this paraphrase of the parable does function as a rationale in the elaboration sequence. It does so not only by making explicit the subject of the παραβολή, i.e., a kind of paideia. It also succeeds in calling the reader's attention to the fact that the way the sowing went in the parable is related to the problem of understanding the parable. The teaching that belongs to this "secret" paideia is a "seed" whose fruition depends upon more than insight and understanding. The list of things that can go wrong is impressive. The issue for the hearers appears to be one of effective participation in a conflict of major cosmic (cf. "Satan"), social (cf. "tribulation," "persecution"), and ethical dimensions (cf. "cares, riches, desires"). Astute critics may already have begun a process of reflection about the difference between this logos, and that of the Greek paideia. "Cultivation," "toil," "achievement," "reward," "virture"—none of these points, traditional to the usual Hellenic comparison of farming to learning, are nuanced anywhere in the story. The kingdom is less a matter of cultivation, more of transformations—seeds sown, destroyed, accepted, bearing fruit. Though it has a logos that gets it started, the "harvest" is still outstanding. The "secret" of the kingdom is thus, appropriately, a parable of fated seed whose harvest the story promises but whose survival is being challenged in the arena of cultural conflict. This paideia is not a "culture." It is a movement in conflict with other cultures, born of a threatened logos that marks the boundary between those who remain in the cultures of convention and those who accept this logos as the secret promise of a harvest.

The contrary (4) picks up on just this theme of the "secret" of the kingdom. It might appear that these sayings in vss 21–23 are badly chosen, unrelated to the Sower parable, because they suddenly introduce the image of a lamp. But the rationale has established the correlation of "seed" with "logos," and the new metaphor of "light" is fully appropriate to the notion of logos as teaching. The discourse that uses analogies has not lost its way.

The contrast developed here is that between the "hidden" and the "manifest." This contrast addresses the main problem under discussion, which has to do with the enigmatic nature of the new paideia—a teaching difficult to accept about a kingdom not yet manifest. The statement of the contrary acknowledges that the problem is severe, as severe as the opposition between things covered in darkness and things obviously manifest. But that, of course, is hardly the point. The contrary takes the occasion to put another, altogether different, construction on the problem of the enigmatic in the parable of the Sower. Since being hidden does not fulfill the *purpose* of lamps, whereas being manifest does, an argument has been won for "everything hidden (eventually) coming to light" (vs 23). As an elaboration of the chreia, this further analogy serves to argue for the inevitable fruition of the seeds as the purpose for which they were sown. We are very close here to an outright statement of prophetic persuasion. Nevertheless, the parabolic mode dominates, and the listener must still be careful how he hears (vs 23).

At this point, Mark inverts the remaining sequence of the elaboration. Instead of following the normal pattern of analogy (5), example (6), and judgment (7), Mark prefers the reverse order which places Jesus' pronouncement in the middle of the discourse. A subtle chiasm results: the contrary (4) has paradigmatic potential, and thus balances the example (6); and the paraphrase (3) explicates the analogy in the Sower parable, thus balancing the analogy proper (5). But this structural playfulness is not sufficient to account for the inversion of the sequence and the resulting emphasis upon the judgment (7) at this point in the elaboration.

The contrary has introduced the categories of purpose and inevitability. Now the discourse can use direct address, since from this point on the subject under consideration will have to do with what those who have received the teaching are to be *doing* in the light of this instruction about the ways of the kingdom: "Take heed what *you* hear."

For the judgment, Mark uses the image of the "measure." It is appropriate to the harvest scene of the Sower parable, and works now to explicate how one's own participation in the sowing-reaping activity of the logos of the kingdom determines one's stake in the eventual manifestation of the kingdom itself. Now the categories of "giving" and "getting" come to the fore, since they are more capable of stating the principle of reciprocity involved. The mixed metaphor gives rise to several complex subtleties that Mark may or may not have intended. They arise because the subject ("you") is simultaneously one who "receives" and must "give" (i.e., the logos); the object of the giving is simultaneously "others" (in the world) and God (at the harvest). But the main point is clear. The one who has received the parable-logos of the kingdom is now being addressed as the one who must pay attention to his role in the process of seed sowing and harvesting.

The example (6) provides a picture of how one is to understand this activity. It makes emphasis upon one thing only—the sowing of the seed. Everything else occurs automatically, i.e., one can leave them to the mysteries of the natural process, i.e., to God. The striking picture of the man sleeping and rising night and day while the seed comes to fruition is fully in keeping with the way in which Mark intended the parable of the Sower to be taken. He cancelled out all of the practices customary to Greek paideia—toil, achievement, reward. He has left only two moments in view: sowing and reaping. Of these two, the disciple is responsible only for one—sowing. "Pay attention (to) the measure you give."

The analogy (5) picks up on the second of the two moments of significance for this strange kingdom, namely that of the harvest. But in order to make the point about the eventual, successful manifestation of the kingdom, the discourse has chosen a mustard seed, not a seed of grain. Mark can now use the topic of "small" and "great" to align all of the preceding points about the seed being "threatened," "hidden," yet "inevitably" and "automatically" coming to fruition. The new point here is now imaginable. This seed will eventually become the "greatest of all shrubs," i.e., successful in its displacement of those cultures with which it is now competing. If the parable of the Sower has been a study in comparison and contrast with Greek paideia, we might view this final parable against the background of traditional Jewish imagery of Israel's destiny.[6] The implicit claim to eventual success in the competition of cultures, which would then be the point of this elaboration, is quite complete and startling. It was a singular achievement to win this claim in the elaboration of a parable by means of other parables.

The conclusion (8) marks the period by returning to the narrative setting, reiterating that the "hearing" of the parables makes the difference, and that the parables themselves are not merely about the logos. The logos is spoken by means of them (τοιαύταις παραβολαῖς πολλαῖς). One wonders, though, whether it is not Mark's elaboration that achieves the specific logos he has in mind.

---

6. Cf. Jeremias, *Parables of Jesus*, 147.

6. The Rhetoric of Early Christian *Paideia*

Mark demonstrated the proposition that "Jesus taught in parables" by elaborating a seed parable. To anyone acquainted with Hellenistic discourse at all, this parable would immediately be understood as an illustrative comparison that intended to make some point about paideia. But the parable does not draw the comparison, and this omission introduces the element of mystery or curiosity. This lack of reference also opens the way for a complex elaboration that can creatively play with referentially ambiguous images. As it turns out, however, there is more than artful play involved, since the subject under consideration (kingdom of God) is an entity that resists comparison with Hellenistic forms of culture, including Judaism. Nevertheless, the discourse names the kingdom of God as the subject, and the topics of teaching, logos, understanding, *ethos* boundary, ethics, and cultural history are all present, just as one might expect in an elaboration about paideia. But none of these components of a culture is made specific, as normal discourse would do. Instead, the elaboration consists only of suggestive comparisons to unnamed referents. It achieves the sense that there is a subject under consideration by the way in which the elaboration compares and contrasts the images of the several παραβολαί with one another. The elaboration pattern provides the logic that compounds these associations. Not only is the sequence of the arguments in the pattern helpful for making certain connections among images, the notion of elaboration itself also allows for key words to recur, giving the impression of thematic development. Thus it is that one has the sense of learning something about the mystery throughout the course of the elaboration.

But, upon reflection, one has not learned anything at all in the normal sense of the term. Instead, the elaboration has simply given those within the new Jesus movement the opportunity to reflect on the ways in which their ethos is *not* like a culture of paideia. And the exercise has supported them in certain anti-cultural attitudes, as well as challenged them to persevere in these attitudes. The new ethos that hopes for the kingdom of God is still strongly oriented to experiences that take place on the borders of conflicting cultural systems and their values. These critical encounters are not moments of development, toil, achievement, or performance that can manifest virtue and bring honor. Only "sowing" and "reaping" are in view, and they are understood as ruptures. The community of the kingdom of God is still in the process of definiton as a culture. And it does not yet know what it will become. But this community does know that it is being born in social conflict, and that it is different from both of the cultural systems over against which it must win its identity by contrast.

Given these circumstances, it is truly amazing that a reflection on Christian paideia has taken place at all, much more that it occurs as an elaboration of Jesus' teaching. In conflict with alternative cultural systems, and lacking clear substitutes of its own for the common standards of cultural identification and formation, it is hardly thinkable that arguments could be found for an elaboration, much less a recognizable thesis. All of the arguments in the elaboration pattern of Greco-Roman culture assume topics that gain their persuasive power by reference to authorities, traditions, legal codes, social conventions, views of the world, and patterns of inference that are common coin within an established order. If one runs down the list of the arguments required for an elaboration, it is clear immediately that the normal resources for most of them would be problematic if not dangerous for an early Christian author to use. But Mark found a way to put them all under partial erasure. He discovered the possibility of παραβολή-without-express-reference. His achievement, given the odds against it, is remarkable. He succeeded in elaborating the enigmatic, μῆτις-like character of the Jesus tradition. One probably needs to read his gospel story as a whole in order to learn what the (narrative) logos of Mark's parable of the Sower is really about in terms of social conflict.[7]

7. See Mack, *A Myth of Innocence.*

SEVEN

Rhetorical Composition & the Beelzebul Controversy

Vernon K. Robbins

In this chapter, we explore the four units in the synoptic gospels that feature an assertion that Jesus casts out demons by the ruler (or prince) of demons (Matt 9:32–34; 12:22–37; Mark 3:19a-30; Luke 11:18–28). In rhetorical terminology, these units contain a high degree of epideictic rhetoric. By its nature, epideictic rhetoric is not as clearly defined as judicial and deliberative rhetoric.[1] It is commonly known as the oratory of praise and censure, and it treats members of the audience as spectators or observers rather than judges.[2] The goal is to confirm already held values rather than to call forth a decision about the legality of a past action or the expediency of a future action.

Whereas the dominant tradition of epideictic rhetoric features its positive side (praise, laudation, or encomium), the four units we are analyzing give prominence to a negative view of Jesus and his activity in a setting where many have exhibited a positive view. For the most part, ancient treatises suggest that negative epideictic rhetoric—censure and blame ($\psi\acute{o}\gamma o\varsigma$), or invective and vituperation (Greek: $\kappa\alpha\kappa o\lambda\acute{o}\gamma\iota o\nu$;[3] Latin: *vituperatio*)—applies the same techniques as praise or encomium for an opposite effect. In certain circles after Aristotle it became fashionable to distinguish between "praise" ($\check{\epsilon}\pi\alpha\iota\nu o\varsigma$), which expresses the greatness of virtue, and "encomium" ($\dot{\epsilon}\gamma\kappa\acute{\omega}\mu\iota o\nu$), which programatically displays

---

1. Kennedy, *New Testament Interpretation*, 73–78.
2. See Aristotle, *Rhet*. I.iii.1258a.
3. See *Rhet. ad Alex*. III.1440b.5.

noble deeds and qualities of people.[4] Rhetoricians did not distinguish censure from vituperation in a similar manner, because they did not give such detailed attention to negative epideictic rhetoric.[5] Careful use of the short passages and passing comments about negative epideictic rhetoric, however, may advance our analysis and interpretation of the four units in the synoptic gospels that feature an assertion that Jesus casts out demons by the ruler of demons.

The general procedure of epideictic rhetoric is to develop topics through amplification ($a\check{v}\xi\eta\sigma\iota s$).[6] This procedure displays good and bad qualities in a framework that confirms generally held values. The most common place for epideictic rhetoric was at a civil ceremony, like a funeral or a birthday celebration.[7] But epideictic rhetoric regularly appears in judicial oratory,[8] and the negative use of epideictic rhetoric easily creates a judicial situation.[9] Also, epideictic rhetoric occurs in deliberative rhetoric to inspire a person or group toward good actions in the future. The flexibility of epideictic rhetoric is observable in the use of topics associated with the Beelzebul controversy in the gospels. This chapter will explore this flexibility through analysis of the common synoptic tradition, the hypothesized earliest version, and each of the synoptic versions.

1. The Common Synoptic Tradition

In accordance with the flexible nature of epideictic rhetoric, the synoptic tradition of the Beelzebul Controversy exhibits less verbatim agreement than it does with a unit containing a significant degree of judicial rhetoric like Plucking Grain on the Sabbath. From the perspective of Theon's *Progymnasmata*, the common synoptic ingredients constitute a double chreia ($\delta\iota\pi\lambda\hat{\eta}\ \chi\rho\epsilon\acute{\iota}a$),[10] that is, a chreia containing statements ($\grave{a}\pi o\phi\acute{a}\sigma\epsilon\iota s$) of two characters, either one of which creates a chreia. Theon's example is as follows:

First chreia:

Alexander, the Macedonian king, stood over Diogenes as he slept and said: "To sleep all night ill suits a counsellor"; (Iliad 2.24)

4. See Wilson and Russell, *Menander Rhetor*, xxii–xxix.

5. The treatises by Menander Rhetor and Pseudo-Dionysius (see Wilson and Russell, *Menander Rhetor*) discuss a wide variety of speeches in which praise is the major purpose. They do not, however, discuss situations of invective or vituperation.

6. See Kennedy, *New Testament Interpretation*, 75.

7. See Wilson and Russell, *Menander Rhetor*, 171, 159.

8. See Demosthenes' *On the Crown*.

9. See Matt 21:23–23:39 and Kennedy, *New Testament Interpretation*, 86.

10. See Theon 205,9–19.

Second chreia:

> and Diogenes responded: "On whom the folk rely, whose cares are many." (Iliad 2.25)

Theon's example contains two chreiai by individual people. In Hellenistic tradition, however, including the synoptic tradition, a particular group of people (companions, seers, ambassadors, scribes, Pharisees, Sadducees, crowds) may speak as an individual voice. Through this technique, a narrator creates particular character traits for particular groups of people, and these groups function as role-complements or role-opposites of individual characters. The common synoptic ingredients in the Beelzebul Controversy feature direct speech by scribes, Pharisees, or some people in the crowds. When one of these groups speaks with a single voice, they have uttered a statement (ἀπόφασις) that may function as an individual chreia. This internal nature of the tradition sheds light on the transmission of the Beelzebul Controversy tradition, since the remark by scribes, Pharisees, or some people in the crowds may be transmitted separately as a chreia tradition or it may be coupled with statements by Jesus. The common tradition has the nature of a double chreia, and the second chreia is a refutation of the first chreia, as follows:

(1) *Chreia* (in the form of abbreviation: συστέλλειν):

[They] said, ". . . Beelzebul, . . . By the ruler of demons he casts out demons."

(2) Refutation (ἀνασκευάζειν) through a second, expanded chreia:

He [Jesus] said to them,
(a) A kingdom divided against itself . . .,
(b) and a house . . .,
(c) and if Satan were divided against himself, [he could not] sta[nd].
(d) If a strong man. . . .[11]

The saying in the tradition that could function like a judicial charge

11. The common synoptic Greek text is as follows:

Chreia in the form of abbreviation:
εἶπον/ἔλεγον, Βεελζεβούλ . . . ἐν τῷ ἄρχοντι
τῶν δαιμονίων ἐκβάλλει τὰ δαιμονία.

Refutation through a second, expanded *chreia*:
ἔλεγεν/εἶπεν αὐτοῖς,
(a) βασιλεία μερισθ [passive voice] ἐφ'
ἑαυτὴν/καθ᾽ ἑαυτῆς . . .
(b) καὶ οἰκία/οἶκος . . .
(c) καὶ εἰ/εἰ καὶ ὁ σατανᾶς ἐφ᾽ ἑαυτὸν
ἐμερίσθη . . . [οὐ] στ[].
(d) ἐὰν/ἐπάν . . . ἰσχυρο[]. . . .

shows the most verbatim agreement. This part features a slanderous assertion that Jesus casts out demons by the ruler of demons, and this ruler is identified with Beelzebul. According to current scholarly information, the name Beelzebul occurs in no other contemporary Jewish writing.[12] The variant spelling "Beelzebub" comes from assimilation to Baal-zebub in 2 Kgs 1:2, which refers to the god of Ekron and evidently derives from "Lord of Heaven" or "Lord of Temple."[13] The common synoptic tradition takes a decisive swerve as it confronts the name Beelzebul. In truth, the tradition has no way to deal with the accusation as phrased, perhaps because the name means almost nothing to anyone, or perhaps because the Christians who tell the story see the name as a way to make light of the strange things opponents of Jesus said to him.[14]

Instead of working out the implications of associating Jesus with Beelzebul, every elaboration features Jesus rephrasing the title as "Satan." This rephrasing establishes a well-known image, namely an individual personification of "the adversary of God," and the tradition has resources to discredit this adversary. The end result, therefore, is that the initial argument of every elaboration disconfirms an alignment of Jesus with Satan rather than with Beelzebul as the opponents have stated it. But perhaps we should not be amazed at this. We know that chreiai regularly end with a remark for which there can be no adequate response, and the remark of the opponents as featured in the tradition does not leave an open door for disconfirmation. But the common tradition has seen a crack in the door if it is possible to associate Beelzebul with Satan. Through this crack, which opens into a rich arena of understanding concerning "the adversary," the elaboration gets started. Once the elaboration started, the energy focussed upon it by early Christians produced alternative disconfirmations of a remark they considered to be a misguided attempt by opponents to expose Jesus once and for all.

Thus, all the synoptic accounts associate Beelzebul with Satan (Mark 3:23; Matt 12:26; Luke 11:18), and they contain an argument for the implausibility of Jesus' alignment with Satan. There is no agreement in the tradition about who accuses Jesus of casting out demons by Beelzebul, the ruler of demons: Mark attributes it to scribes who came down from Jerusalem (Mark 3:22), Matthew attributes it to Pharisees (Matt 12:24), and Luke attributes it to a group of people in a crowd who saw Jesus cast a demon out of a dumb man (Luke 11:15). No one asserts that Jesus' act was illegal, since the charge is an attack on Jesus' character[15]

---

12. Lane, *Gospel According to Mark*, 141.

13. Lane, *Gospel According to Mark*, 140.

14. According to Lane, *Gospel According to Mark*, 141, the name may be "a passing colloquialism for a demon prince."

15. Fuchs, *Die Entwicklung*, 19.

rather than a legal accusation. The synoptic gospels perpetuate a tradition that Jesus responds to the attack with a sequence of statements about "a kingdom divided against itself," "a house," "Satan not standing if he is divided against himself," and a "strong" man.

In this double chreia material, people say that Jesus casts out demons by the prince of demons, whom they name Beelzebul, but they do not claim that Jesus "possesses" or "has" Beelzebul. Only Mark (Mark 3:22a, 30) and John (John 7:20; 8:48–52; 10:20–21) contain statements concerning Jesus' "having" a demon or Beelzebul. Accordingly, the common synoptic tradition presents an argument about a "kingdom" and a "house" to show the implausibility that Satan would use his evil power against himself and his domain, and it presents an argument about "a strong man" to show that a greater power than Satan casts out the demon. The common tradition, then, contains elaboration in the second chreia which refutes the initial chreia in two steps. The basic logic underlying the two steps may be exhibited in syllogistic form. The logic implied in the initial step is:

> If a kingdom or house is divided against itself, it cannot stand.
>
> If Satan casts out demons, he, his kingdom, and his house are divided against themselves.
>
> Therefore, if Satan casts out demons, he, his kingdom, and his house cannot stand.

This is an argument for implausibility ($\dot{\epsilon}\kappa$ $\tau o\hat{v}$ $\dot{\alpha}\pi\iota\theta\acute{\alpha}\nu o\nu$). It is unlikely that Satan would be willing to cast out an underling, because he would be divided against himself, and this division would destroy him and his domain. The argument is made syllogistic by introducing a rationale through analogy. Analogy with a kingdom or house introduces the rationale that any domain containing hierarchies of authority cannot stand if it is divided against itself. The basic argument from implausibility is similar to the example Theon gives, presupposing a situation of association or alliance with one another. It is unlikely, Theon says, that Antisthenes, who was an Athenian, said that he was coming from women's quarters to men's as he was coming from Athens to Lacedaimon.[16] The reason, of course, is that Antisthenes is associated or allied with Athens. Likewise, it is unlikely that Satan, who is allied with demons, would cast one of his own associates or allies out of a possessed man. The common synoptic tradition adds a rationale through analogy (because a kingdom or house divided against itself cannot stand), and this additional component introduces syllogistic reasoning. Theon's example only implies a rationale (something like: because a person who

---

16. Theon 215,3–6.

lived in Athens knows the meaning of true manliness). Thus, the first step in the second part of the common synoptic tradition is a syllogistic argument for the implausibility of the charge that Jesus casts out demons by Beelzebul, the ruler of demons.

The initial argument in the common tradition is followed by another whose underlying logic is:

> To be able to enter the house "of" (or "protected by") a strong man and plunder his possessions, a person must have the strength to bind (or: must be a stronger man who comes and subdues) the strong man.

> If Jesus can cast out a demon whose strength is from Satan, he has the strength to bind (or: is a stronger man who has come and subdued) a demon whose strength is from Satan.

> If Jesus has the strength to bind (or: is a stronger man who has come and subdued) a demon whose strength is from Satan, then Jesus' strength is *not* from Satan but from a stronger source than Satan.

This is an argument for falsity (ἐκ τοῦ ψεύδους). If Jesus can cast out a demon, he has greater strength than a demon, and if a demon gets his strength from Satan, Jesus gets his strength *not* from Satan but from a power greater than Satan. Theon presents an argument for falsity with a chreia that asserts that it is untruthful that love of money is the mother city of evil, because intemperance is. It is important in an argument for falsity to provide an alternative. Theon's example provides the alternative of intemperance for love of money. The common synoptic tradition provides "a stronger power than Satan" for Satan. Again, however, the synoptic tradition introduces syllogistic reasoning by providing a rationale through analogy. It is untruthful that Satan casts out demons, because a strong man must be overcome before a house can be plundered, which means that a greater power must overcome a lesser power before the possessions he is guarding can be plundered.

Each gospel amplifies the common tradition in different ways. Matthew and Luke put the common tradition in a setting where Jesus casts a dumb spirit out of a man. In contrast, Mark puts the common tradition in the setting of a house around which people gather and to which kinfolk come. The Markan setting and Jesus' response address three topics: "those who are his kinfolk," "being possessed by Beelzebul," and "casting out demons by the ruler of demons." The Markan version uses the common tradition about a house, a kingdom, Satan, and a strong man to show the implausibility and falsity of an argument that Satan casts out Satan. Then Jesus censures "those who blaspheme against the Holy Spirit" and praises "kinfolk who do the will of God." In contrast, after the common tradition about a house, a kingdom, Satan, and a strong man, Matthew and Luke share assertions that the sons of Jesus' opponents cast out unclean spirits, that the kingdom of God has come upon them if he casts out demons by the Spirit or finger of God, and that those who are not with Jesus are against him. After sharing this common tradition, however, Matthew's version adds sayings that produce rhetorical *stasis* and conclude with judicial language concerning "justification" and "condemnation." Luke in contrast, merges the topic of "casting out demons by the ruler of demons" with "seeking signs" to establish a broad epideictic framework for the denunciation of Pharisees and lawyers in the succeeding chapter. Each gospel, therefore, exhibits a different manner of elaborating the common tradition. The association of a basic situation and a series of topics, without extensive agreement on the development of the topics or the conclusion, reflects a tradition that is intrinsically epideictic rather than judicial or deliberative.

2. The Earliest Tradition (Matt 9:32–34)

Some interpreters suggest that the earliest form of the tradition was a short unit in which the saying, "By the prince of demons he casts out demons," was a response to Jesus' successful performance of an exorcism.[17] In the version available to us in Matt 9:32–34, the unit ends with a saying that contradicts a laudation from bystanders who observed the action. Using Theon's perspective, this form of the tradition is a responsive chreia ($\dot{a}\pi o\kappa\rho\iota\tau\iota\kappa\dot{\eta}$ $\chi\rho\epsilon\iota a$). A responsive chreia contains some remark ($\lambda\acute{o}\gamma os$) to which a response is made.[18] In this instance, the crowd makes a remark to which Pharisees respond with a negative assertion:

Situation:

As they were going away, behold, a dumb demoniac was brought to him. And when the demon had been cast out, the dumb man spoke;

Remark by the crowds:

and the crowds marveled, saying, "Never was anything like this seen in Israel."

Response by the Pharisees:

But the Pharisees said, "He casts out demons by the prince of demons."

The description of the situation begins with the conjunction $\delta\acute{e}$ and a genitive absolute ($a\dot{v}\tau\hat{\omega}\nu$ $\delta\grave{e}$ $\dot{e}\xi\epsilon\rho\chi o\mu\acute{e}\nu\omega\nu$) followed by a finite verb ($\pi\rho o\sigma\acute{\eta}\nu\epsilon\gamma\kappa a\nu$) and an accusative object with a descriptive participle ($\ddot{a}\nu\theta\rho\omega\pi o\nu$ $\kappa\omega\phi\grave{o}\nu$ $\delta a\iota\mu o\nu\iota\zeta\acute{o}\mu\epsilon\nu o\nu$). Then it continues with the conjunction $\kappa a\acute{\iota}$, a genitive absolute ($\dot{e}\kappa\beta\lambda\eta\theta\acute{e}\nu\tau os$ $\tauo\hat{v}$ $\delta a\iota\mu o\nu\acute{\iota}o\nu$), and a finite verb

17. See, for example, Fuchs, *Die Entwicklung,* 21–26 and Bultmann, *History of the Synoptic Tradition,* 13.
18. Theon 205,1–3.

with a subject (ἐλάλησεν ὁ κωφός). This is standard procedure for composing a chreia. The remark and the response begin with καί and δέ respectively, and they continue with direct speech preceded either by the participal λέγοντες or the finite verb ἔλεγον. Such straightforward paratactic composition is characteristic of chreia composition.[19]

The rhetorical situation in Matt 9:32–34 is epideictic, featuring both praise and censure. Immediately after Jesus has cured the dumb man, the crowds praise Jesus' activity as beyond comparison to all other acts in Israel's history:

> And the crowds marvelled, saying, "Never was anything like this seen in Israel" (9:33b).

In turn, Pharisees censure Jesus' activity with a dissenting opinion:

> But the Pharisees said, "By the prince of demons he casts out demons." (9:34)

The situation depicted in this unit has positive and negative dynamics similar to the situation that gave rise to the classic epideictic treatises on the "Praise of Helen." In a setting where Homeric epic praised Helen of Sparta as a beautiful and charming heroine, a group of poets voiced a dissenting opinion.[20] Gorgias of Sicily and Isocrates addressed this situation with *Encomia* of Helen that made this topic a favorite in the schools of rhetoric.[21]

It is important to notice that epideictic rhetoric regularly features statements of praise and censure by various people *about* a specific person rather than statements by that person himself or herself. Thus, in contrast to other synoptic tradition which features a situation to which Jesus responds, the version posited to be the earliest form does not feature a response by Jesus himself. The form of the tradition in Matt 9:32–34 is analogous to epideictic units in Greco-Roman literature that contain two interpretations of an event. An approximate analogy, but it is only approximate since the main character makes a response to the situation, exists in Plutarch, *Alexander* 31.10–13:

Situation:

> Meanwhile the older of his companions, and particularly Parmenio, when they saw the plain between the Niphates and the Gordyaean mountains all lighted up with the barbarian fires, while an indistinguishably mingled and tumultuous sound of voices arose from their camp as if from a vast ocean, were astonished at their multitude and argued with one another that it was a great and grievous task to repel such a tide of war by engaging in broad day-light. They therefore waited upon the king when he had finished his sacrifices, and tried to persuade

19. See Robbins, "Pronouncement Stories," 50.
20. See *Isocrates*, X.
21. See Jebb, *Attic Orators*, II, 96–103 on Gorgias.

him to attack the enemy by night, and so to cover up with darkness the most fearful aspect of the coming struggle.

Response:

But he gave them the celebrated answer, "I will not steal my victory";

Remark by some:

whereupon some thought that he had made a vainglorious reply, and was jesting in the presence of so great a peril.

Response by others:

Others, however, thought that he had confidence in the present situation and estimated the future correctly, not offering Dareius in case of defeat an excuse to pluck up courage again for another attempt, by laying the blame this time upon darkness and night, as he had before upon mountains, defiles, and sea.

In this story, one group of people considers Alexander's statement to be driven by vanity and carelessness, whereas another group considers his statement to be wise and well-calculated. The same kind of division of opinion may appear in a shorter unit that contains no speech by the main character, for example, Plutarch, *Alexander* 3.5–7:

Situation:

Alexander was born early in the month Hecatombaeon, the Macedonian name for which is Loüs, on the sixth day of the month, and on this day the temple of Ephesian Artemis was burnt.

Remark by Hegesias:

It was apropos of this that Hegesias the Magnesian made an utterance frigid enough to have extinguished that great conflagration. He said, namely, it was no wonder that the temple of Artemis was burned down, since the goddess was busy bringing Alexander into the world.

Response by Magi:

But all the Magi who were then at Ephesus, looking upon the temple's disaster as a sign of further disaster, ran about beating their faces and crying aloud that woe and great calamity for Asia had that day been born.

In this story, a group of people who have their livelihood endangered by the burning of Artemis' temple contradict an initial assertion which implied that the goddess Artemis was an assistant at Alexander's birth. Even in the setting of Plutarch's more sophisticated style of Greek, the chief grammatical features of the epideictic story in Matt 9:32–34 are present. Plutarch begins the first element with δ᾽ οὖν, the second component with ᾧ γ᾽, and the final component with ὅσοι δέ. The unit emphasizes the speech and action of people other than Alexander, much like Matt 9:32–34 emphasizes the speech of people other than Jesus. In fact, just as Plutarch refers to Alexander's birth in passive voice (ἐγεννήθη) so Matthew refers to Jesus' action in passive voice ("and when the demon was cast out"), since it is simply a presupposition for the unit rather than its center. In contrast, active verbs refer to the action and speech of Hegesias and the magi, as active verbs refer to the action of the people who bring the demonized man to Jesus, the speech of the man from whom the demon is cast out, the comments of the crowds who marvel at Jesus' accomplishment, and the accusation by the Pharisees that Jesus casts out demons by the ruler (or prince) of demons. This compositional procedure exhibits the passive epideictic nature of the unit that focusses on praise and censure of Jesus.

Aelius Theon called attention to the passive nature of certain situations in chreiai, and his illustration, interestingly enough, contains a negative judgment on a person's life:

> Didymon the flute-player, on being convicted of adultery, was hanged by his namesake.

This chreia displays a dimension of epideictic rhetoric that interpreters usually overlook. Epideictic rhetoric regularly is *about* someone, and from this dimension it develops into speech *about* things like cities, etc. Thus, the classic tradition of the encomium began with speech about Helen of Sparta, and most of the epideictic speeches feature speech about a person being honored on a special occasion. The birthday speech (γενεθλιακός), for example, features speech about a person's birth.[22] As Menander says:

> praise the day on which your subject was born. If he was born during a holy month or at some other festival, base the encomium on the circumstances of the day, viz. that he was born in a holy month or at a festival.[23]

This describes, as the reader will recognize, the kind of content found in the unit quoted above about Alexander's birth. Accordingly, the prose introducing the situation features basic information about his birth, and the response contains speech by various people about Alexander's birth. Another well-known epideictic speech is the funeral speech (ἐπι-τάφιος).[24] Menander Rhetor tells us that:

> At Athens, ἐπιτάφιος—funeral speech—is the name of the speech delivered each year over those who fell in the wars. It is so called simply because of its being spoken over the actual grave.[25]

---

22. See Wilson and Russell, *Menander Rhetor*, 158–61.
23. Wilson and Russell, *Menander Rhetor*, 159.
24. Wilson and Russell, *Menander Rhetor*, 170–79.
25. Wilson and Russell, *Menander Rhetor*, 171.

Since the person is dead, someone else, naturally, must rehearse the person's activities and praise his achievements. When this situation is put in chreia-form, however, a prose introduction may present a person's exploits leading up to the situation of death, and the fallen hero may deliver the final line of the tribute. An example is well illustrated in Theon's expansion of the Epameinondas chreia:

Situation:

> Epameinondas, the Theban general, was of course a good man even in time of peace, but when war broke out between his country and the Lacedaemonians, he performed many brilliant deeds of courage. As a Boeotarch at Leuctra, he triumphed over the enemy, but while campaigning and fighting for his country, he died at Mantineia. While he was dying of his wounds

Action and Remark by Friends:

> and his friends were particularly grief-stricken that he was dying childless,

Response by Epameinondas:

> he smiled and said: "Stop grieving, friends, for I have left you two immortal daughters: two victories of our country over the Lacedaemonians, the one at Leuctra, who is the older, and the younger, who has just been born to me at Mantineia."[26]

The opening lines rehearse the valiant exploits of Epameinondas, much like a funeral speech. The chreia form of the tribute, however, puts speech on the lips of the dying general, allowing him to present the climactic line of the tribute. Similarly, the synoptic tradition does not allow the passive nature of Matt 9:32–34 to dominate. Rather, the various synoptic authors compose units that present a situation in which Jesus responds to the divided opinion over his activity in the tradition.

3. The Markan Version (Mark 3:22–30)

The Markan version features a house as the locale, and no one brings a demonized man to Jesus for healing. It embeds the common synoptic material in a sequence that features a segmented response to three issues raised by the situation. The first issue concerns "those akin to Jesus" (οἱ παρ' αὐτοῦ), the second concerns Jesus' possession of Beelzebul, and the third concerns casting out demons by the ruler of demons. The passage contains an intricate network of structural features that makes it pos-

---

26. Theon 213,17–214,4. For a more detailed discussion, see Robbins, "Pronouncement Stories," 50.

sible to outline it or display it in various ways.[27] From the perspective of its overall rhetorical form, a situation occurs in Mark 3:20–22 that introduces three topics:

Situation

Introduction

> Then he went home; and *a crowd* came together again, so that they could not even eat.

Partition or Division

Topic: Kinfolk

> And when *those close to him* heard it, they went out to seize him, for people were saying, "He is out of his mind."

Topic: Possession

> And the scribes who came down from Jerusalem said, "He *possesses* Beelzebul,

Topic: Casting Out

> and by the prince of demons he *casts out* the demons."

First, while Jesus is either "in a house" or "at home" (evidently at Capernaum)[28] and a crowd has gathered so that they cannot even eat, people "akin to Jesus" come to seize him because "people" (or "they themselves")[29] were saying Jesus was out of his mind. Next, scribes come

---

27. Since Jesus responds to the issues in reverse order, we may display the structure chiastically:

A   Those akin to him come to seize him. (Mark 3:20–21)
B   He possesses Beelzebul. (Mark 3:22a)
C   By the prince of demons he casts out demons. (Mark 3:22b)
C′   It is impossible that Satan would cast out demons. (Mark 3:23–27)
B′   Whoever says Jesus possesses an unclean spirit blasphemes. (Mark 3:28–30)
A′   Jesus' kin are those who do the will of God. (Mark 3:31–35)

Since the final scene responds to the first part and since narrative comment divides it from Jesus' response to the scribes' charges, we may display the structure as an *intercalation* as Donahue, *Are You the Christ?*, 58 suggests:

> Those akin to Jesus (Mark 3:20–21)
>   Jesus and scribes from Jerusalem (Mark 3:22–30)
> The kinfolk of Jesus (Mark 3:31–35).

Since the narrator introduces Jesus' response to the scribes with προσκαλεσάμενος ("having called to"), we may display the structure as a three-step progression as we suggested in Robbins, "Summons and Outline":

> I. The situation into which Jesus comes (Mark 3:20–21)
> II. Interaction that calls forth teaching (Mark 3:22)
> III. Jesus "calls to" those around him and teaches them (Mark 3:23–35).

28. Perhaps this house is Jesus' Capernaum home.
29. See Turner, "Marcan Usage," for the meaning of 3d plurals in Mark.

down from Jerusalem and make two statements: (a) Jesus possesses
(ἔχει) Beelzebul, and (b) by the ruler of demons he casts out demons.
Jesus responds to these three topics in three segments of material, beginning with the last topic. First, he argues the implausibility and falsity
that Satan casts out Satan (Mark 3:23–27); second, he pronounces future
judgment on those who say he possesses some other power than the
Holy Spirit (Mark 3:28–30); and third, he defines those who truly are his
kin (Mark 3:31–34):

Response

Topic: Casting Out

Quaestio (paraphrase of the scribes' final remark)
> And *he called them to him*, and said to them in parables, "How can Satan
> *cast out* Satan?"

Argument for Implausibility from Analogies (ἐκ παραβολῶν)
> "If a kingdom *is divided against itself*, that kingdom *cannot stand*."
>
> "And *if* a house *is divided against itself*, that house will *not* be *able to stand*."
>
> "And *if* Satan has risen up *against himself* and *is divided*, he *cannot stand*, but *possesses* an end."

Argument for Falsity from a Contrary (ἐξ ἐναντίον)
> "But no one can enter a strong man's house and *plunder his goods*, unless
> he first *binds* the strong man; then indeed he may *plunder his house*."

First, Jesus summons the scribes and asks a rhetorical question that
introduces the initial topic of his response, which addresses the final
topic. Jesus' rhetorical question "How can Satan cast out Satan?" replaces the scribes' terms "ruler of demons" and "demons" with "Satan,"
and this replacement adapts the scribes' statement so that the arguments
that follow can disconfirm it. Jesus' question, then, paraphrases the
statement by the scribes in a manner that accords with Hermogenes'
recommendation that the first rhetorical act after the recital of the chreia
be a paraphrase of the chreia. Secondly, Jesus presents a three-part
argument for implausibility containing internal repetitive form through
the threefold repetition of "is divided against itself . . . cannot stand."[30]
The expansion of the third statement in characteristic Markan style
places the verb ἔχει ("to have" or "to possess") emphatically at the end,
and this term provides a bridge to the next topic. Before turning to the

---

30. This sequence has the kind of emphatic variation in the third occurrence that
is characteristic of Markan style as we suggested in Robbins, "Summons and Outline":

(a) καὶ ἐὰν . . . ἐφ' ἑαυτὴν μερισθῇ, οὐ δύναται σταθῆναι.
(b) καὶ ἐὰν . . . ἐφ' ἑαυτὴν μερισθῇ, οὐ δυνήσεται . . . σταθῆναι.
(c) καὶ εἰ . . . ἀνέστη ἐφ' ἑαυτὸν καὶ ἐμερίσθη, οὐ δύναται στῆναι ἀλλὰ τέλος ἔχει.

next topic, however, the three-part argument (that contains a three-part center) ends with the argument for falsity. Through the analogy of overcoming a strong man, the Markan version can show the falsity of the assertion that Jesus casts out demons. Mark constructs this saying with an emphasis on plundering (διαρπάσαι) that begins with "plundering his vessels" and ends with "plundering his house." In addition, the Markan version has a tripartite form in which the verbs stand in emphatic final position and the verbs present an alliterative pattern: διαρπάσαι . . . δήση . . . διαρπάσει ("to plunder . . . he binds . . . he will plunder"). The compositional strategy strengthens the assertion that "he will plunder his house" and supports the prior statement that Satan "possesses an end." Thus an irony emerges that, even though it is implausible that Satan would be divided against himself and it is false that Jesus is using the power of Satan to overcome the power of Satan, nevertheless Satan will have an end and his domain will be plundered.

After the argument for implausibility and falsity that the prince of demons would and could cast out demons, the Markan version turns to the second topic, Jesus' possession of Beelzebul:

Topic: Possession

Argument from a Judgment (ἐκ κρίσεως)
"Truly, I say to you, all sins will be forgiven the sons of men, and whatever blasphemies they utter;

but whoever blasphemes against the Holy Spirit never *possesses* forgiveness, but is guilty of an eternal sin."

For they had said, "He *possesses* an unclean spirit."

Jesus counters the assertion by the scribes with an authoritative pronouncement, and with this pronouncement a special characteristic of epideictic rhetoric becomes prominent. One tendency of epideictic oratory, that made it distasteful to many, is its potential for exaggeration. This dimension is already present in the Markan version when some people suggest that Jesus is out of his mind and others suggest he possesses Beelzebul (Mark 3:21). Jesus responds with language that is unusual in the synoptic tradition. Usually, if people seek forgiveness, they will receive it. In this instance, Jesus asserts that even though "all the sins" and "blasphemies" of the sons of men will be forgiven, the person who blasphemes against the Holy Spirit (by saying that Jesus possesses an unclean spirit) will "never" *possess* forgiveness, but is guilty of an "eternal" sin. It is interesting that Jesus employs "extreme censure" to counter "extreme censure." Neither Matthew nor Luke include the topic of Jesus' insanity, possession of Beelzebul, or possession of an unclean spirit. The Markan version focusses the rhetoric epideictically as

Jesus meets censure beyond acceptability with mutual censure. Markan style again is evident in the tripartite structure of the authoritative saying shown above in the three-step quotation. The third line provides the rationale for the saying, and this rationale closes Jesus' argument against the second topic. With this final statement the Markan version creates a sequence that binds the unit together through three occurrences of ἔχει ("he possesses") in final emphatic position: Beelzebul he possesses (3:21); an end he [Satan] possesses (3:26); an unclean spirit he [Jesus] possesses (3:30). With this sequence, the Markan version deflects the possession of Beelzebul by Jesus to Satan's possession of an end and to an absurd idea that Jesus could possess an unclean spirit. When the saying juxtaposes "Holy Spirit" with "unclean spirit," the reader remembers that the Holy Spirit came into Jesus at baptism (1:10) and this spirit gave him the ability to withstand testing by Satan for forty days in the wilderness (1:13). In this instance, then, the language bites, deflects, exposes absurdity, and calls previous settings to remembrance. This step in the argument moves through the door opened by the ironic, syllogistic argument for implausibility and falsity to attack without mercy those who dare to articulate such statements.

After addressing the second topic, the unit returns to the initial topic: the coming of Jesus' kin in response to a belief that Jesus is out of his mind:

Topic: Kinfolk

Argument from Comparison (ἐκ συγκρίσεως)
with Concluding Question and Answer
> And *his mother and his brothers* came; and standing outside *they sent to him and called him*. And *a crowd* was sitting about him; and they said to him, "Your *mother and* your *brothers* are outside, asking for you."

Reply by Jesus
> And he replied, "Who are my *mother and* my *brothers*?"

Conclusion (Judgment with Rationale)
> And looking around on those who sat about him, he said, "Here are my *mother and* my *brothers*! Whoever does the will of God is my *brother*, and sister, *and mother*."

The Markan version links the final topic with the initial topic by having Jesus' mother and brothers "call to him" (Mark 3:31) in a manner reminiscent of Jesus' "calling to" the scribes (Mark 3:23). In addition, there may be a play on the assertion, in final emphatic position, that Jesus is ἐξέστη ("out of his mind") and that Jesus' mother and brothers are ἔξω στήκοντες ("standing outside"). This suspicion arises, because the episode is characterized by repetition that persists from the beginning to the end.[31] Jesus focusses the topic in the final unit with a rhetorical question in a manner similar to his focussing of the initial topic. The introductory section had referred to "those near to him" (οἱ παρ᾽ αὐτοῦ). The introduction (3:31), the speech of the crowd (3:32), and then Jesus' rhetorical question (3:33) change "those near him" to "his mother and brothers." Again the rhetorical technique is tripartite repetitive form. After the rhetorical question, Jesus identifies his true mother and brothers, and ends with a tripartite reference to "my brother, sister, and mother" who do the will of God. For Jesus, the question is whether those who stand outside, who think he is out of his mind, and who call for him (or come to seize him: Mark 3:20) are truly his kin. When Jesus replies that whoever does the will of God is his brother, sister, and mother, he is addressing the initial topic. His true kin act according to the will of God, and this implies that he himself has his mind on the will of God. Thus, instead of being "out of his mind," he and his kin have their minds on God and are seeking to do his will.

Thus, through the juxtaposition of good and bad, Jesus confirms the good and exposes the bad. Toward the end of the second topic Jesus says, "Whoever blasphemes against the Holy Spirit does not have forgiveness forever, but is guilty of eternal sin." In contrast, "Whoever does the will of God is my brother, sister, and mother." Judicial language emerges in Mark 3:28–29, and the conclusion in Mark 3:35 has a gener-

---

31. Repeated terms in the Markan version are as follows:

καὶ ἔρχεται (vss 20, 31)
οἶκον/οἰκία (vss 21, 25 [twice], 27 [twice]
ὄχλος (vss 20, 32)
ἐξέστη/ἔξω στήκοντες (vss 21, 31)
ἔχει (vss 22, 26, 29, 30)
ἐκβάλλει (vss 22, 23)
προσκαλεσάμενος αὐτούς/πρὸς αὐτὸν καλοῦντες αὐτόν (vss 23, 31)
δύναται (vss 23, 24, 25, 26, 27)
Σατανᾶς (vss 23 [twice], 26)
βασιλεία (vs 24 [twice])
ἐφ᾽ ἑαυτήν/ἑαυτόν (vss 24, 25, 26)
μερισθῆναι (vss 24, 25, 26)
σταθῆναι (vss 24, 25, 26, and 31)
ἀλλά (vss 26, 27, 29)
ὁ ἰσχυρός (vs 27 [twice])
ἀφεθήσεται/ἔχει ἄφεσιν (vss 28, 29)
βλασφημίαι/βλασφημεῖν (vss 28 [twice], 29)
ἁμάρτημα (vss 28, 29)
πνεῦμα (vss 29, 30)
μήτηρ (vss 31, 32, 33, 34 [twice])
ἀδελφοί (vss 31, 32, 33, 34 [twice])
κάθημαι (vss 32, 34)
ἔξω (vss 31, 32)

ally deliberative orientation toward action in the future. But epideictic rhetoric dominates from beginning to end as the topics, which are filled with invective, are met with statements filled both with invective and with praise.

4. The Version in Matt 12:22–37

As we begin the analysis of Matt 12:22–37, it may be good to reflect a moment on Matthew's use of the short version of the accusation that Jesus casts out demons by the ruler (or prince) of demons (Matt 9:32–34), which we analyzed earlier. The short version stands at the end of two Matthean chapters that are well known to interpreters for their presentation of Jesus as the Messiah of Deed (Matthew 8–9) after three chapters that present the Messiah of Word (Matthew 5–7).[32] Matthew introduces the Pharisees to the reader in Matt 3:7 when they come with Sadducees to be baptized by John the Baptist. Then, after the introduction to the Sermon on the Mount, Matthew formulates what Betz calls his "fourth and final hermeneutical principle"[33] by comparing the righteousness that will make it possible for his disciples to enter the kingdom of Heaven with the righteousness of the scribes and Pharisees, which is not sufficient for entrance. Then, in the stories that present Jesus' practices and mighty works, the Pharisees object to Jesus' eating with tax collectors and sinners (Matt 9:11), and they fast during times when the disciples of Jesus do not fast (Matt 9:14–17). In other words, the actions of Jesus and his disciples differ from the actions of the Pharisees, and the actions of the Pharisees are not deemed appropriate to provide entrance into the kingdom. At the end of Matthew's portrayal of Jesus' practices and mighty works, the crowds marvel that Jesus' action exceeds any action prior to it in Israel (Matt 9:33). In contrast, the Pharisees attempt to defame his career by assigning his exorcistic power to "the prince (or ruler) of demons" (Matt 9:34). The short version of the Pharisees' attack serves as the conclusion to the section. This means that there is no attempt to respond to the Pharisees' assertion in the section that exhibits Jesus' mighty works and deeds. Rather, Jesus continues his work (Matt 9:35–36) and commissions the Twelve to help him carry out the work (Matt 9:37–11:1). In other words, whereas the Matthean Jesus develops a complete argument to support his understanding of righteousness in the Sermon on the Mount,[34] he does not present a rebuttal to the charge by the Pharisees at the end of the section on his actions and practices. Matthew will not, however, allow the charge to remain unan-

---

32. See Held, "Matthew as Interpreter," 246–47.
33. Betz, *Essays*, 51–53.
34. Kennedy, *New Testament Interpretation*, 39–63.

swered by Jesus. We turn now to the unit where Matthew presents Jesus' response.

In Matt 12:22–37, Jesus responds with a complete argument against the Pharisees. Whereas the basic principles of epideictic rhetoric and elaboration of the chreia seemed sufficient for explicating the Markan version, the Matthean version breaks the bounds of these models as it counters—carefully, intricately, and powerfully—the case presented by the Pharisees. Once again, then, we will use Hermogenes' *On Stases* to guide the analysis of the Matthean version of the tradition.

From a perspective informed by Hermogenes' *On Stases*, the Matthean version of the Beelzebul Controversy has the nature of a political question with an epideictic focus. A political question (πολιτικὸν ζήτημα) is a reasoned disputation (ἀμφισβήτησις λογική) on a particular item from the standpoint of customs arising from ordinary notions of justice (δίκαιος), honor (καλός), or expediency (συμφέρον). In this instance, the question arises from ordinary notions of honor (καλός) and calls forth praise (ἔπαινος) of the good and censure (ψόγος) of the bad.[35] According to Hermogenes, this kind of disputation arises not only from persons (πρόσωπα) but also from deeds (πράγματα). The disputation naturally begins with reference to persons, since "the mention of a person does generally present an object for scrutiny."[36] Moreover, those references "which are specific and definite have the greatest force."[37] A disputant also will use terms indicating relation, like master and slave or father and son,[38] and statements that combine a person with an act.[39]

The beginning of the Matthean version of the Beelzebul Controversy contains the rhetorical features characteristic of a political disputation. The opening clauses introduce Jesus' healing of a demonized man, and the crowds present a *quaestio* ("question") that focusses on Jesus' personal identity:

Situation:

> Then a blind and dumb demoniac was brought to him, and he healed him, so that the dumb man spoke and saw.

Quaestio:

> And all the people were amazed, and said, "Can this be the Son of David?"

35. See Aristotle, *Rhet.* I.iii.5 for the rhetorical sphere of καλός ("honor").
36. See Hermogenes 29,12–13 and the English translation in Nadeau, "Hermogenes' *On Stases*," 389.
37. See Hermogenes 29,14–15 and the English translation in Nadeau, "Hermogenes' *On Stases*," 389.
38. See Hermogenes 29,16–17 and the English translation in Nadeau, "Hermogenes' *On Stases*," 389.
39. See Hermogenes 29,22–30,2 and the English translation in Nadeau, "Hermogenes' *On Stases*," 389.

The quaestio ("question") makes reference to a specific name, David, and a special relation to David, son. According to Jewish tradition, the son of David, namely Solomon, attained a knowledge of healing that was handed down to others.[40] The crowds raise a question of Jesus' identity and relationship as a "son" that makes it possible for him to heal the demonized man.

Immediately after the quaestio ("question") of the crowds, the Pharisees (perceived as a specifically defined group of people) present a case against Jesus:

Statement of the Case (προβολή):

> But when the Pharisees heard it they said, "It is only by Beelzebul, the prince of demons, that this man *casts out* demons."

With this statement of the case, an issue of stasis emerges. According to Hermogenes, a question (ζήτημα) is capable of stasis (συνεστώς) if either a person or an act can be judged (κρινόμενον). From either source (person or act), a disputant must have statements that are not only "apt for persuasion" (σὺν τῷ πιθανῷ διαφόρους) but also "strong in proofs" (ταῖς πίστεσιν ἰσχυρούς), and the issue to be judged must be uncertain and not pre-judged in such a manner that it is not capable of being judged.[41]

The Matthean version presupposes that the issue can be argued and a decision can be reached. In Hermogenes' terminology, the situation presents a stasis of definition (περὶ ὅρον).[42] As the Pharisees make their statement, they attempt to stop (bring stasis to) the thought that Jesus can heal the demonized man because he is the Son of David. Their statement of the case establishes an issue of stasis by introducing a definition (ὅρος) of Jesus' act as a "Beelzebul exorcism." They define the act when they say that "he casts out demons by Beelzebul the ruler of demons." In contrast to the Markan version, therefore, the reader does not encounter a series of topics including insanity and being possessed by Beelzebul. Rather, there is one, and only one, charge: "It is only by Beelzebul, the prince of demons, that this man casts out demons."

Hermogenes suggests that after the statement of the case and the definition, the stasis of definition contains counterdefinition (ἀνθορισμός). Jesus presents the counterdefinition in Matt 12:25–28. Interestingly, the narrator begins this section with a comment that Jesus "knew their thoughts (ἐνθυμήσεις)."[43] From the perspective of rhetorical

---

40. See Duling, "Solomon."

41. See Hermogenes 31,19–32,9 and the English translation in Nadeau, "Hermogenes' *On Stases*," 390–91.

42. See Hermogenes 59,10–65,8 and the English translation in Nadeau, "Hermogenes' *On Stases*," 404–6.

43. I am grateful to Prof. Morton Smith, Columbia University, for suggesting that I pursue the significance of this comment by the narrator.

analysis, this comment suggests that Jesus knew the essential propositions (ἐνθυμήματα) the Pharisees would use to supply the proofs (πίστεις) for their definition of his act. Matthew's choice of Greek is fascinating, since the noun ἐνθύμησις ("thought") is amazingly close to the noun ἐνθύμημα ("enthymene"), which is the rhetoricians' term for the kind of deductive argument that is most powerful in disputation. Matthew's comment suggests that Jesus is able to intercept and preempt the Pharisees' argument, because he knows the essential components of their argument.

After the comment by the narrator, Jesus presents an argument from analogy and quality in common which sets the stage for a counterdefinition (ἀνθορισμός). The argument moves deftly and intricately through a series of steps to attain this end:

Transitional Comment:

    Knowing their thoughts, he said to them,

Argument from Analogies for the Implausibility of the Pharisees' Definition:

    "Every *kingdom* divided *against itself* is laid waste,

    and no city or *house divided against itself* will stand;

    and if Satan *casts out* Satan, he is *divided against himself.*

    How then will his *Kingdom* stand?"

Argument from Quality in Common (ἡ κοινὴ ποιότης):

    "And if I *cast out* demons by Beelzebul, by whom do your sons *cast* them *out*? Therefore, they shall be your *judges.*

Counterdefinition (ἀνθορισμός):

    But if it is by the Spirit of God that I *cast out* demons, then the *kingdom* of God has come upon you.

Restatement of the Counterdefinition by Analogy:

    Or how can one enter a strong man's *house* and plunder his goods, if he does not first bind the strong man? Then indeed he may plunder his *house.*"

With the argument from analogy with a kingdom, a city, and a house, Jesus begins to refute the claim of the Pharisees. Here we see the common tradition in a new form. Instead of presenting three if-clauses (ἐάν, ἐάν, εἰ) in a sequence, the Matthean version presents a *parallelismus membrorum* followed by a simple conditional clause and a rhetorical question. This compositional procedure creates a progressive form that leads to the question: How then will his kingdom stand? Instead of simply changing the language of the opponents from "the prince of demons" to "Satan," as the Markan version does, the Matthean version moves through the change into language about "kingdom." This move prepares the way for the counterdefinition that follows ("if I . . ., then the Kingdom of God has come upon you"). But before the counterdefinition, the Matthean version presents an argument from quality in common. Sons of the Pharisees cast out demons. Would the Pharisees suggest that their own sons cast them out by Beelzebul? With this argument, Jesus produces a judicial indictment of the Pharisees by their own kin. According to Hermogenes, an argument from quality in common is used in a second (answering) speech,[44] which this speech is perceived to be in Matthew. The appeal to "sons" is not only a skillful transference of "Son" of David to "sons" of the Pharisees, but, again according to Hermogenes, it attacks whatever advantage the opponents may have by presenting "children, wives, friends, and devices of this kind."[45] This presentation may draw on the topics of "the lawful, the just, the expedient, the possible, and the honorable."[46] At this point in the argument, the Matthean Jesus draws on the topic of the just: the Pharisees' own sons will judge them as unjust, since they would not accuse their own sons of casting out demons by Beelzebul. With the argument from quality in common, the judicial dynamics that began when the Pharisees presented the case against Jesus continue as Jesus presents a counter case against the Pharisees. Jesus reverses the indictment so it applies to the Pharisees rather than himself. This is a form of argument from the contrary, and it opens the way for a counterdefinition (ἀνθορισμός):

> But if it is by the spirit of God that I cast out demons, then the kingdom of God has come upon you.

Jesus, in contrast to the Pharisees, defines his exorcisms as "Spirit of God exorcisms." This is the proper definition, he argues, whereas the Pharisees' claim is implausible, inappropriate, and unjust. In addition, the counterdefinition refers to kingdom, and its use exhibits the principle that the kingdom of God is not divided against itself, but asserts its power against a strong one that it can subdue, namely Satan and his kingdom.

The counterdefinition is followed by a restatement of it that concludes the section. In other words, since Matthew has already introduced a counterdefinition, the statement about the strong man does not show the falsity of the opponents' argument, as it does in Mark, but confirms the assertion already made in the counterdefinition. The restatement moves from the analogy of kingdom, which was used in the

44. See Hermogenes 52,6–7 and the English translation in Nadeau, 'Hermogenes' *On Stases*," 401.

45. See Hermogenes 52,17–18 and the English translation in Nadeau, "Hermogenes' *On Stases*," 401.

46. See Hermogenes 52,20–53,1 and the English translation in Nadeau, "Hermogenes' *On Stases*," 401.

first stich of the *parallelismus membrorum*, to the analogy of house in the second stich. If the casting out of demons by the Spirit of God exhibits the coming of the Kingdom of God, then the strong man has been bound and his house is being plundered.

After the counterdefinition and its restatement in terms of "house" analogy, a series of sayings establishes the counter-case against the Pharisees. According to Hermogenes,[47] a speaker can establish the case by drawing an inference, showing the gravity of the issue, and showing the better alternative through comparison. Matthew adds a judicial feature with a statement of law, then in the tradition of epideictic he presents the comparison that establishes a diairesis between good and bad. In Matthew, then, there are four steps as follows:

Inference ($\sigma v \lambda \lambda o \gamma \iota \sigma \mu \acute{o}s$):

"He who is not with me is *against* me, and he who does not gather with me scatters.

Gravity ($\acute{\eta} \pi \eta \lambda \iota \kappa \acute{o} \tau \eta s$):

Therefore, I tell you, every sin and blasphemy *will be forgiven* men, but the blasphemy *against* the Spirit *will not be forgiven*.

Statement of the Law:

And whoever says a *word against* the Son of man *will be forgiven*; but whoever speaks *against* the Holy Spirit *will not be forgiven*, either in this age or in the age to come."

Diairesis through Analogy:

"Either make the *tree good*, and its *fruit good*; or make the *tree bad*, and its *fruit bad*; for the *tree* is known by its *fruit*."

In the stasis of definition, according to Hermogenes, the inference draws the definition and the counterdefinition together. In Matthew, Jesus begins with an inference that the Pharisees are "against" him. This use of "against" changes the "against itself" of the *parallelismus membrorum* to "against me" through inference that emerges from the Pharisees' definition of his action as "Beelzebul exorcism." In other words, since Jesus casts out demons by the Spirit of God, the Pharisees' statement that he casts them out by Beelzebul means that they are "against" Jesus and not "with" him.

After the inference, Jesus describes the gravity of the issue: blasphemy against the spirit will not be forgiven. This statement begins with $\pi \hat{a} \sigma a$ ("every") that opens both lines of the first *parallelismus membrorum*. This time, instead of synthetic parallelism, the lines contain antithetical parallelism:

---

47. See Hermogenes 60,8–14 and the English translation in Nadeau, "Hermogenes' *On Stases*," 404.

every sin and blasphemy will be forgiven men, but blasphemy against the spirit will not be forgiven.

After the statement of the gravity of the issue, Jesus states the law that is operative in the situation. Since he gives the punishment for the act, the statement takes the form of casuistic rather than apodictic law:

> and whoever speaks a word *against* the Son of man,
>> it shall be forgiven him;
> but whoever speaks *against* the Holy Spirit,
>> it shall not be forgiven him either in this age or
>> in the coming age.

After the statement of the law, the Matthean version presents an epideictic diairesis through analogy, a division between that which is good and that which is bad. This rhetorical figure suggests that there are only two alternatives—a good tree with good fruit and a bad tree with bad fruit—and the analogy suggests that "the tree is known by its fruit." With the inference, the issue becomes "those who are against," and with the statement of the gravity of the offense and the law, it develops into "those who speak against." Then the epideictic diairesis characterizes "those who speak against" as "bad." This progression employs both judicial and epideictic rhetoric to impugn the character of the Pharisees who spoke against Jesus after he had performed a good action. The argument shows that the action of the Pharisees is shameful. It is so shameful that it shall not be forgiven, either now or in the future. Then a new arena of analogy, the tree and its fruit, associates the Pharisees with production of evil that reveals evil character as its source. The conclusion maintains the diairesis between good and evil but shifts the image from production of fruit to "bringing forth treasure":

Conclusion (Heightening Emotion through Direct Attack):

Direct Address:

> "Brood of vipers!

Quaestio:

> How can *you* speak *good*, when *you* are *evil*?

Rationale:

> For out of the abundance of the heart the mouth speaks; the *good* man out of his *good* treasure *brings forth* (ἐκβάλλει) *good*, and the *evil* man out his *evil* treasure *brings forth* (ἐκβάλλει) *evil*."

Judgment with Rationale:

> "I tell *you*, on the day of *judgment* men will render account for every careless *word* they utter."

> "For by *your words you* will be justified, and by *your words you* will be condemned."

Now the exhortation has worked through "that which the mouth speaks" to "that which is brought forth (ἐκβάλλει)." At this point a word play takes place on the "casting forth" at the beginning of the unit. How can an evil man cast out evil? The answer is that an evil man may bring forth evil words and deeds, but a good man brings forth good words and deeds. Building on the diairesis ("division") between the good and the bad and the analogy that a tree is known by its fruit, the answer indicts the "heart" of those who speak against Jesus and his deeds. When the Pharisees cast out a word, it was an evil word out of their evil treasures. In contrast, when Jesus cast out (ἐκβάλλει) the demon, it was a good action out of his good treasure.

Direct address that intensifies emotion is a characteristic feature in a conclusion: "Brood of vipers!" Then the quaestio reiterates the diairesis achieved in the previous section: "How can you speak good, when you are evil?" The rationale summarizes the argument that a good person who uses his words carefully in exorcism and in refutation has just made. The judgment is introduced with "I tell you" and is general in character as it speaks in third person about "men" and "they." Then, returning to second person plural, Jesus concludes with a διαίρεσις ("division") containing judicial language: "By your words you will be justified, and by your words you will be condemned." With this move, the argument leaves the Pharisees as subjects whose words exonerate or condemn them. Epideictic oratory, then, has brought forth highly judicial language. A special touch of the Matthean composition appears in the use of the preposition κατά for "against" throughout the elaboration. The discussion of a kingdom divided "against" itself, a house divided "against" itself, and Satan divided "against" himself leads to an inference about he who is "against me." Then a discussion of "speaking against" the Holy Spirit and the Son of man leads to the concluding statement that "by your words you will be justified and by your words you will be judged against" (καταδικασθήσῃ). The compound verb with κατά stands in final emphatic position at the end of the unit. This leaves the final comment on the negative side of praise and censure, in contrast to the Markan version that ended on the positive side with "my brother, sister, and mother who do the will of God" (Mark 3:35). The Matthean version has not officially pronounced a verdict, but it has made eminently clear the manner in which it will reach the verdict. The author of the Matthean version has lined us up on the side of Jesus against the Pharisees whom Jesus has been addressing.

4.1 Conclusion

When we apply insights from ancient rhetoric to Matt 9:32–34 and Matt 12:22–37, we see not only techniques analogous to the preliminary stage of rhetorical composition but also techniques discussed in advanced stages of rhetorical training. Analysis from the perspective of chreia composition reveals how Matthew has composed a brief epideictic unit to conclude a section that depicts the mighty acts of the Messiah. Alternatively, a chreia may be the beginning point for an elaboration which contains significant dimensions of rhetorical stasis. If the elaboration is designed to defend one person's career and defame another entire group, one will not be surprised to discover that the argument contains most or all of the steps Hermogenes recommends for a complete rhetorical argument.

5. The Version in Luke 11:18–28

The internal epideictic nature of the Beelzebul controversy emerges in full form in the Lukan version. In contrast to the Matthean version, which presents a well-organized stasis argument, the Lukan version has a topical organization reminiscent of the Markan principle of organization. Instead of a chiastic tripartite structure like the Markan version, however, the Lukan version strings together a series of units with a topical relationship much like some of the sections in Plutarch's *Parallel Lives*, where a list of apophthegms occur in a loosely-organized progression.[48] The Lukan version merges the request for a sign with the Beelzebul Controversy, and this prepares the way for a series of units concerning censure, an unclean spirit, praise, and testing. The opening chreia prepares the stage for these developments through four responses to Jesus' action at the beginning:

Situation

> Now he was casting out a demon that was dumb;

Topic: Exit

> when the demon had gone out, the dumb man spoke,

Topic: Praise

> and the *crowds* marveled.

Topic: Censure

> But some of them said, "He casts out demons by Beelzebul, the prince of demons";

Topic: Test

> while others, to test him, *sought* from him a *sign* from heaven.

In contrast to the Matthean version that uses aorist tense for Jesus' action in the opening scene, the Lukan version begins with a peri-

---

48. See Perrin, *Plutarch's Vita Alexandrorum*, XXXIX.1–7.

phrastic imperfect construction: "Now he was casting out a demon that was dumb" (Luke 11:14). In turn, the demon comes out, the dumb man speaks, and the crowd marvels. The unit begins, then, with direct action by Jesus, the demon, and the crowds. Before the unit ends, however, there are two more actions: (a) some people in the crowd say that Jesus casts out demons by Beelzebul, and (b) others test him seeking a sign from heaven. The end result of this composition is a complex, active situation.

Once the scene is set up in this complex, active way, the Lukan version depicts Jesus in response to the variety of activities going on. First, Jesus responds to the people who say he casts out demons by Beelzebul. This response has the same basic steps as the Matthean version:

Topic: Censure

Transitional Comment:

> *But* he, knowing their thoughts, said to them,

Argument from Analogy for the Implausibility of the Beelzebul Definition:

> "Every *kingdom* divided *upon* itself is laid waste, and *house upon house* falls. And if Satan also is divided *upon* himself, how will his *kingdom* stand?"

Counterdefinition:

> "For *you* say that I cast out demons *by* Beelzebul . And if I cast out demons *by* Beelzebul,
> > *by* whom do *your* sons cast them out?
> > Therefore they shall be *your judges.*
> *But* if it is *by* the finger of God that I cast out demons,
> > then the *kingdom* of God has come upon *you.*"

Argument from Analogy:

> "When a strong man, fully armed, *guards* his own palace,
> > his goods are in peace;
> *but* when one stronger than he comes *upon* him and
> > conquers him, he takes away his armor *upon* which he
> > trusted, and divides his spoil."

Inference:

> "He who is not with me is against me, and he who does not gather with me scatters."

This section of the Lukan version is similar to the Matthean version. Yet it contains touches that give a slightly different style of integration to the unit. Instead of using κατά for "against" so that "divided against" leads through "he who is against" and "whoever speaks against" to "by your words you will be judged against (καταδικασθήσῃ)," the Lukan version discusses a kingdom or a house that dissipates its power "upon itself" and a stronger man who uses his power "upon someone else" and takes away that "upon which" the other person trusted. In addition, the Lukan version of the stronger man does not refer to "entering the strong man's house." Rather, the Lukan version focusses on the strong man who "guards" his palace but then is conquered by a stronger person. Since these terms and images re-emerge almost playfully as the elaboration proceeds, the overall composition differs noticeably from the more severe judicial tone of the Matthean version.

After addressing the group which censures his activity, Jesus addresses the activity of the unclean spirit who went out of the man:

Topic: Exit

Argument from Fable ($\mu\hat{v}\theta os$):

> "When the unclean spirit has gone out of a man, he passes through waterless places *seeking* rest; and finding none he says, 'I will return to my *house* from which I came.' And when he comes he finds it swept and put in order. Then he goes and brings seven other spirits more *evil* than himself, and they enter and dwell there; and the last state of that man becomes worse than the first."

This little fable ($\mu\hat{v}\theta os$) applies the analogy of a house to a man with an unclean spirit. Up to this point the elaboration has explored the possible forces at work in the casting out of a demon. Therefore, the discussion concerned the action in the first clause of the section: "and he was casting out a demon" (Luke 11:14a). In the exorcism itself we were told that the demon went out (Luke 11:14c), but then we were told about the actions of the healed man, the crowds who marveled, some who censured Jesus, and some who tested him. Now we are told about the potential activity of an unclean spirit once he has gone out of a man. First he "seeks rest," but then he decides to return to "his house" and brings seven other spirits "more evil than himself" into the swept and well-ordered abode. We must see the conception at work here. The house that he left has been well-kept while he was away. In fact, it reminds a person of the house in which the possessions were at peace because they were guarded by a fully-armed strong man (Luke 11:21). It is surprising, of course, that the house is not guarded when the unclean spirit returns with seven others. But instead of pursuing this angle, it seems to be a commentary on "he who does not gather with me scatters." Those who turn against Jesus will go out and wander around seeking a place of rest. In contrast, those who gather to Jesus will be with him, his kingdom, and his house. When those who have scattered become aware of their situation, they will return home, much like the Prodigal Son returns in Luke 15:17–20. But, instead of being greeted by an overjoyed father, they will find a clean house, go out and bring others more evil than themselves and put the house in greater disorder than it was at first. This fable appears to relate Jesus' exorcism to the action of the group who turned against him and will scatter to cause even greater disorder than they presently have caused. With the fable a new term, namely "evil," appears in the elaboration. We will see this term again before the elaboration ends.

Immediately after Jesus' statement that associates people who censure good activity with demons who gather even more evil associates around themselves, a woman in the crowd, representing those who praise Jesus' activity, raises her voice and pronounces a blessing. The unit is as follows:

Topic: Praise

Epideictic *Chreia* with Appropriate Redirection of the Praise

> As he said this, a woman in *the crowd* raised her voice and said to him, "Blessed is the womb that bore you, and the breasts that you sucked!" *But* he said, "Blessed rather are those who hear the word of God and *guard* it!"

The composition of this unit keeps the activity of the scene in motion. While Jesus is speaking, the woman speaks out. Thus, whatever Jesus may have been inclined to say after the fable has been interrupted, now he must address people who praise him. It may appear, at first blush, that Jesus should be happy with the woman's statement of praise. But auditors in Mediterranean society know the danger of flattery,[49] and Jesus immediately removes any suspicion that he might be susceptible to it. The woman speaks out of the world of blessing she knows. A mother who bore such a capable, gifted, and articulate son would certainly consider herself blessed. Thus the woman praises Jesus through his mother: "Blessed is the woman that bore you and the breasts that you sucked" (Luke 11:27). Jesus responds from the perspective of the adult male role for which he was anointed (Luke 4:18–19). In his view, her statement may encourage him to think about fame and glory rather than the tasks that lie ahead. Thus Jesus directs attention to the word of God, much as he responded to Satan with words of God during the temptations in the wilderness (Luke 4:1–13). In the same mode in which he knew the word of God and kept it in the wilderness, he asserts that those are blessed who "hear the word of God and guard it." In the Lukan sequence, the wording of this response has an interesting relationship to Jesus' earlier statement about the strong man: "When the strong man, fully armed, *guards* his own palace, his possessions are in peace." Likewise, "Blessed are those who hear the word of God and *guard* it." In the midst of censure, flattery, and temptation, the only safeguard is, as Jesus

49. See, for example, Plutarch, *On Friends*.

explained at the end of his paraphrase of the parable of the sower, to "hear the word, hold it fast in an honest and good heart, and bring forth fruit with patience" (Luke 8:15).

In the Lukan version, Jesus' response to both the censure and praise sets the stage for his response to testing. When tested, Jesus might not only fail by being unable to perform a special sign, but he might be lured into an exhibition of his power that would persuade more people in the crowd to praise him. Thus, Jesus now presents an elaborate response to those who test him by seeking from him a sign from heaven:

Topic: Test

Thesis:

> When *the crowds* were increasing, he began to say, "This *generation* is an *evil generation*; it *seeks* a *sign*,
>
> *but* no *sign* shall be given to it except the *sign* of Jonah."

Rationale:

> For as Jonah became a *sign* to the men of Nineveh, so will the Son of man be to this *generation*.

Argument from Example:

> The queen of the South will arise at the *judgment* with the men of this *generation* and *condemn* them;
>
> for she came from the ends of the earth to hear the wisdom of Solomon,
>
> and behold, something greater than Solomon is here.
>
> The men of Nineveh will arise at the *judgment* with this *generation* and *condemn* it;
>
> for they repented at the preaching of Jonah,
>
> and behold, something greater than Jonah is here.

Argument from Analogy:

Contrary:

> No one after lighting a *lamp* puts it in a cellar or under a bushel, *but* on a stand, that those who enter may see the *light*.

Application:

> *Your eye* is the *lamp* of *your body*;

Diairesis:

> when *your eye* is sound, *your whole body* is full of *light*; *but* when it is not sound, *your body* is full of *darkness*.

Concluding Exhortation:

> Therefore be careful lest the *light* in *you* be *darkness*.
>
> If then *your whole body* is full of *light*, not having any part *dark*, it will be *wholly* bright, as when a *lamp* with its rays gives *you light*.

Again this section begins with a statement that continues the activity with which the unit began. In the midst of increasing crowds, referred to by a present genitive absolute, Jesus begins to speak to those who wish to test him by seeking a sign from heaven. They shall receive no sign except the sign of Jonah, namely the action and speech of the Son of man that functions like the action and speech of Jonah to the men of Nineveh. This reference provides the opportunity to introduce exemplary people from the past who proclaimed and repented of evils and who embodied and sought wisdom. What those people heard, saw, and did prepared the way for the greater things people hear, see, and need to do now. The argument from analogy suggests that the signs of Jesus' mission and greatness are clearly visible—on a lamp stand. Thus, it is foolish to seek some other sign. If a person cannot see how Jesus functions, that person is full of darkness. Returning to the image of the house, the elaboration envisions the body of a person as a house that needs to have light in it. Earlier, the house out of which the unclean spirit went was the body of a man who had been healed through exorcism, and the return of the unclean spirit produced a worse state than his first dwelling there. As the body is envisioned as a house at the end of the elaboration, the eye is a lamp, and all who enter see the light when the lamp is put on a stand rather than in the cellar or under a bushel. This leads to the exhortative conclusion.

The unit ends with the observation that if your whole body is full of light, it will be possible for you to see clearly. A true picture of things will reveal that Jesus casts out demons by the finger of God, that he is not susceptible to flattery but keeps the word of God, and that he resists the temptation to seek fame and glory to continue the work for which he was anointed. The elaboration has moved from an assertion about "the finger of God" and the "kingdom of God" to an assertion to "hear the word of God and guard it" like the queen of the South who heard the wisdom of Solomon and the men of Nineveh who repented at the preaching of Jonah. It ends with an exhortation to let the "entire" body be full of light so that any darkness in the body will be replaced by light.

Thus, the Lukan version ends with a positive image which envisions the body as a house. In Mark, the final scene envisioned people sitting in a house, sharing a kinship relation because they do the will of God. In Luke, the image concerns lighting the house. If there is no lamp in the house, it will be dark. In Luke, then, the elaboration ends with attention to the eye as the lamp of the body whereas in Mark it ended with an interest in people who do the will of God and in Matthew it ended with concern about the words that come out of a person's mouth. From Luke's perspective, all of the hearing in the elaboration has been seeing. And if the eye is sound, the person will not seek further signs and will not enter into misguided censure or praise, but will see God's work both in Jesus' activity and in the activity of Solomon, Jonah, and the queen of the South in the past.

With this sequence, Luke has brought the topics of the casting out of demons and the seeking of signs to a conclusion. He moves to the next topic with the conjunction δέ ("and") and a dative infinitive (Luke 11:37: ἐν δὲ τῷ λαλῆσαι), which is one of his favorite constructions. He has been building to a full-scale encounter of Jesus with Pharisees and lawyers. The series that follows establishes a setting where Jesus' statement about those who blaspheme against the Holy Spirit emerges as an authoritative pronouncement against Pharisees and lawyers (Luke 12:10).

6. Conclusion

The shortest version of the Beelzebul controversy is in Matt 9:32–34. Whether this is actually the earliest version is difficult to say, since it functions in Matthew as a conclusion to the section on Jesus as the Messiah of Deed. Outside of this unit, all the synoptic gospels feature a response by Jesus that argues the implausibility of Jesus being aligned with Satan.

The epideictic nature of the tradition suggests that it is perpetuated by people who already know what values are accepted by the Christian community, and they are promulgating those values. Epideictic rhetoric intensifies values we already hold by lining us up on the side of the good against the bad. Through the power of rhetorical composition, the "authors" of these elaborations feature Jesus as "author" of a value system perpetuated within the Christian community at the expense of "opponents" of the community. Who are these opponents? It is not clear. One thing we can see. The tradition perpetuates an ideology of "opponents" to Jesus as a way of intensifying attitudes of the good versus the bad.

The Markan version perpetuates the most exaggerated form of opposition as unnamed people and scribes from Jerusalem say that Jesus is "out of his mind" and "possesses Beelzebul," and Jesus says that people who say such things are "guilty of an eternal sin." The Markan version embeds this in a positive epideictic framework, however, as Jesus looks at those sitting around him in a circle and says, "See my mother and my brothers. Whoever does the will of God, this is my brother, sister, and mother" (Mark 3:35). But what does it mean to do the will of God in Mark? This section only tells us it is necessary to have our attitudes and actions on the side of Jesus' attitudes and actions. And most of the Gospel of Mark proceeds in a similar manner. For the most part, anti-values are nurtured as a person learns *not* to be scandalized by a message that brings tribulation and persecution (Mark 4:17) and *not* to be lured by cares of the world, delight in riches, and desire for other things

(Mark 4:18–19). Also, a person learns *not* to be associated with evil thoughts, fornication, theft, murder, adultery, coveting, wickedness, deceit, licentiousness, envy, slander, pride, and foolishness (Mark 7:21–22). What then does a person do? A person develops the attitudes and will to act according to the presupposition that "Whoever loses his life for my sake and the gospel's will save it" (Mark 8:35). This is epideictic rhetoric, intensifying attitudes and the will to act through positive and negative characterization of persons and groups.

The Matthean version uses judicial rhetoric to intensify epideictic rhetoric. Skillful rhetorical composition creates a scene in which Pharisees define Jesus' action as a "Beelzebul exorcism." Jesus presents a counterdefinition of his action as a "Spirit of God exorcism" and introduces a law about "speaking against" that indicts the Pharisees. This indictment is intensified by analogies about "knowing a tree by its fruit" and "bringing forth good and bad treasure," analogies that impugn the character of the Pharisees. As the unit ends with a diairesis between being justified and being condemned "by your words," the reader again is aligned on the side of good against evil. What then is "good" character? Again with this procedure the reader sees what is *not* good character. The perpetuation of images of "anti-character" is a primary means of building and maintaining character. The reader should *not* be like the Pharisees, should *not* be allied with Satan and demons, should *not* be against Jesus or scattered from him, and should *not* speak against the Holy Spirit. What, then, are the characteristics of "good" character? The Gospel of Matthew undertakes, especially in the Sermon on the Mount (Matt 5–7), to articulate a system of deliberative rhetoric that will nurture good character and guide one's actions.[50] As it does this, however, it also nurtures and deepens the epideictic "anti-rhetoric." The righteousness nurtured by the Gospel of Matthew is to be understood as a righteousness that "exceeds the righteousness of the scribes and Pharisees" (Matt 5:20), and people are to understand that whereas the scribes and Pharisees preach this righteousness, "they do not practice it" (Matt 23:3). Why this need to cultivate an anti-rhetoric with such intensity? This anti-rhetoric exhibits intensive anxiety about the claim to possess the benefits of a religious heritage in which the people always have had difficulty receiving the benefits promised to them. In the Gospel of Matthew, a system has been "authored" that intensifies virtues which have been "authored" by people within Jewish heritage. But this system is "authored" by turning it against its "originators." The anxiety of "taking over" a system in this way appears to be exhibited in a need to suppress the "true authorship" of that system through intense rhetoric against those "authors." Only at moments does the true authorship appear as

---

50. See Kennedy, *New Testament Interpretation*.

the reader hears that "the scribes and Pharisees sit on Moses' seat" (Matt 23:2) and that he/she should "practice and observe whatever the scribes and Pharisees tell you" (Matt 23:3). But these things cannot be said apart from the anti-rhetoric, because the anti-rhetoric maintains the identity over against the true transmitters of this social, cultural, and religious way of life.

The Lukan version perpetuates this anti-rhetoric, but in an environment of artistry, mythology, domesticated imagery, and some playfulness. For Luke, many things happen on an active day among the crowds. As you send a demon out of a man, you have to be ready to deal with people who will use your good actions against you, the demon himself who will gather his friends and return to the man, people who will lure you away from your commitments through praise, and people who will seek more from you simply to test you. A person can live in the midst of such activity by nurturing the imagery of a strong man who guards his palace and keeps his possessions in peace, a mythology of unclean spirits who travel around seeking a place of rest, a system of obedience to the word of God that gives greater priority to articulated culture than articulated sentiments of family, a heritage of men and women who knew and sought wisdom and who proclaimed and responded to a call for repentance, and an architecture of the body that makes the eye a lamp that lights up the entire body so there is no dark place in it. The Lukan version provides the seedbed for a Christian culture that uses the resources of human society to live in a complex world. One of the characteristics of such an approach is to let the images play more freely, to let various stories emerge in the midst of a major story, to personify evil characters and let them receive our sympathy for a moment as they wander about seeking a place of rest, to give some female characters a place among male characters, and to imagine our eye as a lamp or our body as a house that can have dark and light places in it. In Luke, Christian rhetoric begins to find a home. In the language of our previous discussion, a Cynic-style rhetoric that leaves people in silence as they stand before unburied dead and muse on the prospects of following a person who has nowhere to lay his head has developed into a domesticated rhetoric where people willingly put their hand to the plow without looking back and attentively guard the word of God with an eye which illumines their entire body like a lamp brightens every corner of a house.

EIGHT

Conclusion

Burton L. Mack & Vernon K. Robbins

The authors of this volume have analyzed early traditions about Jesus in the light of rhetorical theory and practice common to the Hellenistic culture of the time. Five detailed studies present the results of different types of composition in the gospels. The studies are examples of what might be learned in the pursuit of a rhetorical investigation of the Jesus traditions, and they illustrate application to a range of issues encountered in the synoptic texts and their traditions.

The express aim has been to demonstrate rhetorical composition in clusters of sayings not normally regarded as patterned, much less as patterned in forms of argumentation that were current in conventional discourse of the first century. In the course of these studies, however, more than exegetical demonstration has occurred. The investigations contain important observations both about the culture of rhetoric at large and about the implications of rhetorical practice for the transmission of the teachings of Jesus in the movements stemming from him. It is appropriate to summarize these observations now as a conclusion to this set of studies. We can organize what has been learned by focusing upon (a) the rhetoric of chreia elaboration, (b) the composition of pronouncement stories, and (c) the creation of a Christian *paideia*. We will indicate where new perspectives on Christian origins have been won in relation to more conventional scholarly views. At the end the authors will make some suggestions for further research, since these studies are intended to chart an arena of investigation yet to be thoroughly explored.

1. The Rhetoric of Chreia Elaboration

The point of departure for the studies as a whole was the discovery that the pronouncement stories in the gospels could be defined as chreiai in keeping with Hellenistic practice. Robbins has discussed the significance of this discovery in chapter 1. New Testament scholars have been aware that the pronouncement stories in the gospels bore some relation to the Hellenistic anecdote, but very little work had been done on the form and function of chreiai in Hellenistic literature, and none at all on the phenomenon of elaboration as practiced in the schools. The authors of this volume had to take seriously what the teachers of rhetoric said about chreiai and their elaboration before they could give a fresh assessment of the pronouncement stories.

Mack has discussed in chapter 2 what has been learned about chreiai from studies in the progymnasmata. He pointed out that rhetors regarded chreiai as examples of persuasive speech and submitted them to rigorous rhetorical analysis. Rhetors could describe types of response to situations, with moral maxims on one end of a gradient curve and aphoristic rejoinders on the other. They understood all the chreiai as ways of making "arguments," and they classified them accordingly. Viewed in this way, chreiai did not cease to be anecdotes of memorable occasions in which humor, sagacity, or wisdom was evoked, but they did take on a distinctly new nuance. They also regarded chreiai as evidence for a person's rhetorical skills in argumentation.

To regard aphoristic speech as rhetorical performance may seem strange to many New Testament scholars. That is because proverbs, pithy rejoinders, and clever applications of similes and metaphors among the sayings of Jesus have not usually been thought of as chreiai that contained "arguments." The view has been that the sayings of Jesus were more like maxims with didactic and ethical intent. Nevertheless, collecting chreiai for comparison by using the rhetors' descriptions did garner many pronouncement stories about Jesus along with a very large number of stories about other men of note in the biographic literatures of the time. When surveyed, Jesus' responses in the pronouncement stories did not appear to be much different in style from those characteristic for Hellenistic chreiai. If the rhetors were right about chreiai, so the question came to be posed, Could the nature of Jesus' responses also fit their rhetoric? A closer look at the logic of Jesus' responses was in order.

The survey of the pronouncement stories in comparison with chreiai undertaken in this book stumbled upon a feature of some significance. Not many of the stories about Jesus were brief, snappy "textbook" chreiai. Most were stories that joined not one, but several sayings. The point of expanded chreiai, moreover, was frequently difficult to isolate, or the way to the point difficult to trace. In the progymnasmata, to be sure, there were references to "paraphrasing" and "amplifying" brief narratives, including chreiai. And some of this discussion could help us understand the ways in which sayings accrued and changes occurred in the transmission of chreiai about Jesus. But we needed something more to grasp the logic behind the phenomenon of clustered sayings.

Mack's discovery of the pattern and logic of elaboration in Hermogenes' progymnasmata provided a model for investigating the rationale of sayings units in which there was little discursive guidance. In his elaboration of a chreia, Hermogenes used proverbial material and conventional metaphors to develop a thesis. The astute interpreter could infer the logic of elaboration from the functions Hermogenes indicated for each additional saying in his patterned example, and could follow the theme by paying attention to the composition of the unit as a whole. Tracing the functions back to discussions of theory in the classical handbooks of rhetoric, two conclusions could be drawn. One was that the list of functions Hermogenes suggested for the elaboration was actually an outline of the major moves in the construction of a "complete argument," a reduction of the classical speech of deliberation to its basic components. The other conclusion was that a reader could explain the logic behind this outline. A given case (or chreia) was "confirmed" when the speaker could demonstrate alignment among the various orders of discourse common to the culture. Agreement among cultural conventions was the basis of the logic of persuasion.

The pattern of elaboration, the notion of inventing an argument, and the use of comparative imagery for supporting the logic of a thesis, should now be understandable concepts to the reader. To clarify these concepts and their usefulness for the rhetorical analysis of proverbial material has been one of the major subsidary aims of the book. The authors selected pericopae with the elaboration pattern in mind, but also for the purpose of illustrating a variety of compositional techniques made possible by that pattern. In Mack's study of the anointing of Jesus, for instance, it could be shown that an author could elaborate a simple chreia by specifying the point of the challenge and developing the response into a full argumentation. In this case, a very sophisticated logic was concentrated within five tightly knit sayings that compressed an elaboration into a single, interlocking response. Robbins' study of the discipleship sayings, on the other hand, analyzed the phenomenon of a cluster of chreiai as a compositional technique with rhetorical intention. There, and in his study of the Beelzebul stories, Robbins pointed out that the addition of a very few items was sufficient to change the rhetorical focus of a chreia. In his study of the variants of the chreia about plucking grain on the sabbath, moreover, Robbins could show various ways in which several authors pressed the elaboration pattern to accommodate judicial as well as deliberative argumentation. And Mack's study of the set of parables in Mark 4 disclosed another compositional arrangement. In this case, it was a composition that followed the elaboration pattern, yet consisted only of analogies.

These studies, however, have touched upon aspects of rhetorical theory and practice other than those easily illustrated by the pattern of elaboration. This was especially clear in Robbins's analyses of the Beelzebul pericopae where various synoptic authors had made different decisions when making their first moves to reinterpret the story. Robbins was able to distinguish among these decisions only by reference to discussions of different speech types and their issues or circumstances found in the more advanced handbooks. The complexity of rhetorical theory and the intricacies of rhetorical composition need to be emphasized if the usefulness of the pattern of elaboration is not to be misunderstood. The pattern is extremely helpful as an introduction to the practice of rhetoric in the composition of gnomic, thematic, and biographic writings, but it cannot illustrate all of the options possible for any given elaboration, nor serve as a decoder for determining the precise rhetorical function of any given component of an elaboration. An elaboration need not to have contained all of the items in Hermogenes' pattern in order to have been effective. Items need not always to have followed Hermogenes' order. And an elaboration might duplicate arguments of a given type, *parabolai* for instance, in order to underscore a single point, or develop a theme, rather that to move the argument ahead as was the case in Hermogenes. The value of the elaboration pattern has been to demonstrate argumentation at work in aphoristic material, not to exhaust the possibilities of rhetorical composition that used such material. We should not think of it as a wooden outline, but as a grammar.

In chapter 2 Mack made the point that the pattern of elaboration reproduced the major sections of the traditional speech form. He pointed out the distinction between those items that established the thesis and those that offered supporting arguments. The items that established the thesis included (1) a restatement of the chreia in paraphrase, (2) a statement of the rationale, and (3) a statement of the contrary. By means of these items, an author could translate a chreia into a proposition and establish it by stating its reasonableness in the rationale and by clarifying it in the contrary. The author could then support the proposition by means of (1) an analogy, (2) an example, and (3) a judgment. Hermogenes used the term elaboration to designate the exercise as a whole, even though, technically, the term best described the function of the supporting arguments rather than the establishment of the proposition.

In his work, Robbins has emphasized the logic of argumentation involved in the establishment of a thesis. He has noted that all of the items in the pattern of elaboration need not be present in order to formulate and support a proposition and that analysis must begin by making certain of the proposition and its primary rationale. From his studies we can see that the three major techniques for translating a chreia into an arguable issue were: (1) restating (or paraphrasing) the chreia as a proposition that could be argued, (2) supporting the proposition through one or more reasons, in effect creating what Aristotle called an enthymeme, and (3) clarifying the proposition by means of a contrary statement, a restatement of the issue from an angle that would *not* be true or acceptable. This finding suggests that rhetors gave particular attention to the first moves required in the elaboration of a chreia. These moves correspond to the first set of items in Hermogenes' elaboration, those that establish the proposition to be supported further by analogy, example, and citation. Since, however, according to Aristotle, analogies and examples were primary means for creating propositional enthymemes, the rhetorical function of figurative material within an elaboration may be quite complex, analogies and examples serving now to establish a proposition, now to support it with reasons, and now to develop its definition, theme, or application. Often, moreover, a single saying can serve two or more rhetorical functions. The studies in this volume illustrate complexities of this kind.

In the Lukan version of the sayings about foxes, birds, and burying the dead, for instance, the addition of the saying about plowing provides a rationale for leaving the dead to bury their own dead and for leaving parents without saying farewell. The presence of this rationale gives the argument an enthymematic form that interrelates deductive and inductive reasoning. Nevertheless, the saying also presents an argument from analogy, an argument from the contrary, and an argument from example. The analogy, taken from the arena of agriculture and the circumstances of plowing, gives substantial support to the proposition that a person should follow Jesus without compromise. The way Luke phrases it, however, makes the point by means of the contrary statement that no one who puts his hand to a plow and looks back is fit for the kingdom of God. This is an argument from that which is *not* acceptable, used to clarify what *should* be done. The analogy actually produces two images: (1) looking back, which should *not* be done, and (2) looking ahead, which *should* be done. Viewed from yet another perspective, the analogy of a person who puts his hand to the plow can function as an argument from example by depicting someone who starts a task and pursues it with unfaltering commitment. Even though the example is not a named person from the past in the mode of Hermogenes' reference to Demosthenes, it is a social example that provides the elaboration with the same kind of supporting argument. The presence of an argument from analogy, an argument from the contrary, and an argument from example in this saying does not disqualify it from its primary function as a rationale for the exhortations to follow Jesus without hesitation and without compromise. Because the imagery is so clear and the rhetorical possibilities so manifest, however, another author could easily build upon it and thus develop a new elaboration. The author of the new elaboration would have to decide how to take the saying, whether as the rationale, or as an argument from the contrary, from analogy, from example, or even as a judgment. In the analysis of this elaboration in chapter three, Robbins identified the function of this saying as a rationale because, when viewed within the elaboration given, it formed an enthymeme and served as a proposition.

Thus the set of studies in this book have positioned the elaboration pattern as a bridge from the larger field of advanced rhetorical theory to the rhetoric of gnomic and biographic compositions. The elaboration pattern has made it possible to travel back and forth, now analyzing curious concentrations of proverbial imageries for rhetorical coherence, and now exploring the technical handbooks for discussions of rhetorical practice not clarified by reference to the pattern of elaboration alone. The hope is that the pattern can serve as sufficient introduction to the rhetoric of the pronouncement stories in spite of the complex twists and turns encountered in their many combinations of rhetorical techniques. Advanced knowledge of classical rhetoric and its influence upon Greco-Roman literatures would greatly enhance, no doubt, the further investigation of synoptic compositions. Even within the limits of the present set of studies, the surprise has been that the more the investigations gave the culture of rhetoric its due, the greater the sophistication of the synoptic tradents and authors appeared. The discovery of such intention and finesse in the composition of pronouncement stories presents something of a challenge to traditional scholarly views of the Jesus traditions. Observations on the nature of this challenge can now be made.

2. The Composition of Pronouncement Stories

In chapter 1, Robbins reviewed the history of scholarship on apophthegms, paradigms, and pronouncement stories in the synoptic tradition. The review set the stage for a redefinition of pronouncement stories as chreiai. Robbins emphasized the importance of this recognition, for with it far reaching questions about the early reminiscences of Jesus gain new specificity. If the pronouncement stories are chreiai, and if chreiai were familiar vehicles for depicting the character and teaching of noteworthy persons, the incidence of pronouncement stories in the Jesus tradition means that his followers remembered Jesus in much the same way as other persons of importance. Thus, pronouncement stories take their place among sayings, parables, miracle stories, and other biographical materials as a distinct but common form of memory and imagination. The integrity of the chreia means that interpreters should not separate saying and scene, and that behavior as well as statements belong to the primary form of rehearsal. Robbins's critique of the form-critics thus deserves reiteration: in our quest for the earliest traditions, we cannot privilege sayings over scenes or narratives in which actions make the point.

A study of the rhetorical intention of the Hellenistic chreia thus introduces a reassessment of traditional assumptions about the language of the Jesus traditions. The bifurcation of the sayings of Jesus into apocalyptic (or prophetic and eschatological) "announcements" on the one hand, and sapiential (or parabolic and aphoristic) "teachings" on the other, a scholarly convention in the wake of Bultmann, was partially overcome when Taylor coined the term "pronouncement." The notion of making pronouncements catches up both aspects of the sayings of Jesus as a whole even while suggesting a sense of the speaker's authority. Thus, the new term befits a comfortable compromise. The term seemed especially appropriate, moreover, as definitive for the function of the sayings in those units of tradition distinguished as pronouncement stories. Since, by definition, these stories depict Jesus making an authoritative pronouncement on a situation. For many scholars, Jesus' authority to make pronouncements has not appeared strange, and they have regarded the term pronouncement as descriptive for the nature of the sayings of Jesus in general.

If the pronouncement stories are elaborated chreiai, however, the question of the speaker's authority involves an assessment of the speaker's rhetoric. One suspects that Taylor coined the term pronouncement largely with respect to sayings we have identified as judgments in the elaborated chreiai. Jesus' authoritative pronouncements are certainly a noteworthy feature of these stories and thus justify the designation of the literary form and function. In many instances, however, analysis can show that the particular saying serving as an authoritative pronouncement entered the textual tradition at the point of elaboration. If one starts instead with the rhetoric characteristic for unelaborated chreiai, often still at the core of the pronouncement stories, retort rather than pronouncement would be the better description. The significance of this observation should not be overlooked, for a clever rejoinder implies a rhetoric and an authority quite different from that assumed for the Jesus who makes authoritative pronouncements.

The studies in this volume have not forced the question of the use of unelaborated chreiai at some early stage of a Jesus movement, nor argued for a reconstruction of the mode of speech used by the historical Jesus on the basis of the incidence of chreiai. We have pursued these studies at the level of redaction criticism, working with the textual units in their several literary contexts. The suspicion might well be, however, that, in general, it was an originally aphoristic response that was later elaborated. If so, the earlier form of wisdom attributed to Jesus in these traditions would best be described as aphoristic. The logic would not be that of pronouncements, whether "prophetic," or grounded in the self-referential authority of a superior sage, but of critical insight gained by the practice of μῆτις. It would be wrong, therefore, to regard the wisdom attributed to Jesus in the unelaborated stories as proclamatory, programmatic, revelatory, or unique. It would be an occasional wisdom, inviting assent and assessment by redescribing situations. Taking the lead from the chreiai attributed to him, Jesus' wisdom would have included penetrating insight into the critical moments of life in a society held to be deserving of critique. Critique, however, appears to have been offered generally, not directed at specific institutions, and in the aphoristic mode, that is, rhetorically astute per occasion.

Nevertheless, chreiai should not be taken as historical reminiscences merely because of their authenticity as a primary form of memory in Greco-Roman society. That is because chreiai bear the marks of being crafted. The meaning of an action or saying is assured only when the response is constructed to fit a carefully construed situation. In the quest to locate a chreia among differing traditions, we must discern the issue engaged by that scene plus response. Knowledge of the use of chreiai in philosophical school traditions and in Hellenistic literature makes it possible to understand why attributions of only a certain kind might collect around a founding figure. It also suggests that participants in a given movement regarded only certain characteristics as important for the founder of that movement with its particular practices. Knowledge of the use of chreiai in the common schools of Hellenistic education and rhetoric makes it possible to imagine how the ancients produced such chreiai. It was "speech-in-character," not the "authenticity" of a historical reminiscence, that counted in the cultivation of memory and mimesis. Thus, we must imagine incremental shifts both in "speech" and in "character" for the transmission of chreiai, just as change in the rhetorical focus of a chreia is the rule for the history of a chreia's elaboration.

This perspective on the transmission of the early Jesus traditions presents a challenge to customary views. Scholars have usually thought of tradents as copyists, collectors, or "interpreters" of sayings that originated with Jesus. They frequently speak of "floating" λόγια and imagine the sayings of Jesus to have travelled at first in the oral tradition independently of one another and of narrative context. This view has allowed a composite characterization of Jesus as the original speaker of many types of sayings that, even in isolation, are understood to have been charged with intrinsic meaning and to have created their own trajectories. To account for the appearance of these sayings in the literay contexts in which we now find them, scholars have made various proposals about the reasons for written collections and the principles of their composition. These proposals thus view many of the sayings that occur in the pronouncement stories as originally independent λόγια and regard the clusters that formed as the result of collecting λόγια by type or theme. A saying thought to be valuable would have been preserved, accordingly, simply by adding it to the collection.

The studies in this volume have shown that thematic selection is indeed a feature of composition in the clusters of sayings in pronouncement stories. Nevertheless, the underlying principle of selection was undoubtedly rhetorical. Again, we might still imagine early followers of Jesus making their selections in some cases from a fund of sayings already attributed to Jesus. But, in other instances, they appear to have created new sayings and to have domesticated proverbs and metaphors common to the times. Variants at the redactional level illustrate the wide-ranging authorial activity of those involved in portrayals of Jesus as a powerful speaker. When one sees, moreover, that the issues addressed by these elaborations fit best in circumstances of concern to the tradents themselves, grounds for such authorial activity are not difficult to imagine, though they need to be worked out in studies yet to be accomplished. The lesson from the chreia and its patterns of elaboration is a call to revise prevailing views of the teachings of Jesus, and a challenge to research the early history of the traditions of those teachings.

3. The Creation of a Christian *Paideia*

In chapter 1, Robbins rehearsed the history of New Testament scholarship in which only a few scholars brought some awareness of classical rhetoric to bear upon studies of the pronouncement stories. He analyzed the reasons for repeated hesitations to explore thoroughly the similarities that these scholars had noted between pronouncement stories and Hellenistic chreiai. Some of the reasons for turning away from Hellenistic models are quite understandable. Many stem from the observation that, in comparison to Hellenistic modes of discourse, the language of the Jesus traditions brings a new ethos to expression. The novelty of the Jesus movements seemed to require a distinctive articulation, so that the differences between the synoptic materials and their Hellenistic counterparts appeared more important than the similarities.

The set of studies presented here has emphasized the correspondence between pronouncement stories and Hellenistic chreiai elaborated according to rhetorical conventions. The high degree of correspondence is surprising, however, in light of the claims to novelty and distinctiveness characteristic for the new movements. The reason it is surprising can be stated quite precisely. A logic of persuasion that was culturally conditioned was the basis of the rhetoric of elaboration in Hellenistic provenance. Argumentation rested ultimately upon cultural conventions and traditions that were shared and in force. Orators had to show that their propositions agreed with the values, logic, world-view, historic exemplifications, and literate wisdom of the culture in order for their audiences to confirm them. One of the functions of the pattern of elaboration was to list the topics from which an orator could make just such an appeal to culture as a comprehensive system. Items in the pattern were not invitations to invent a new system of values, but to find strong and convincing figures from the reservoir of commonly accepted truisms. That being the case, neither the pattern nor the lore indexed by the components of the pattern would seem to be appropriate vehicles for a social movement in the process of marking its differences from that larger cultural context.

Noting that the domestication of the pattern of elaboration must have presented a challenge for early Jesus movements, two kinds of questions emerge. The first seeks to account for the circumstances under which the early followers of Jesus pursued elaborations on the Hellenistic model in spite of the lack of agreement between the cultural assumptions inherent in the model and the contrastive values emerging in the new social experiment. The second question asks whether the elaborations achieved bear the marks of accommodation to their new social context. Both questions call for investigation more detailed than that of the present studies. But on the basis of the studies as presented we can make a few preliminary observations nonetheless. The ultimate answers to these questions may prove to be an important contribution to studies in Christian origins.

Taking the second question first, we can begin by noting that four items of Hermogenes' pattern were frequently missing from the pronouncement stories: (1) the introductory encomium, (2) the well-known example from history, (3) the literary citation from the ancient sages, and (4) the final exhortation. Because the pronouncement stories occur in a larger narrative context in distinction from the speech situation assumed by Hermogenes' exercise, the general lack of introductory encomia and final exhortations on the part of the synoptic authors is not a serious problem. The matter is different with the infrequency of examples and authoritative citations. The fact that synoptic authors did not refer to well-known examples from cultural history, whether Greek or Jewish, and did not cite traditional literatures, whether Greek or Jewish, is, of course, quite understandable. A group at pains to distinguish itself from other cultural traditions could not afford to appeal to the history and literature of those cultures to make its novel points. Only the Matthean version of the story about plucking grain on the Sabbath gives a citation from ancient authority as an argument ("I desire mercy and not sacrifice," Matt 12:7). As for well-known examples from history, we have encountered only the figure of David in the story about plucking grain, and the figures of Jonah, the Ninevites, the Queen of the South, and Solomon in the Lukan version of the Beelzebul controversy. Of great significance is the fact that the stories used all of these references, not to marshal positive precedent for a Jesus proposition, but to argue the contrast between the Jesus movement and the Jewish tradition. They used them as "negative examples" that used the scriptures to tell against the force of Jewish culture as determining for Christian propositions.

It now becomes understandable why the synoptic elaborations are heavy with rationales, contraries, and analogies. Rationales were absolutely necessary for discourse of any kind to emerge. Contraries were required in the nature of the case if difference from others was the issue to be addressed. And analogies were the one form of argument that need not imply culturally specific values, for the members of this burgeoning movement could easily have found or invented new figures and new applications for conventional figures in order to support novel propositions. A survey of the analogies encountered in the studies shows that we must attribute astonishing ingenuity to those who invented them. We immediately notice in these stories applications of proverbial images, sayings, and metaphors. And the depiction of striking and unusual circumstances and events is also frequent. By definition, the παραβολή would capture the usual occurrence of general practice in support of a particular proposition or case. In the synoptic elaborations, however, the unusual circumstance often serves to illustrate a proposition calling for another order of things.

For example, one story uses plowing a field, which presupposes a commitment to home life, to illustrate the willingness to leave home, family, and even an unburied father to begin an itinerant life (Luke 9:62). Likewise, another story uses the activity of priests with the burnt offering, an example that presupposes careful observance of sabbath laws, to illustrate "violation of the sabbath without guilt" (Matt 12:5). Moreover, when the analogy of planting seeds is primary in Mark 4, there is no reference to "preparing the ground beforehand" (Hippocrates II), "plowing the seed into the ground" (Antiphon fr. 60), or "cultivating it so it will bear fruit" (Quintilian, *Inst. Orat.* V.xi.24). Instead of supporting "regular, disciplined" activity, the analogy depicts "sleeping and rising night and day" until a process occurs that is "out of the hands" of the sower.

Both Robbins and Mack have remarked on the preponderance of analogies that argue for the novel or unusual, as well as the use of analogies where one would expect to find an example. We have already suggested why classical examples are missing in early Christian elaborations. But it is now also obvious that a fund of examples from the early histories of the Jesus movements also is not in evidence. This lack of lore specific to exemplary Christian behavior compounded the problem of argumentation by paradigm. Early Jesus believers, however, found a very interesting solution to this problem. Where the rhetoric required paradigms, synoptic authors invented a non-specific example. The large number of sayings that describe the activity or character of "the one who . . ." fit the needs of the new argumentation perfectly. It visualized a particular case, but without the usual name, location, and place in the roster of well-known persons. This type of example, which can be called a general example, gave an added advantage as well. The example need not claim that anyone actually had lived as suggested, only that it was possible and/or necessary that one do so. Thus, the lack of examples, either from the culture at large or from the group's own tradition, did not prevent the construction of arguments from example. The synoptic authors simply made them up in keeping with the ideals held to be exemplary for the new social movement.

The substitute for ancient witnesses, to which we have given the technical label judgment, worked out another way. No elaboration studied lacked a strong authoritative pronouncement, but the sources of these pronouncements were not the poets, sages, and authors of traditional literatures. All were attributed to Jesus except the quotation from Hosea in Matthew's version of the Plucking of the Grain. So Jesus became the sole source of judgments within the movements stemming from him. That has always seemed reasonable to those who have studied the stories, since the singular authority of Jesus for Christians has appeared to be self-evident. Now it is clear, however, that the needs of those engaged in elaborations may have contributed to the attribution of such authority to Jesus. How could that have happened?

Returning to the first question posed above, and recalling an earlier discussion about the probability of a development from brief chreiai about Jesus to elaborated pronouncement stories, a history of the chreia tradition can be imagined. The chreia about the physician in Mark 2:15–17 is a fine example of a brief chreia slightly elaborated. Assuming that the elaboration consisted of (1) amplifying the setting in order to specify those who objected to Jesus' eating with "tax collectors and sinners," and of (2) adding the statement that "I came not to call the righteous, but sinners," we can see the change in social circumstance from chreia rehearsal to chreia elaboration. The chreia originally made its point teasingly, subverting the logic assumed by the objection merely by means of witty juxtaposition of two incongruous instances of contact with uncleanness. The social circumstance that supported the rehearsal of such a chreia must have called for awareness of some tensions between the practice of the Jesus people and certain Jewish codes, but the tensions need not have escalated to the point of extravagant claims and painful separations. The addition of the self-referential statement and the specification of the objectors tells another tale. A division of the house has taken place and an absolute seriousness has displaced the humor.

If one assumes that the process of elaborating chreiai took place in tandem with the social histories of early Jesus movements, one might imagine a development from simpler forms of argumentation to full elaborations of precise propositions. One of the results of the studies in this volume is the discovery that Matthew and Luke contain the more highly developed patterns, and that each experimented not only with elaboration on the deliberative model, but with judicial issues and epideictic topics as well. In the case of the Markan elaboration of the chreia about the physician mentioned above, a single statement was sufficient to establish the rationale. We might note, however, that the addition of the statement about calling not the righteous, but sinners, also functions as a paraphrase or restatement of the chreia and thus retains something of the original sense of enigma. It also, however, functions as contrary, example, and judgment. In the story about fasting that follows the chreia about the physician, a somewhat larger elaboration is in evidence (Mark 2:18–22). The story about fasting uses a separate statement to provide the contrary (vs 20), and it gives two additional analogies (vss 21–22). Thus, there is evidence for experimentation with simple forms of elaboration at a relatively early stage in the history of chreia transmission.

It is clear, however, that we cannot chart the stages of chreia transmission in early Jesus movements on the basis of the studies presented in this volume. Clean distinctions may not be possible in any case merely on formal grounds, since "complete elaborations" were not a sufficient mark of "later" developments. In order to control such an investigation, we would need additional considerations, including the correlation of issues addressed with junctures of social histories identified, as well as with changes that occur in the characterization of Jesus and the grounds for his authority. Nevertheless, the present investigations do marshal sufficient evidence to make a final observation of some importance. The nature of Jesus' authority for those who cultivated his memory with chreiai changed in the course of elaboration. The Jesus of the unelaborated chreia does not speak with the same kind of authority as the Jesus who goes on to argue for its principle. And the Jesus who turns a witty rejoinder into a serious proposition does not speak with the same kind of authority as the Jesus who concludes an elaboration with a self-referential pronouncement or a "christological" claim. One might be able to understand the process by which Jesus became the sole authority for early movements stemming from him, given the novel nature of these social experiments and the lack of other authorities to which they could appeal. But we should not take for granted the phenomenal concentration of authority in the single figure of Jesus that resulted. In the course of creating a new *paideia*, tradents of the Jesus traditions did not come to speech as authors of their own elaborations of chreiai about Jesus, commenting on his wisdom and adding their own reasons and exhortations for paying heed. Instead, they retold the stories and let the founder of their new movements speak for them in order to avoid any appeal to the claims and logics of the cultures at large. By subverting in this way the logic of Hellenistic culture, the Jesus movements created a teacher whose authority no one could question, a teacher whose statements were final. The elaboration of chreiai characterized by μῆτις produced a rhetoric of sheer pronouncement.

Works Consulted

Aalen, S., "'Reign' and 'House' in the Kingdom of God in the Gospels." *New Testament Studies* 8 (1962): 215–40.

Aichinger, H., "Quellenkritische Untersuchung der Perikope vom Ährenraufen am Sabbat: Mk 2,23–28 par, Mt 12,1–8 par, Lk 6,1–5." Pp. 110–53 in *Jesus in der Verkündigung der Kirche*. Ed. Albert Fuchs. Studien zur Umwelt des Neuen Testaments Series A. Vol. 1. Linz: Albert Fuchs, 1976.

Aitken, W. E. M., "Beelzebul." *Journal of Biblical Literature* 31 (1912): 34–53.

Aland, Kurt, *Synopsis Quattuor Evangeliorum*. Stuttgart: Württembergische Bibelanstalt, 1964.

Albertz, Martin, *Die synoptischen Streitgespräche. Ein Beitrag zur Formengeschichte des Urchristentums*. Berlin: Trowitzsch, 1921.

Alexandre, Manuel, Jr., "Argumentação Retórica em Fílon de Alexandria." Ph.D. diss. University of Lisbon, 1986.

Aristotle, *Ars Rhetorica*. Trans. John Henry Freese. Loeb Classical Library. Cambridge: Harvard University Press, 1926.

Aune, David E., "Septem Sapientium Convivium (Moralia 146B–164D)." Pp. 51–105 in *Plutarch's Ethical Writings and Early Christian Literature*. Ed. Hans Dieter Betz. Studia ad Corpus Hellenisticum Novi Testamenti 4. Leiden: E. J. Brill, 1978.

———, "Magic in Early Christianity." Pp. 1507–57 in *Aufstieg und Niedergang der römischen Welt*. Band II.23.1. Ed. Hildegard Temporini and Wolfgang Hasse. Berlin and New York: Walter de Gruyter, 1980.

Baldwin, Charles S., *Medieval Rhetoric and Poetic*. New York: Macmillan Press, 1928.

Banks, Robert, *Jesus and the Law in the Synoptic Tradition*. Cambridge: Cambridge University Press, 1975.

Beare, F. W., "The Sabbath was Made for Man?" *Journal of Biblical Literature* 79 (1960): 130–36.

Benoit, Piere, "Les epis arraches (Mt 12,1–8 et par.)." *Studii Biblici Franciscani Liber Annuus* 13 (1962): 76–92.

Best, Ernest, "Mark 3:20, 21, 31–35." *New Testament Studies* 22 (1976): 309–19.

Betz, Hans Dieter, "Jesus as Divine Man." Pp. 114–33 in *Jesus and the Historian: Written in Honor of Ernest Cadman Colwell*. Ed. F. Thomas Trotter. Philadelphia: The Westminster Press, 1968.

———, *Der Apostel Paulus und die sokratische Tradition. Eine exegetische Untersuchung zu seiner "Apologie" 2 Korinther 10–13*. Beiträge zur historischen Theologie 45. Tübingen: J. C. B. Mohr, 1972.

_____, "The Literary Composition and Function of Paul's Letter to the Galatians." *New Testament Studies* 21 (1975): 353–79.

_____, "In Defense of the Spirit: Paul's Letter to the Galatians as a Document of Early Christian Apologetics." Pp. 99–114 in *Aspects of Religious Propaganda in Judaism and Early Christianity*. Ed. Elizabeth Schüssler Fiorenza. Notre Dame: University of Notre Dame Press, 1976.

_____, *Galatians: A Commentary on Paul's Letter to the Churches in Galatia*. Hermeneia. Philadelphia: Fortress Press, 1979.

_____, "The Sermon on the Mount: Its Literary Genre and Function." *Journal of Religion* 59 (1979): 285–97.

_____, *Essays on the Sermon on the Mount*. Philadelphia: Fortress Press, 1984.

Black, Matthew, *An Aramaic Approach to the Gospels and Acts*. 3d ed. Oxford: The Clarendon Press, 1967.

Blomberg, Craig L., "The Law in Luke-Acts." *The Journal for the Study of the New Testament* 22 (1984): 53–80.

Boismard, M.-É., *Synopses des quatre évangiles en français. Tome II: Commentaire par M.-É. Boismard*. Ed. Piere Benoit and M.-É. Boismard. Paris: Éditions du Cerf, 1972.

Bonner, Stanley F., *Education in Ancient Rome*. Berkeley and Los Angeles: University of California Press, 1977.

Bowker, John W., "Mystery and Parable: Mark iv.1–20." *Journal of Theological Studies* 25,2 (1974): 300–17.

Braun, Herbert, "Erwägungen zu Markus 2,23–28 Par." Pp. 53–56 in *Entscheidung und Solidarität: Festschrift für Johannes Harder*. Beiträge zur Theologie, Politik, Literatur and Erziehung. Ed. Hermann Horn. Wuppertal: Hammer, 1973.

Bultmann, Rudolf, *Die Geschichte der synoptischen Tradition*. Göttingen: Vandenhoeck und Ruprecht, 1931.=*The History of the Synoptic Tradition*. Trans. John Marsh. New York: Harper & Row, 1963. Rev. ed. New York: Harper & Row, 1976.

Busse, Ulrich, *Die Wunder des Propheten Jesus. Die Rezeption, Komposition und Interpretation der Wundertradition im Evangelium des Lukas*. Forschung zur Bibel 24. Stuttgart: Verlag Katholisches Bibelwerk, 1977.

Butts, James R., "The *Progymnasmata* of Theon: A New Text with Translation and Commentary." Ph.D. diss. Claremont Graduate School, 1987.

_____, "The Voyage of Discipleship: Narrative, Chreia, and Call Story." Pp. 199–219 in *Early Jewish and Christian Exegesis: Studies in Memory of William Hugh Brownlee*. Ed. William Steinspring and Craig A. Evans. Atlanta: Scholars Press, 1987.

Butts, James R. and Ronald F. Hock, "The Chreia Discussion of Aphthonius of Antioch: Introduction, Translation, and Comments." Pp. 209–34 in *The Chreia in Ancient Rhetoric. Volume I: The Progymnasmata*. Eds. Ronald F. Hock and Edward N. O'Neil. Society of Biblical Literature Texts and Translations 27. Atlanta: Scholars Press, 1986.

Calloud, Jean, "Toward a Structural Analysis of the Gospel of Mark." *Semeia* 16 (1979): 133–65.

Cameron, Ron, "'What Have You Come Out to See?' Characterizations of John and Jesus in the Gospels." *Semeia* 51 (forthcoming).

Carson, D. A., "Jesus and the Sabbath in the Four Gospels." Pp. 57–97 in *From Sabbath to Lord's Day*. Ed. D. A. Carson. Grand Rapids: Zondervan, 1982.

Chilton, Bruce, "A Comparative Study of Synoptic Development: The Dispute between Cain and Abel in the Palestinian Targums and the Beelzebul Controversy in the Gospels." *Journal of Biblical Literature* 101 (1982): 553–62.

Church, F. Forrester, "Rhetorical Structure and Design in Paul's Letter to Philemon." *Harvard Theological Review*. 71 (1978): 17–33.

Cicero, *Orator*. Trans. Harry M. Hubbell. Loeb Classical Library. Cambridge: Harvard University Press, 1939.

———, *De Oratore*. Books I–II. Trans. E. W. Sutton and H. Rackham. Loeb Classical Library. Cambridge: Harvard University Press, 1942.

———, *De Oratore*. Book III and *De Partitione Oratoria*. Trans. H. Rackham. Loeb Classical Library. Cambridge: Harvard University Press, 1942.

———, *De Inventione, De Optimo Genere Oratorum, Topica*. Trans. Harry M. Hubbell. Loeb Classical Library. Cambridge: Harvard University Press, 1949.

Clark, Donald L., *Rhetoric in Greco-Roman Education*. New York: Columbia University Press, 1957.

Cohen, B., "The Rabbinic Law Presupposed by Mt. xii.1 and Lk. vi.1." *Harvard Theological Review* 23 (1930): 91–92.

Cohn-Sherbok, D. M., "An Analysis of Jesus' Arguments concerning the Plucking of Grain on the Sabbath." *The Journal for the Study of the New Testament* 2 (1979): 31–41.

Conley, Thomas M., "The Enthymeme in Perspective." *Quarterly Journal of Speech* 70 (1984): 168–87.

Crossan, John Dominic, *In Parables: The Challenge of the Historical Jesus*. New York: Harper & Row, 1973.

———, "The Seed Parables of Jesus." *Journal of Biblical Literature* 92 (1973): 244–66.

———, *In Fragments: The Aphorisms of Jesus*. New York: Harper & Row, 1983.

Daube, David, "The Anointing at Bethany." Pp. 311–24 in *The New Testament and Rabbinic Judaism*. London: Athlone Press, 1956.

———, *The New Testament and Rabbinic Judaism*. London: Athlone Press, 1956.

———, "Responsibilities of Master and Disciples in the Gospels." *New Testament Studies* 19 (1972): 1–15.

Delebecque, Édouard, "Les épis 'égrenés' dans les Synoptiques." *Revue des Études Grecques* 88 (1975): 133–42.

Derrett, J. D. M., "The Anointing at Bethany and the Story of Zacchaeus." Pp. 266–85 in *Law in the New Testament*. London: Darton, 1970.

———, "Judaica in St. Mark." *Journal of the Royal Asiatic Society* [no vol. number] (1975): 2–15. Reprinted as pp. 85–100 in *Studies in the New Testament I: Glimpses of the Legal and Social Presuppositions of the Authors*. Leiden: E. J. Brill, 1977.

Detienne, Marcel and Jean-Pierre Vernant, *Cunning Intelligence in Greek Culture and Society*. Atlantic Highlands, NJ: Humanities Press, 1978.

Dewey, Joanna, *Markan Public Debate: Literary Technique, Concentric Structure, and Theology in Mark 2:1–3:6*. Society of Biblical Literature Dissertation Series 48. Chico, CA: Scholars Press, 1980.

Dibelius, Martin, *Die Formgeschichte des Evangeliums*. Tübingen: J. C. B. Mohr, 1919.

———, *Die Formgeschichte des Evangeliums*. 2d ed. Tübingen: J. C. B. Mohr, 1933.

———, *From Tradition to Gospel*. Trans. Bertram Lee Wolf. 2d ed. New York: Charles Scribner's Sons, 1935.

Diogenes Laertius, *Lives of Eminent Philosophers*. Trans. R. D. Hicks. 2 vols. Loeb Classical Library. London: William Heinemann and Cambridge: Harvard University Press, 1972.

Doeve, J., *Jewish Hermeneutics in the Synoptic Gospels and Acts*. Assen: Van Gorcum, 1954.

Donahue, John, *Are You the Christ?* Society of Biblical Literature Dissertation Series 10. Missoula, MT: Scholars Press, 1973.

Döring, Klaus, *Exemplum Socratis. Studien zur Sokrates-nachwirkung in der Kynisch-stoischen Popularphilosophie der frühen kaiserzeit und in frühen Christentum*. Vol. 42. Hermes Einzelschriften. Wiesbaden: Steiner, 1979.

Dormeyer, D., *Die Passion Jesu als Verhaltensmodell*. Münster: Aschendorff, 1974.

Doughty, D. J., "The Authority of the Son of Man (Mk 2:1–3:6)." *Zeitschrift für neutestamentliche Wissenschaft* 74 (1983): 161–81.

Droge, Arthur, "Call Stories in Greek Biography and the Gospels." *Society of Biblical Literature Seminar Papers* 22 (1983): 245–57.

Duling, Dennis C., "Solomon, Exorcism, and the Son of David." *Harvard Theological Review* 68 (1975): 235–52.

Edwards, Richard A., *A Theology of Q: Eschatology, Prophecy, and Wisdom*. Philadelphia: Fortress Press, 1976.

Ehrhardt, A. A. T., "Lass die Toten ihre Toten begraben." *Studia Theologica* 6 (1952): 128–64.

Evans, O. E., "The Unforgivable Sin." *Expository Times* 68 (1957): 240–44.

Farenga, Vincent, "Periphrasis on the Origin of Rhetoric." *Modern Language Notes* 94 (1979) 1033–55.

Farmer, William R., "Notes on a Literary and Form-Critical Analysis of Some of the Synoptic Material Peculiar to Luke." *New Testament Studies* 8 (1962): 301–16.

Fitzer, G., "Die Sünde wider den Heiligen Geist." *Theologische Zeitschrift* 13 (1957): 161–82.

Flender, Helmut, *St. Luke: Theologian of Redemptive History*. Trans. Reginald H. and Ilse Fuller. Philadelphia: Fortress Press, 1967.

Foerster, Werner and Knut Schäferdiek, "σατανᾶς." Pp. 151–65 in *Theological Dictionary of the New Testament*. Vol 7. Ed. Gerhard Friedrich. Trans. and ed. Geoffrey W. Bromiley. Grand Rapids: Wm. B. Eerdmans, 1971.

Fridrichsen, Anton, "Le péché contre le Saint-Esprit." *Revue d'histoire et de philosophie religieuses* 3 (1923): 367–72.

Fuchs, Albert, *Die Entwicklung der Beelzebul Kontroverse bei den Synoptikern*. Studien zur Umwelt des Neuen Testaments Series B. Vol. 5. Göttingen: Vandenhoeck und Ruprecht, 1980.

Gamba, G. G., "Struttura letteraria e significato dottrinale di Marco 2,23–28 e 3,1–6." *Salesianum* 40 (1978): 529–82.

Gaston, Lloyd, "Beelzebub." *Theologische Zeitschrift* 18 (1962): 247–55.

Gemoll, Wilhelm, *Das Apophthegma: Literarhistorische Studien*. Vienna: Hölder, Pichler, Tempsky, 1924.

Georgi, Dieter, "The Records of Jesus in the Light of Ancient Accounts of Revered Men." Pp. 527–42 in *Society of Biblical Literature Seminar Papers*. Vol. 2. Ed. Lane C. McGaughy. Missoula, MT: Scholars Press, 1972.

Gils, F., "'Le sabbat a été fait pour l'homme et non l'homme pour le sabbat' (Mc II,27). Reflexions á propos de Mc II,27–28." *Revue Biblique* 69 (1962): 506–23.

Gnilka, J., *Das Evangelium nach Markus*. 2 vols. Neukirchen: Neukirchener Verlag, 1978–79.

Grundmann, W., *Das Evangelium nach Lukas*. Berlin: Evangelische Verlag, 1961.

———, *Das Evangelium nach Markus*. Berlin: Evangelische Verlag, 1962.

Hadas, Moses and Morton Smith, *Heroes and Gods: Spiritual Biographies in Antiquity*. Religious Perspectives 13. New York: Harper & Row, 1965.

Haenchen, Ernst, *Der Weg Jesu*. Berlin: Topelmann, 1966.

Hamerton-Kelly, Robert G., "A Note on Matthew XII.28 par. Luke XI.20." *New Testament Studies* 11 (1965): 167–69.

Hay, L. S., "The Son of Man in Mark 2:10 and 2:28." *Journal of Biblical Literature* 89 (1970): 69–75.

Held, Heinz Joachim, "Matthew as Interpreter of the Miracle Stories." Pp. 165–299 in *Tradition and Interpretation in Matthew* by Günther Bornkamm, Gerhard Barth, and Heinz Joachim Held. Trans. Percy Scott. Philadelphia: The Westminster Press, 1963.

Hengel, Martin, *Nachfolge und Charisma*. Beihefte zur Zeitschrift für die neutestamentliche Wissenschaft 34. Berlin: Töpelmann, 1968.

Hermogenes, *Peri Staseon*. Pp. 28–92 in *Hermogenis Opera*. Ed. Hugo Rabe. Rhetores Graeci VI. Leipzig: Teubner, 1913.

———, *Progymnasmata*. Pp. 1–27 in *Hermogenis Opera*. Ed. Hugo Rabe. Rhetores Graeci VI. Leipzig: Teubner, 1913.

Hiers, R. H., "Satan, Demons, and the Kingdom of God." *Scottish Journal of Theology* 27 (1974): 35–47.

Hill, Forbes T., "The Rhetoric of Aristotle." Pp. 19–76 in *A Synoptic History of Classical Rhetoric*. Ed. James J. Murphy. Davis, CA: Hermagoras Press, 1983.

Hock, Ronald F. and Edward N. O'Neil, eds., *The Chreia in Ancient Rhetoric. Volume I: The Progymnasmata*. Society of Biblical Literature Texts and Translations 27. Atlanta: Scholars Press, 1986.

Holladay, Carl R., *Theios Aner in Hellenistic Judaism: A Critique of the Use of this Category in New Testament Christology*. Society of Biblical Literature Dissertation Series 40. Missoula, MT: Scholars Press, 1977.

Holmer, Paul L., *The Grammar of Faith*. San Francisco: Harper & Row, 1978.

———, *Making Christian Sense*. Philadelphia: The Westminster Press, 1984.

Hook, Larue van, trans., *Isocrates*. Vol. 3. Loeb Classical Library. Cambridge: Harvard University Press and London: William Heinemann, 1968.

Hooker, Morna D., *The Son of Man in Mark*. London: SPCK, 1967.

Horna, K., "Gnome, Gnomendichtung, Gnomologien." *Pauly-Wissowa Realencyclopaedie*. Vol. 6. Stuttgart: J. B. Metzler, 1935.

Hultgren, Arland J., "The Formation of the Sabbath Pericope in Mark 2:23–28." *Journal of Biblical Literature* 91 (1972): 38–43.

———, *Jesus and His Adversaries: The Form and Function of the Conflict Stories in the Synoptic Tradition*. Minneapolis: Augsburg Publishing House, 1979.

Iersel, van, B. M. F. and A. J. M. Linmans, "The Storm on the Lake, Mk iv 35–41 and Mt viii 18–27 in the Light of Form-Criticism, 'Redaktionsgeschichte' and Structural Analysis." Pp. 17–48 in *Miscellanea Neotestamentica*. Vol 2. Ed. T. Baarda, A. F. J. Klijn, and W. C. van Unnik. Novum Testamentum Supplement 48. Leiden: E. J. Brill, 1978.

Isocrates. Trans. L. Van Hook. Vol. 3. Loeb Classical Library. Cambridge: Harvard University Press, 1945.

Jebb, R. C., *The Attic Orators from Antiphon to Isaeos*. 2 vols. New York: Russell and Russell, 1962.

Jeremias, Joachim, "Die Salbungsgeschichte Mk 14:3–9." Pp. 107–15 in *Abba. Studien zur neutestamentlichen Theologie und Zeitgeschichte*. Göttingen: Vandenhoeck und Ruprecht, 1966.

———, *The Parables of Jesus*. 2d rev. ed. Trans. S. H. Hooke. New York: Charles Scribner's Sons, 1972.

Jewett, Robert, "Romans as an Ambassadorial Letter." *Interpretation* 36 (1982): 5–20.

Kaibel, G., *Comicorum Graecorum Fragmenta*. Berlin, 1889.

Kee, Howard C., "Aretalogy and Gospel." *Journal of Biblical Literature* 92 (1973): 402–22.

Kelber, Werner H., *The Oral and the Written Gospel*. Philadelphia: Fortress Press, 1983.

Kennedy, George A., *The Art of Persuasion in Greece*. Princeton: Princeton University Press, 1963.

———, *The Art of Rhetoric in the Roman World*. Princeton: Princeton University Press, 1972.

———, *Classical Rhetoric and Its Christian and Secular Tradition from Ancient to Modern Times*. Chapel Hill: University of North Carolina Press, 1980.

———, *New Testament Interpretation Through Rhetorical Criticism*. Chapel Hill and London: The University of North Carolina Press, 1984.

Kernaghan, Ron, "History and Redaction in the Controversy Stories in Mark 2:1–3:6." *Studia Biblica et Theologica* 9 (1979): 23–47.

Kertelge, K., "Jesus, seine Wundertaten und der Satan." *Concilium* 11 (1975): 168–73.

Kimbrough, S. T., "The Concept of Sabbath at Qumran." *Revue de Qumran* 5 (1966): 483–502.

Klauck, Hans-Josef, *Allegorie und Allegorese in synoptischen Gleichnistexten*. Münster: Aschendorff, 1978.

Klemm, H. G., "Das Wort von der Selbstbestattung der Toten." *New Testament Studies* 16 (1969): 60–75.

Klostermann, E., *Das Markusevangelium*. 2d ed. Handbuch zum Neuen Testament 3. Tübingen: J. C. B. Mohr, 1926.

———, *Das Lukasevangelium*. Handbuch zum Neuen Testament. 2d ed. Tübingen: J. C. B. Mohr, 1929.

Kruse, H., "Das Reich Satans." *Biblica* 58 (1977): 29–61.

Kuhn, Heinz-Wolfgang, *Ältere Sammlungen im Markusevangelium*. Studien zur

Umwelt des Neuen Testaments 8. Göttingen: Vandenhoeck und Ruprecht, 1971.

Lambrecht, Jan, *Marcus Interpretator. Stijl en Boodschap in Mc. 3,20–4,34*. Utrecht: Descle'e de Brouwer, 1970.

Lane, William L., *The Gospel According to Mark*. New International Commentary on the New Testament 2. Grand Rapids: Wm. B. Eerdmans, 1974.

Lategan, Bernard C., "Structural Interrelations in Matthew 11–12." *Neotestamentica–Die Nuwe-Testamentiese Werkgemeenskap van Suid-Afrika* 11 (1977): 115–29.

Lausberg, Heinrich, *Handbuch der literarischen Rhetorik*. 2 vols. München: Max Hueber Verlag, 1973.

Lefkowitz, Mary R., "The Poet as Hero: Fifth-Century Autobiography and Subsequent Biographical Fiction." *Classical Quarterly* 28 (1978): 459–69.

Leitch, J. W., "Lord Also of the Sabbath." *Scottish Journal of Theology* 19 (1966): 426–33.

Limbeck, M., "Beelzebul—eine ursprüngliche Bezeichnung für Jesus?" Pp. 31–42 in *Wort Gottes in der Zeit*. Eds. Helmut Feld and J. Nolte. Düsseldorf: Patmos Verlag, 1973.

_____, "Satan und das Böse im Neuen Testament." Pp. 271–388 in *Teufelsglaube*. Ed. Herbert Haag. Tübingen: J. C. B. Mohr, 1974.

_____, "Jesus und die Dämonen. Der exegetische Befund." *Bibel und Kirche* 30 (1975): 7–11.

_____, "Die Wurzeln der biblischen Auffassungen vom Teufel und den Dämonen." *Concilium* 11 (1975): 161–68.

Lindemann, Andreas, "'Der Sabbat ist um des Menschen willen geworden . . .' Historische und theologische Erwägungen zur Traditionsgeschichte der Sabbatperikope Mk 2,23–28 parr." *Wort und Dienst* 15 (1979): 79–105.

Lohmeyer, Ernst, *Das Evangelium des Markus*. Meyer Kommentar 2. Göttingen: Vandenhoeck und Ruprecht, 1967.

Lohse, Eduard, "σάββατον." Pp. 1–35 in *Theological Dictionary of the New Testament*. Vol. 7. Ed. Gerhard Friedrich. Trans. and ed. Geoffrey W. Bromiley. Grand Rapids: Wm. B. Eerdmans, 1971.

Long, William R., "The *Paulusbild* in the Trial of Paul in Acts." *Society of Biblical Literature Seminar Papers* 22 (1983): 87–105.

Lucian. Trans. A. M. Harmon. Loeb Classical Library. Vol. 1. New York: Macmillan, 1913.

Lührmann, Dieter, *Die Redaktion der Logienquelle*. Wissenschaftliche Monographien zum Alten und Neuen Testament 33. Neukirchen und Vluyn: Neukirchener Verlag, 1969.

MacLaurin, E. C. B., "Beelzeboul." *Novum Testamentum* 20 (1978): 156–60.

Mack, Burton L., "Decoding the Scriptures: Philo and the Rules of Rhetoric." Pp. 81–115 in *Nourished with Peace: Studies in Hellenistic Judaism in Memory of Samuel Sandmel*. Eds. F. E. Greenspahn, E. Hilgert, and Burton L. Mack. Denver: University of Denver (Colorado Seminary), 1984.

_____, *A Myth of Innocence: Mark and Christian Origins*. Philadelphia: Fortress Press, 1988.

_____, *Rhetoric in the New Testament*. Guides to Biblical Scholarship. Minneapolis: Augsburg-Fortress (in press).

Manson, Thomas W., *The Sayings of Jesus*. London: Cambridge University Press, 1949.

Marsh, T., "Holy Spirit in Early Christian Teaching." *Irish Theological Quarterly* 45 (1978): 101–16.

Marshall, I. Howard, *The Gospel of Luke: A Commentary on the Greek Text*. New International Greek Testament Commentary. Grand Rapids: Wm. B. Eerdmans, 1978.

McCall, Marsh H., Jr., *Ancient Rhetorical Theories of Simile and Comparison*. Cambridge: Harvard University Press, 1969.

Metzger, Bruce M., *A Textual Commentary on the Greek New Testament*. New York: United Bible Societies, 1971.

Meyer, H. A. W., *Kritisch-exegetisches Handbuch über die Evangelien des Markus und Lukas*. 1st ed. Göttingen: Vandenhoeck und Ruprecht, 1832.

Moo, Douglas J., "Jesus and the Authority of the Mosaic Law." *The Journal for the Study of the New Testament* 20 (1984): 3–49.

Morgan, C. S., "'When Abiathar was High Priest' (Mark 2:26)." *Journal of Biblical Literature* 98 (1979): 409–10.

Murmelstein, B., "Jesu Gang durch die Staatfelder." *Angelos* 3 (1930): 111–20.

Nadeau, Ray, "The Progymnasmata of Aphthonius." *Speech Monographs* 19 (1952): 264–85.

_____, "Hermogenes' *On Stases*: A Translation with an Introduction and Notes." *Speech Monographs* 31 (1964): 361–424.

Nauck, August, ed., *Tragicorum Graecorum Fragmenta*. 2d ed. Leipzig: B. G. Teubner, 1889.

Neirynck, Franz, "Jesus and the Sabbath: Some Observations on Mark II,27." Pp. 227–70 in *Jesus aux origines de la christologie*. Ed. J. Dupont. Bibliotheca ephemeridum theologicarum lovaniensium 40. Gembloux and Louvain: Duculot and Leuven University, 1975.

Neyrey, Jerome H., "The Thematic Use of Isaiah 42.1–4 in Matthew 12." *Biblica* 63 (1982): 457–73.

Nineham, D. E., *Saint Mark*. Pelican Gospel Commentaries. Harmondsworth: Penguin Books, 1963.

Perelman, Ch. and L. Olbrechts-Tyteca, *The New Rhetoric: A Treatise on Argumentation*. Notre Dame: University of Notre Dame Press, 1969.

Pesch, Rudolf, "Die Salbung Jesu in Bethanien (Mk 14.3–9): Eine Studie zur Passionsgeschichte." Pp. 267–85 in *Orientierung an Jesus*. Ed. Paul Hoffmann. Freiberg: Herder, 1973.

_____, *Das Markusevangelium*. Herders theologischer Kommentar zum Neuen Testament I. Freiburg, Basel, and Vienna: Herder, 1977.

Philostratus, *The Life of Apollonius of Tyana*. 2 vols. Trans. F. C. Conybeare. Loeb Classical Library. Cambridge: Harvard University Press and London: William Heinemann, 1969.

Philostratus, *Lives of the Sophists*. Trans. Wilmer C. Wright. Loeb Classical Library. London: William Heinemann and Cambridge: Harvard University Press, 1921.

Plutarch, *Alexander*. Trans. Bernadotte Perrin. Loeb Classical Library. Vol. 7. Cambridge: Harvard University Press, 1919.

_____, *Moralia*. 16 vols. Loeb Classical Library. Cambridge: Harvard University Press, 1926–69.

Quintilian, *Institutio Oratoria*. 4 vols. Trans. H. E. Butler. Loeb Classical Library. Cambridge: Harvard University Press, 1920.

Rabe, Hugo, ed., *Hermogenis Opera*. Rhetores Graeci VI. Leipzig: B. G. Teubner, 1913.

_____, *Aphthonii Progymnasmata*. Rhetores Graeci X. Leipzig: B. G. Teubner, 1926.

Raymond, James, "Enthymemes, Examples, and Rhetorical Method." Pp. 140–51 in *Essays on Classical Rhetoric and Modern Discourse*. Eds. R. Connors, L. Ede, and A. Lunsford. Carbondale and Edwardsville: Southern Illinois University Press, 1984.

Rhetorica ad Alexandrum. Trans. H. Rackham. Rev. ed. Loeb Classical Library. Cambridge: Harvard University Press, 1965.

Rhetorica ad Herennium. Trans. Harry Caplan. Loeb Classical Library. Cambridge: Harvard University Press, 1954.

Rice, George E., "Luke 5:33–6:11: Release from Cultic Tradition." *Andrews University Seminary Studies* 20 (1982): 127–32.

Robbins, Vernon K., "The Healing of Blind Bartimaeus (Mark 10:46–52) in the Marcan Theology." *Journal of Biblical Literature* 92 (1973): 224–43.

_____, "Classifying Pronouncement Stories in Plutarch's *Parallel Lives*." *Semeia* 20 (1981): 29–52.

_____, "Summons and Outline in Mark: The Three-Step Progression." *Novum Testamentum* 23 (1981): 97–114.

_____, "Pronouncement Stories and Jesus' Blessing of the Children: A Rhetorical Approach." *Semeia* 29 (1983): 42–74.

_____, *Jesus the Teacher: A Socio-Rhetorical Interpretation of Mark*. Philadelphia: Fortress Press, 1984.

_____, "Picking Up the Fragments: From Crossan's Analysis to Rhetorical Analysis." *Forum* 1,2 (1985): 31–64.

_____, "Pragmatic Relations as a Criterion for Authentic Sayings." *Forum* 1,3 (1985): 35–63.

_____, The Woman who Touched Jesus' Garment: Socio-Rhetorical Analysis of the Synoptic Accounts." *New Testament Studies* 33 (1987): 502–15.

_____, "Rhetorical Argument about Lamps and Light in Early Christian Gospels." Pp. 177–95 in *Context. Essays in Honour of Peder Johan Borgen*. Eds. P. W. Bøckman and R. E. Kristiansen. Relieff 24. University of Trondheim: Tapir, 1987.

_____, "The Chreia." Pp. 1–23 in *Greco-Roman Literature and the New Testament: Selected Forms and Genres*. Ed. David E. Aune. Sources for Biblical Study 21. Atlanta: Scholars Press, 1988.

_____, "The Crucifixion and the Speech of Jesus." *Forum* 4,1 (1988): 33–46.

_____, "Pronouncement Stories from a Rhetorical Perspective." *Forum* 4,2 (1988): 3–32.

_____, *Ancient Quotes and Anecdotes: From Crib to Crypt*. Sonoma, CA: Polebridge Press, 1989.

Robbins, Vernon K. and John H. Patton, "Rhetoric and Biblical Criticism." *The Quarterly Journal of Speech* 66 (1980): 327–37.

Robinson, James M. and Helmut Koester, *Trajectories through Early Christianity*. Philadelphia: Fortress Press, 1971.

Roloff, Jürgen, *Das Kerygma und der irdische Jesus*. Göttingen: Vandenhoeck und Ruprecht, 1970.

Ross, J. M., "The Rejected Words in Luke 9:54–56." *Expository Times* 84 (1972): 85–88.

Roulin, P., "Le péché contre l'Esprit-Saint." *Bible et vie chrétienne* 29 (1959): 38–45.

Samain, P., "L'accusation de magie contre le Christ dans les évangiles." *Ephemerides theologicae lovanienses* 15 (1938): 449–90.

Schenke, L., *Studien zur Passiongeschichte des Markus*. Forschung zur Bibel 4. Wüzburg: Echter, 1971.

Schille, Gottfried, *Die urchristliche Wundertradition. Ein Beitrag zur Frage nach dem irdischen Jesus*. Arbeiten zur Theologie 29. Stuttgart: Calwer Verlag, 1967.

Schmid, Josef, *Das Evangelium nach Markus*. Regensburger Neues Testament 2. Regensburg: Friedrich Pustet, 1954.

Schneider, Gerhard, "Jesu überraschende Antworten. Beobachtungen zu den Apophthegmen des dritten Evangeliums." *New Testament Studies* 29 (1983): 321–36.

Schottroff, Luise and W. Stegemann, "Der Sabbat ist um des Menschen willen da. Auslegung von Markus 2,23–28." Pp. 58–71 in *Der Gott der kleinen Leute. Sozialgeschichtliche Bibel Auslegungen*. Band 2: Neues Testament. Ed. W. Schottroff and W. Stegemann. Munich: Christian Kaiser Verlag, 1979.

Schürmann, Heinz, *Das Lukasevangelium*. Herders theologischer Kommentar zum Neuen Testament. Freiburg: Herder, 1969.

Schwarz, Günther, "ἄφες τοὺς νεκροὺς θάψαι τοὺς ἑαυτῶν νεκρούς." *Zeitschrift für die neutestamentliche Wissenschaft* 72 (1981): 272–76.

Schweizer, Eduard, *The Good News According to Mark*. Atlanta: John Knox Press, 1976.

Shuler, Philip, "The Greisbach Hypothesis and Gospel Genre." *Perkins School of Theology Journal* 33 (1980): 41–49.

———, *A Genre for the Gospels: The Biographical Character of Matthew*. Philadelphia: Fortress Press, 1982.

Silberman, Lou H., "Schoolboys and Storytellers: Some Comments on Aphorisms and *Chriae*." *Semeia* 29 (1983): 109–15.

Smith, Jonathan Z., "Towards Interpreting Demonic Powers in Hellenistic and Roman Antiquity." Pp. 425–39 in *Aufstieg und Niedergang der römischen Welt*. Band 2.16.1. Ed. Wolfgang Hasse. Berlin and New York: Walter de Gruyter, 1978.

Smith, Morton, "Prolegomena to a Discussion of Aretalogies, Divine Men, the Gospels, and Jesus." *Journal of Biblical Literature* 90 (1971): 174–99.

Spencer, Richard A., "A Study of the Form and Function of the Biographical Apophthegms in the Synoptic Tradition in Light of their Hellenistic Background." Ph.D. diss. Emory University, 1976.

Spengel, Leonard von, *Rhetores Graeci ex recognitione Leonardi Spengel*. Ed. C. Hammer. Leipzig: B. G. Teubner, 1854.

Strack, Herman L. and Paul Billerbeck, *Kommentar zum Neuen Testament aus Talmud und Midrasch*. 4th ed. 5 vols. Munich: Beck, 1965.

Suhl, Alfred, *Die Funktion der alttestamentlichen Zitate und Anspielungen im Markusevangelium*. Gerd Mohn: Gütersloh, 1965.

Talbert, Charles H., "The Concept of Immortals in Mediterranean Antiquity." *Journal of Biblical Literature* 94 (1975): 419–36.

———, *What Is a Gospel? The Genre of the Canonical Gospels*. Philadelphia: Fortress Press, 1977.

———, "Biographies of Philosophers and Rulers as Instruments of Religious Propaganda in Mediterranean Antiquity." Pp. 1619–51 in *Aufstieg und Niedergang der römischen Welt*. Band II.2. Berlin and New York: Walter de Gruyter, 1978.

———, "Prophecies of Future Greatness: The Contribution of Graeco-Roman Biographies to an Understanding of Luke 1:5–4:15." Pp. 129–41 in *The Divine Helmsman: Studies on God's Control of Human Events Presented to Lou H. Silberman*. Ed. James L. Crenshaw and Samuel Sandmel. New York: KTAV, 1980.

Tannehill, Robert C., *The Sword of His Mouth: Forceful and Imaginative Language in Synoptic Sayings*. Philadelphia: Fortress Press; Missoula, MT: Scholars Press, 1975.

———, ed., *Pronouncement Stories*. *Semeia* 20 (1981).

———, "Introduction: The Pronouncement Story and Its Types." *Semeia* 20 (1981): 1–13.

———, "Varieties of Synoptic Pronouncement Stories." *Semeia* 20 (1981): 101–19.

———, "Types and Functions of Apophthegms in the Synoptic Gospels." Pp. 1792–1829 in *Aufstieg und Niedergang der römischen Welt*. Band II.25.2. Ed. Hildegard Temporini and Wolfgang Hasse. Berlin and New York: Walter de Gruyter, 1984.

Taylor, R. O. P., *The Groundwork of the Gospels*. Oxford: Basil Blackwell Publishers, 1946.

Taylor, Vincent, *The Formation of the Gospel Tradition*. London: Macmillan, 1933.

———, *The Gospel According to Mark*. London: Macmillan, 1959.

Theissen, Gerd, *Urchristliche Wundergeschichten. Ein Beitrag zur formgeschichtlichen Erforschung der synoptischen Evangelien*. Studien zum Neuen Testament 8. Gütersloh: Gütersloher Verlagshaus Gerd Mohn, 1974.

Theon, Προγυμνάσματα. Ed. Christianus Walz. *Rhetores Graeci*. Vol. 1. Stuttgart: Cottae, 1832.

Tiede, David L., *The Charismatic Figure as Miracle Worker*. Society of Biblical Literature Dissertation Series 1. Missoula, MT: Scholars Press, 1972.

Turner, C. H., "Marcan Usage: Notes, Critical and Exegetical, on the Second Gospel." *Journal of Theological Studies* 25 (1923): 377–86.

Turner, Max M. B., "The Sabbath, Sunday, and the Law in Luke-Acts." Pp. 99–157 in *From Sabbath to Lord's Day*. Ed. D. A. Carson. Grand Rapids: Zondervan, 1982.

Veltman, Fred, "The Defense Speeches of Paul in Acts." Pp. 243–56 in *Perspectives on Luke-Acts*. Perspectives in Religious Studies, Special Studies 5. Ed. Charles H. Talbert. Macon, GA: Mercer University Press and Edinburgh: T. & T. Clark, 1978.

Vermes, Geza, "Appendix E: The Use of *bar nasha/bar nash* in Jewish Aramaic." Pp. 310–30 in *An Aramaic Approach to the Gospels and Acts* by Matthew Black. Oxford: The Clarendon Press, 1967.

_____, *Jesus the Jew*. London: Williams Collins' Sons, 1973.

_____, *Jesus and the World of Judaism*. London: SCM, 1983.

Volkmann, R., *Die Rhetorik der Griechen und Römer in systematischer Übersicht*. Hildesheim: Olms, 1963 (reprint of 1885 edition).

Waibel, Maria, "Die Auseinandersetzung mit der Fasten- und Sabbatpraxis Jesu in urchristlichen Gemeinden." *Quaestiones Disputatae* 87 (1979): 63–96.

Walz, Christian, *Rhetores Graeci*. 7 vols. Stuttgart and Tübingen: J. G. Cottae, 1832–36.

Weber, Joseph C., "Jesus' Opponents in the Gospel of Mark." *Journal of Bible and Religion* 34 (1966): 214–22.

Wechssler, E., *Hellas im Evangelium*. Berlin: Metzner, 1936.

Weeden, Theodore J., "Recovering the Parabolic Intent in the Parable of the Sower." *Journal of the American Academy of Religion* 47,1 (1979): 97–120.

Weiss, Johannes, "Die Verteidigung Jesu gegen den Vorwurf des Bündnisses mit Beelzebul." *Theologische Studien und Kritiken* 63 (1890): 555–69.

Wenham, J. W., "Mark 2,26." *Journal of Theological Studies* New Series. 1 (1950): 156.

West, M. L., *Hesiod: Works & Days*. Oxford: The Clarendon Press, 1978.

Westerholm, Stephen, *Jesus and Scribal Authority*. Coniectanea biblica, New Testament 10. Lund: Gleerup, 1978.

Wilkinson, John Gardiner, *A Popular Account of the Ancient Egyptians*. 3 vols. London: J. Murray, 1878.

Wilson, Nigel G. and Donald A. Russell, *Menander Rhetor*. Oxford: Oxford University Press, 1979.

Wilson, Stephen G., *Luke and the Law*. Cambridge: Cambridge University Press, 1983.

Wuellner, Wilhelm H., "Paul's Rhetoric of Argumentation in Romans: An Alternative to the Donfried-Karris Debate over Romans." *Catholic Biblical Quarterly* 38 (1976): 330–51.

_____, "Der Jakobusbrief im Licht der Rhetorik und Textpragmatik." *Linguistica Biblica* 43 (1978): 5–66.

_____, "Greek Rhetoric and Pauline Argumentation." Pp. 177–88 in *Early Christian Literature and the Classical Intellectual Tradition: In honorem Robert M. Grant*. Theologie historique 53. Ed. William R. Schoedel and Robert L. Wilken. Paris: Beauchesne, 1979.

Yates, R., "Jesus and the Demonic in the Synoptic Gospels." *Irish Theological Quarterly* 44 (1977): 39–57.

Ziffer, W., "Two Epithets for Jesus of Nazareth in Talmud and Midrash." *Journal of Biblical Literature* 85 (1966): 356–57.

Index of Authors

Index of Passages

Old Testament and Apocrypha

Old Testament Pseudepigrapha and Other Jewish Literature

New Testament

Greek and Latin Authors

Egyptian Authors

Index of Subjects

Index of Greek & Latin Words

Greek Words

Latin Words